SPELLING
THE WORD

Other Books by Chana Bloch

A Dress of Fire: Selected Poems of Dahlia Ravikovitch,
  1978 (translations)
The Secrets of the Tribe, 1981 (poems)

SPELLING
THE WORD

GEORGE HERBERT
AND THE BIBLE

CHANA BLOCH

University of California Press

Berkeley
Los Angeles
London

University of California Press
Berkeley and Los Angeles, California
University of California Press, Ltd.
London, England
© 1985 by
The Regents of the University of California

Library of Congress Cataloging in Publication Data
Bloch, Chana, 1940–
    Spelling the word.
    Includes index.
    1. Herbert, George, 1593–1633—Criticism and
interpretation.   2. Bible in literature.   3. Christian
poetry, English—History and criticism.   I. Title.
PR3508.B5 1985   821'.3   84-123
ISBN 0-520-05121-1

Printed in the United States of America
1 2 3 4 5 6 7 8 9

*for Ariel
Benjamin
and Jonathan*

THE H. SCRIPTURES

I

Oh Book! infinite sweetnesse! let my heart
 Suck ev'ry letter, and a hony gain,
 Precious for any grief in any part;
To cleare the breast, to mollifie all pain.
Thou art all health, health thriving till it make
 A full eternitie: thou art a masse
 Of strange delights, where we may wish & take.
Ladies, look here; this is the thankfull glasse,
That mends the lookers eyes: this is the well
 That washes what it shows. Who can indeare
 Thy praise too much? thou art heav'ns Lidger here,
Working against the states of death and hell.
 Thou art joyes handsell: heav'n lies flat in thee,
 Subject to ev'ry mounters bended knee.

II

Oh that I knew how all thy lights combine,
 And the configurations of their glorie!
 Seeing not onely how each verse doth shine,
But all the constellations of the storie.
This verse marks that, and both do make a motion
 Unto a third, that ten leaves off doth lie:
 Then as dispersed herbs do watch a potion,
These three make up some Christians destinie:
Such are thy secrets, which my life makes good,
 And comments on thee: for in ev'ry thing
 Thy words do finde me out, & parallels bring,
And in another make me understood.
 Starres are poore books, & oftentimes do misse:
 This book of starres lights to eternall blisse.

Contents

5
Singing to God 231

Acknowledgments

It is a pleasure to name the many friends and colleagues who have enabled me to write better than I could have managed on my own. Paul Alpers, Donald Friedman and Robert Alter guided my first research on Herbert and have been unfailingly generous with advice and encouragement. So have Elizabeth Pope, Norman Rabkin and Brendan O Hehir, who read the manuscript at various stages, and Noel Kinnamon, who read the chapter on Herbert and the Psalms. Donald Friedman took time when he had none to comment on parts of the "final" version and spurred me to yet another effort at rewriting. Janice Knight, my student in name only, was one of my best teachers: stimulating, rigorous and not easily satisfied. To all these I owe thanks for penetrating criticism that helped me discover what I wished to say.

Moshe Greenberg let me draw upon his profound knowledge of the Bible. Richard Strier kindly permitted me to read the manuscript of *Love Known: Theology and Experience in George Herbert's Poetry* while it was still in press. Amy M. Charles, Richard Crocker, J. S. Held, Drora Pershing-Maynard, Patrick Diehl, Connie Stroud and Susan Summerfield answered queries in their respective fields. For help with specific bibliographical problems I am obliged to Anne-Marie Bouché, Eva Kreshka and Eda Regan of the Mills College Library; John Emerson of the Music Library, University of California at Berkeley; Katherine F. Pantzer of the Houghton Library, Harvard University; Thomas V. Lange of the Huntington Library; and

Robert L. Volz of the Chapin Library, Williams College. Roussel Sargent entrusted me with her valuable 1604 Prayer Book which, to my good fortune, was bound up with a 1604 Psalter and a 1602 Sternhold-Hopkins—a rare book collection in one volume.

I am indebted to the Graves Foundation and the National Endowment for the Humanities for fellowships that gave me the gift of time. Mills College supported this project by allowing me two leaves of absence and providing for secretarial expenses. Florence Myer typed and retyped the manuscript with undismayed good humor and a loving devotion to Order: where she has labored "all is neat." Doris Kretschmer, Marilyn Schwartz and Alice Rosenthal of the University of California Press handled the manuscript with meticulous care. Finally, I wish to thank the readers chosen by the Press for their very helpful suggestions.

An abridged version of chapter 1, entitled "Spelling the Word: Herbert's Reading of the Bible," was included in *"Too Rich to Clothe the Sunne": Essays on George Herbert,* ed. Claude J. Summers and Ted-Larry Pebworth (Pittsburgh, 1980), 15–31; the final section of chapter 2 appeared as "George Herbert and the Bible: A Reading of 'Love (III)' " in *English Literary Renaissance* 8 (Autumn 1978): 329–40; and a few scattered paragraphs come from my review article, " 'Dehumanizing' Herbert," *Seventeenth-Century News* 37 (Spring–Summer 1979): 1–5. Permission to reprint is gratefully acknowledged.

This book is dedicated to my husband, Ariel, who helped in his gracious way with criticism and wise counsel, and to my children, Benjamin and Jonathan, who for as long as they can remember have lived with a presence they called George Sherbet.

A Note on Sources

All quotations of Herbert's poetry and prose, unless
otherwise specified, are from *The Works of George Herbert*,
ed. F. E. Hutchinson (Oxford, 1941; corr. ed., 1945), hereafter cited as *Works*. Quotations from the poems are identified by line number, and from the prose by page number. Poems bearing the same title are distinguished by
Roman numerals without the customary parentheses.
Two collections of critical essays are frequently mentioned
in the notes: *Essential Articles for the Study of George Herbert's Poetry*, ed. John R. Roberts (Hamden, Conn., 1979)
and *"Too Rich to Clothe the Sunne": Essays on George Herbert*, ed. Claude J. Summers and Ted-Larry Pebworth
(Pittsburgh, 1980).

Where the Bible is concerned, I have made a point of
citing chapter and verse to allow readers to examine for
themselves the texts I think were present in Herbert's
mind. My references are necessarily selective, often
chosen from among many that would have answered the
purpose. Quotations from the Bible come primarily from
the Authorized, or "King James," Version (hereafter AV),
published in 1611, when Herbert was a student at Trinity
College. This was the official church Bible throughout his
adult life and is obviously the one he would have known
best, though he would have been familiar with earlier
versions as well, in particular the Geneva Bible, popular
as a household Bible, and the Bishops' Bible, used in
church before 1611.

In the case of the Psalms, however, it is the Prayer Book
versions with which Herbert would have been most famil-

iar. Coverdale's translation of the Psalms from the Great
Bible of 1540, adopted in the 1549 Prayer Book of Edward
VI, was retained even after the publication of the more
accurate AV because of the conservatism of liturgical practice. The Psalms were read through once each month in
church, and as a clergyman Herbert would have heard
them recited daily at matins and evensong in the Prayer
Book versions. There are many instances (the epigraph
from Psalm 29 on the 1633 title page of *The Temple* being the
best known) where Herbert draws upon Coverdale's translation. Both because this is the Psalter that Herbert himself
would have used and because it is not generally available
today, I consistently quote from the Prayer Book version of
the Psalms unless otherwise noted. Unfortunately the
numbering of verses in this Psalter does not always agree
with that of the AV; where there is a deviation, the reader
will find the corresponding AV verse numbers in brackets
in the Index of Biblical References.

For contemporary interpretations of biblical texts, I turn
most often to Calvin. As an expositor Calvin had no peer
in his own day. His commentaries were widely known in
England, and not only in Puritan circles. In *Biathanatos*
(II.iv.1) Donne compares Calvin with Augustine "for
sharpe insight, and conclusive judgement, in exposition
of places of Scripture, which he alwaies makes so liquid,
and pervious," noting that "(where it concernes not
points in Controversie,) I see the *Jesuits* themselves often
follow, though they dare not name him." While the theology of the pre-Laudian church and the precise character
of Herbert's Protestantism are still subject to debate—a
debate I do not engage in—there is no question about the
value of Calvin's exegesis, and I name him frequently.
When quoting from sixteenth- and seventeenth-century
texts I have followed modern usage in transcribing *u* and
v, *i* and *j*; I have expanded contractions, and occasionally
modified punctuation or italics where noted, for the sake
of clarity.

Introduction

There is scarcely a poem in Herbert's *Temple*—one might say scarcely a line—that does not refer us to the Bible. The readers of *The Temple* are assumed to be readers of the Bible as well, a group of initiates with a history and a dialect in common. We cannot get past the title page of the volume without some knowledge of Scripture, and readers had better have the Bible at their fingertips (or at least at their elbow) if they expect to enjoy Herbert's poetry with anything like its full resonance.

As a Protestant and a clergyman, Herbert knew the Bible so intimately, and as a poet used it so extensively, that it will not do to call it an "influence," certainly not just a "literary" influence. For Herbert and his contemporaries the Bible was not merely a work of literature— though it was one of the signal achievements of the Renaissance to be able to see it in that light, too[1]—but the living Word of God. The preface to the Authorized Version speaks for Herbert's day:

> It is not onely an armour, but also a whole armorie of weapons, both offensive, and defensive; whereby we may save our selves and put the enemie to flight. It is not an herbe, but a tree, or rather a whole paradise of trees of life, which bring foorth fruit every moneth, and the fruit thereof is for meate,

1. Israel Baroway, "The Bible as Poetry in the English Renaissance: An Introduction," *Journal of English and Germanic Philology* 32 (1933): 447–80; "The Hebrew Hexameter: A Study in Renaissance Sources and Interpretation," *ELH* 2 (1935): 66–91; "'The Lyre of David': A Further Study in Renaissance Interpretation of Biblical Form," *ELH* 8 (1941): 119–42; "The Accentual Theory of Hebrew Prosody," *ELH* 17 (1950): 115–35.

and the leaves for medicine. It is not a pot of *Manna*, or a cruse of oyle, which were for memorie only, or for a meales meate or two, but as it were a showre of heavenly bread sufficient for a whole host, be it never so great; and as it were a whole cellar full of oyle vessels; whereby all our necessities may be provided for, and our debts discharged.[2]

In his two sonnets on the Scriptures, which I have taken as my epigraph and starting point, Herbert calls the Bible a medicinal honey, a mirror that mends the looker's eyes, a well that cleanses what it reflects, heaven's ambassador, a pledge of joy, a book of stars that lights the way to heaven. Nicholas Ferrar, in his preface to *The Temple*, confirms what we could guess at from the poems:

> Next God, he loved that which God himself hath magnified above all things, that is, his Word: so as he hath been heard to make solemne protestation, that he would not part with one leaf thereof for the whole world, if it were offered him in exchange.[3]

Herbert doesn't simply read the Bible, he believes in it; and it marks his poetry so distinctively because it first molds his life. Hence his allusions to the Bible have a more-than-literary motivation. *The Temple* incorporates the words of Scripture in much the same way that the New Testament summons up the Old: to affirm its continuity with the tradition from which it springs, and to validate its discoveries with the seal of ancient authority. My title alludes to a line from "The Flower": "Thy word is all, if

---

2. "The Translators to the Reader," *The Holy Bible* (London, 1611), sig. A4$_v$. The Preface to *The Reader's Digest Bible,* published in 1982, may be permitted to speak for our own day: "The device of repetition—in word, thought, and incident—and the multiplying of words for rhetorical effect were practices favored in ancient times. Today they tend to confuse and exhaust the reader's attention. . . . In this condensed version the Biblical text has been reduced by an overall figure of some forty percent" (p. x).

3. "The Printers to the Reader," *Works,* 4.

we could spell" (21). In this context "word" means the will of God,[4] but elsewhere in *The Temple* it means the Bible, and the two senses belong together. The poems of *The Temple* are about learning to "spell" God's will; and the Word of God, the Holy Scriptures, is Herbert's spelling school.

Although most of Herbert's critics acknowledge his indebtedness to the Bible as a matter of course, there is no detailed, full-length study of this subject. The varying interpretations of Herbert—Rosemond Tuve's loving traditionalist, Louis Martz's disciplined student of meditation, Arnold Stein's meticulous craftsman, Stanley Fish's self-consuming artificer, Helen Vendler's audacious innovator, to name but a few—all have something of consequence to teach us.[5] Yet each seems to me often to miss the essential Herbert. I believe that if we take as our guide the Bible, we can come closest to the very center of *The Temple*. This point of view informs the seminal work of Joseph Summers, as well as the introduction and notes to C. A. Patrides' edition of the English poems, and it is developed at length in Barbara Lewalski's magisterial

---

4. Richard Strier, *Love Known: Theology and Experience in George Herbert's Poetry* (Chicago, 1983), glosses this line: "Everything that happens, whether in the inner or the outer world, is a direct result of a specific—and benevolent—act of divine decision. . . . The word-spelling conceit seems to function as a guarantee of ultimate intelligibility and, perhaps, of benevolence" (248, cf. 62). See also Northrop Frye, *The Great Code: The Bible and Literature* (New York, 1981), 76–77, on the metaphorical identification of the Bible and the person of Christ in the phrase "word of God."

5. Rosemond Tuve, *A Reading of George Herbert* (Chicago, 1952), and "George Herbert and *Caritas*," *Journal of the Warburg and Courtauld Institutes* 22 (1959): 303–31; Louis L. Martz, *The Poetry of Meditation: A Study in English Religious Literature of the Seventeenth Century* (New Haven, 1954; rev. ed. 1962); Arnold Stein, *George Herbert's Lyrics* (Baltimore, 1968); Stanley E. Fish, *Self-Consuming Artifacts: The Experience of Seventeenth-Century Literature* (Berkeley and Los Angeles, 1972); Helen Vendler, *The Poetry of George Herbert* (Cambridge, Mass., 1975).

study.[6] How much I have learned from these critics will be apparent in the following pages.

The thesis of this book—that the poems of *The Temple* owe their distinctive character to Herbert's immersion in Scripture—is by no means controversial, though for the most part it is understood today only in a limited way. One would not expect otherwise, given that the Bible has become peripheral to our culture: in Herbert's day an uneducated layman would have known the Scriptures a good deal better than a reasonably literate one in our own. By presenting the various ways that Herbert's debt to the Bible is manifested, I wish to suggest how the poems would have been understood by the seventeenth-century reader.

The first chapter, "Doctrine and Life," considers what the poems tell us about the place of the Bible in Herbert's life—the authority it holds for him, his sense of personal identification with the text. When he pronounces a biblical verse in reply to the voices of the world, Herbert reveals his faith in the power of Scripture to protect and sustain the believer; indeed, the Bible is so central to his existence that he reads God's Word as "my words." In what follows I take for granted these fundamental insights, assuming that if the reader is aware of Herbert's attitude toward the Bible, he will be more disposed to accept the evidence of its shaping force in his poems. Each of the next four chapters studies that evidence from a different point of view.

"The Rhetoric of Allusion" deals with borrowings from Scripture at the level of word or phrase—that is, with the kind of indebtedness most commonly recognized by readers today. My concern is with Herbert's creative use

---

6. Joseph H. Summers, *George Herbert: His Religion and Art* (Cambridge, Mass., 1954); C. A. Patrides, ed., *The English Poems of George Herbert* (Totowa, N.J., 1974); Barbara Kiefer Lewalski, *Protestant Poetics and the Seventeenth-Century Religious Lyric* (Princeton, 1979).

of these materials: how he explores the distinctive properties of biblical language as a resource for poetry; how he
brings together texts in new configurations to uncover
latent possibilities of meaning; and how he transforms
what he borrows to reflect his own experience.

Of course Herbert finds a good deal more in Scripture
than a vocabulary of words and phrases: its governing
assumptions have helped to form his characteristic way of
looking at the world. Herbert learned from the Bible, for
example, to define human experience by correspondences
(the Exodus and the Redemption, the Temple of Solomon
and the temple of the heart) and contraries (flesh and
spirit, sin and love, Old and New); to think of himself not
as a unique individual but as part of a community of
believers; and to locate the present moment in relation to
an unfolding historical drama whose chief actor is God.
The third chapter focuses on the relations of Old and
New in the history of salvation and the life of the individual—a central preoccupation both in the Bible and in *The
Temple*. Here I examine the typological poems, in which
Herbert comes to understand his life in historical perspective, and poems of discovery in which he puts off the
"old man" and puts on the new.

"Talking to Man," the fourth chapter, concerns the didactic intent of Scripture as it is reflected in *The Temple*.
Arguing that the didactic impulse is at work in a great
variety of poems, even those we are accustomed to thinking of as "expressive," I discuss a number of strategies for
effective teaching—proverbial sayings, dramatic symbols
and homely images—that are commonly found in Scripture. In employing these in his poems, Herbert takes the
biblical position that what is true of one will be true of
others as well; that we learn best by "tasting" or experi-
encing; and that the most profound truths may be so
framed that they are accessible to all.

The final chapter, "Singing to God," identifies three

types of poems in "The Church" that resemble Old Testament psalms in their formal structures: the hymns that are pure celebration, the complaints that begin in grief and end in assurance, the thanksgivings that rejoice in the experience of God's love, even as they keep a memory of pain. My study of Herbert and the Bible concludes with the psalms of *The Temple* not only because they form such a large and coherent group but also because they reveal the essential temper of Herbert's poetry in their loving dialogue with God, their truth to the emotions, their stubborn expression of faith and, above all, their intent to praise.

Since what I hope to demonstrate can best be shown in close readings of individual poems, a great part of this book is occupied with such readings. These are, by design, limited in scope: my aim is to single out representative poems and to read them attentively in the light of the Bible. Where the material lends itself, I proceed from obvious parallels and close imitations of biblical materials to more inventive transmutations; this ordering should not be taken to imply a theory of artistic development. I have often borrowed phrases from one poem in talking about another, since *The Temple* is a unified work and its parts are mutually illuminating. This practice may be justified also on the grounds that it offers an illustrative analogue to the way Herbert uses phrases from Scripture. And should the reader find it playful on occasion, that too is not unintended: a book on Herbert need not be unflinchingly sober.

One would wish, as an aid to reading *The Temple*, for an edition that recorded every debt, large and small, to the Bible. Part of my task has been to supply information of this kind, with the hope of clarifying passages that have been wrongly or inadequately understood. I must emphasize, however, that the recovery of Herbert's biblical sources is my starting point, not my goal. I am interested not only in tracking down Herbert's materials but also in understanding how he succeeds in making them speak with his own voice—that process by which the past is recovered and put to use. Seeing what a poet works with and what he does with it, we are afforded some insight into the mystery we call poetic creation. When the sources are as clearly marked as they are in Herbert's case, it is possible to glimpse the mind of the poet in the very act of creation, choosing among alternatives, elaborating or excluding, making something out of something. We have only recently begun to recognize that Herbert belongs to the very first rank of English poets; I hope to provide fresh evidence to corroborate that judgment.

I came to the study of Herbert by a rather different route, I suspect, than that taken by many of my colleagues. As a poet and translator, I wished to serve an apprenticeship with "a master at [his] trade." I admired Herbert's beauty of spirit, wisdom, candor, precision, wit, deftness, control—the list is long—but apart from that I was fascinated by the use he made of biblical materials. I began to read *The Temple* with essentially practical questions: Why does this or that passage of Scripture interest Herbert? How does he wrest from it a clearer image of himself, one that will "mend" his eyes? Finally, how does he transform it in the act of claiming it for his own? My special interests will account for the bent of this investigation, which keeps asking of the master: Why? and How?

Although I believe that the Bible offers a particularly helpful way of approaching Herbert's poems, I do not offer this study as a key to *The Temple*. Anyone who knows how poems come to be written, certainly any poet who has watched himself at work, can vouch for the variety of perceptions and experiences that come to bear on every choice of word or phrase. No single perspective can reveal everything we wish to know about the beautifully subtle and complex lyrics of *The Temple*. Recalling his

words in *A Priest to the Temple*, I think Herbert himself
would say "Amen":

> As one Countrey doth not bear all things, that there may be a
> Commerce; so neither hath God opened, or will open all to
> one, that there may be a traffick in knowledg between the
> servants of God, for the planting both of love, and humility.[7]

7. *A Priest to the Temple*, *Works*, 229.

Doctrine and Life

LIVING BY THE BOOK: "BIBLES LAID OPEN"

In his first sonnet on the Scriptures, Herbert sounds like a mountebank hawking a miraculous cure-all. "Ladies, look here," he cries; "Who can indeare / [Its] praise too much?" ("The H. Scriptures, I," 8, 10–11). The Bible works, he claims; it produces real effects: it clears the breast, it mends the eyes, it neutralizes death and hell, it tastes of heaven. "Precious for any grief in any part," it is positively guaranteed "to mollifie all pain" (3, 4). The Bible performs its magic of healing and inner transformation with no apparent effort on the believer's part: like a little child, one may "suck," may "wish & take" (2, 7).

Herbert's second sonnet on the Scriptures explores from a subjective point of view the truths proclaimed in the first. The speaker is a diligent student of Scripture, who yearns to know "how all [its] lights combine" ("The H. Scriptures, II," 1) and who collates passages and hunts down allusions in his efforts to make sense of the text:

> This verse marks that, and both do make a motion
> Unto a third, that ten leaves off doth lie:
> Then as dispersed herbs do watch a potion,
> These three make up some Christians destinie:
> Such are thy secrets, which my life makes good,
> And comments on thee: for in ev'ry thing
> Thy words do finde me out, & parallels bring,
> And in another make me understood.
>
> (5–12)

Again the Bible is presented as powerfully active. Its words call out for connection ("This verse marks that"); what is more, they go in pursuit of the reader ("Thy words do finde me out"). But here the lines of force move in two directions: Herbert writes not only "thy words . . . make me understood" but also, perhaps to our surprise, "my life . . . comments on thee." Calvin speaks of this process of reciprocal illumination in the preface to his commentary on the Psalms. The mirror of Scripture shows him who he is: "yit did it greatly availe mee to beholde as it were in a Glasse, bothe the beginnings of my vocation, and also the continuall race of my ministerie." At the same time, his own experience helps him to see what the Bible means: "To thintent I might the fuller understand [David's] complaints concerning the inward mischeeves of the Church, it availed mee not a litle that I had abiden the same things that he bewaileth or much like."[1] For Herbert, as for Calvin, the understanding of Scripture is bound up with self-understanding.

Herbert's sonnets on the Scriptures, like the paired sonnets entitled "Love," were clearly intended to be read together. These sonnets reflect two fundamental beliefs about Scripture that were at the very heart of the Protestant Reformation. First, the Reformers insisted that the Bible's authority sets it apart from all merely human books or traditions or institutions, making it the final source of truth in Christianity and the supreme guide in human affairs. This belief was a rallying cry of the Reformation, "an essential ingredient," historians tell us, "of its revolutionary *élan*": "Opposing an entrenched institutionalism by appeal to an older and purer truth before and beyond it, Protestantism was forced by the very logic of its position into a peculiar reliance upon Scripture."[2] John Jewel's is a typical voice, with its note of triumphant assurance:

1. John Calvin, *The Psalmes of David and others*, trans. [Arthur Golding] (London, 1571), sig. *[vii$_v$].
2. Charles H. George and Katherine George, *The Protestant Mind of the English Reformation, 1570–1640* (Princeton, 1961), 341.

We receive and embrace all the canonical Scriptures, both of the Old and New Testament, . . . whereunto all ecclesiastical doctrine ought to be called to account; and that against these Scriptures neither law, nor ordinance, nor any custom ought to be heard; no, though Paul himself, or an angel from heaven, should come and teach the contrary.[3]

Moreover, the Reformers claimed—and this claim is quite as radical in its implications—that the ordinary believer, with God's help, can be trusted to discern the true meaning of Scripture. Hence the numerous translations of the Bible into the vernacular, the work of Protestant scholars all over Europe. This was an age in which Bibles were "laid open,"[4] made accessible by translation and commentary. The translators of the AV were explicit about their intentions: "We desire that the Scripture may speake like it self, as in the language of *Canaan*, that it may bee understood even of the very vulgar."[5]

The remarkable power of the Bible to fortify and sustain, and the readers who grasp its meaning for their lives— these subjects, set forth briefly in the sonnets on the Scriptures, will furnish our point of departure. In this chapter, I would like to consider two groups of poems in which these subjects are dramatized. In the first, Herbert quotes or paraphrases a verse of Scripture, summoning its more-than-human authority to silence the voices of the world that trouble or distract him. In the second, taking a verse of Scripture for his title, he proceeds to spell out not its plain sense, as we might expect, but rather his own deep-felt

3. John Jewel, *An Apology of the Church of England,* ed. J. E. Booty (Ithaca, 1963), 30.
4. "Sinne, I," 8. An early commentator, George Ryley, explains: "in our own tongue" ("Mr Herbert's Temple & Church Militant explained and improved," Houghton Library, Her. 2.3, p. 58). I am referring to a photocopy of this manuscript copy of the original (Bodleian, MS. Rawlinson D 199, 1714/15) kindly loaned to me by Prof. Donald Friedman. Ryley's text is also available in a critical edition by J. M. Heissler, Ph.D. diss. (Univ. of Illinois, 1960).
5. "The Translators to the Reader," *Holy Bible* (1611), sig. [B2ᵥ].

response to it. From both we learn how "doctrine and life" come together in the experience of the true Christian.[6] When we start with a moment of self-definition in the speaker's life, we find him reaching for a biblical text for support; when we start, on the other hand, with a biblical text, we are thrust at once into the life of the man who identifies with it. The high claims that Herbert makes for Scripture are given a kind of documentation in these poems, which show what it means to live by the Book.

THE POWER OF SCRIPTURE: "THY BOOK ALONE"

Herbert speaks as a Protestant when he insists on the authority of Scripture in his life: "Not a word or look / I affect to own, / But by book, / And thy book alone" ("Discipline," 9–12). Reliance on Scripture, he believes, is man's surest defense, even before God. In "Judgement" he proclaims that when called to his final accounting he will "thrust a Testament into thy hand," Christ's own will and testament (Heb. 9:15–17), and face the "dreadfull look" of the "Almightie Judge" without fear (13, 1–2). In "Complaining" Herbert holds up the mirror of Scripture to an angry God:

> Art thou all justice, Lord?
> Shows not thy word
> More attributes?
>
> (11–13)

And in "Longing" he pointedly quotes God's Word to God:

---

6. "The Windows," 11. "Doctrine" and "life" are linked in this way also in *A Priest to the Temple:* "A Priest is to do that which Christ did, and after his manner, both for Doctrine and Life," *Works,* 225; the first means to the understanding of the Scriptures is "a holy Life," for "*if any do Gods will, he shall know of the Doctrine, John 7,*" *Works,* 228; "God cannot be wanting to them in Doctrine, to whom he is so gracious in Life," *Works,* 263.

Lord heare! *Shall he that made the eare,*
                    Not heare?

(35–36)

The italics set off the verse from the surrounding context,
giving it a qualitatively different force from "Bow down
thine eare!" in line 21, quoted verbatim from the Bible
(Pss. 31:2, 86:1, etc.), which passes for Herbert's own
voice. The italicized verse is a close paraphrase of Psalm
94:9: "He that planted the eare, shall he not heare: or he
that made the eye, shall he not see?" In its original context it is a rebuke to fools who think they can escape
punishment for their crimes, but Herbert directs it with a
telling logic to God himself.

If Herbert makes bold to quote Scripture at God, he
cites it with a steady assurance when threatened with
human voices. In "The Quip," "The Posie," "Divinitie,"
"Jordan, I" and "The Forerunners," he invokes a verse of
Scripture as a rejoinder to the voices of the world or a
talisman to sustain himself, and we see the Word of God,
in all its massive authority, prevail against the pretensions
of human speech. Paul distinguishes between the "entis-
ing words of mans wisedome" and "the word of God,
which effectually worketh also in you that beleeve" (1
Cor. 2:4, 1 Thess. 2:13). Herbert takes up this distinction,
opposing the simple power of God's Word to the "trim,"
"rich," "enchanting" language of men.

The quotations from Scripture in these poems differ
from the frequent allusions to the Bible that merge almost
indistinguishably with Herbert's own voice. In each case
the verse is marked out for special notice by italics, repetition or emphatic placement. The context lends it prominence—usually by way of opposition—and once the verse
is pronounced, we recognize that it contains in brief the
point of the passage or poem. Herbert takes relatively few
freedoms with the wording of these emphatic quotations.
His restraint here is significant for, as we shall observe, he

can be quite free with biblical texts when it suits his purpose. Here he adds a word or two at most, modifying the word order or rephrasing the text in simpler language, motivated by prosodic considerations or by the desire to present the verse in a concise, memorable form.

In "The Quip," where a verse from the Book of Psalms furnishes a strategem of defense, Herbert shows us what the power of Scripture means in the life of the believer:

> The merrie world did on a day
> With his train-bands and mates agree
> To meet together, where I lay,
> And all in sport to geere at me.
>
> First, Beautie crept into a rose,
> Which when I pluckt not, Sir, said she,
> Tell me, I pray, Whose hands are those?
> *But thou shalt answer, Lord, for me.*
>
> Then Money came, and chinking still,
> What tune is this, poore man? said he:
> I heard in Musick you had skill.
> *But thou shalt answer, Lord, for me.*
>
> Then came brave Glorie puffing by
> In silks that whistled, who but he?
> He scarce allow'd me half an eie.
> *But thou shalt answer, Lord, for me.*
>
> Then came quick Wit and Conversation,
> And he would needs a comfort be,
> And, to be short, make an Oration.
> *But thou shalt answer, Lord, for me.*
>
> Yet when the houre of thy designe
> To answer these fine things shall come;
> Speak not at large; say, I am thine:
> And then they have their answer home.

Beauty, Money, Glory, Wit and Conversation belong to those troops of worldly temptations (they never seem to arrive singly) that would usurp God's prerogative: Learning, Honor and Pleasure in "The Pearl," beauty, wisdom, honor and pleasure in "The Pulley," honor, riches or fair eyes in "Frailtie," invention, comparisons and wit in "The

Posie," all the splendid appurtenances of court life in "The Quidditie." They address themselves to the clever and elegant young man that Herbert was known to be— the Herbert who, in his student days, as Walton tells us, "kept himself . . . at too great a distance with all his inferiours: and his cloaths seem'd to prove, that he put too great a value on his parts and Parentage"—though it would be naive to suppose, as Walton does, that such temptations ceased to disturb Herbert once he "chang'd his sword and silk Cloaths into a Canonical Coat."[7]

The speaker of "The Quip" makes no attempt to match the scoffers' repartee with the "quick returns of courtesie and wit,"[8] as he might have done. He declines to speak in his own defense, and even in declining he does not choose his own words. His reply, repeated four times over—*"But thou shalt answer, Lord, for me"*—is a quotation from one of the Penitential Psalms: "For in thee, O Lord, have I put my trust: thou shalt answere for me, O Lord my God" (Ps. 38:15).[9] Herbert adds the adversative "But" and modifies the word order very slightly for the sake of emphasis and rhyme, but he preserves the sober plainness of the verse. What Joseph Summers calls "the marvellous wit and playfulness"[10] of the poem is confined to the lines about the "merrie world": the mocking condescension of Beauty, Money, and Wit, and the bustling arrogance of Glory, whose silks speak louder than words. The quiet dignity of the psalm verse offers a deliberate contrast. In "Frailtie" Herbert considers "both Regiments; / The worlds, and thine":

7. Izaak Walton, *The Life of Mr. George Herbert* [1670], in *The Lives of John Donne, Sir Henry Wotton, Richard Hooker, George Herbert, and Robert Sanderson*, intro. George Saintsbury (London, 1927), 270, 291.

8. "The Pearl," 12.

9. This is one of the many instances where, as noted in the Preface, Herbert uses the Prayer Book version of the Psalms. The AV reads: "For in thee, O LORD, doe I hope: thou wilt heare, O Lord my God."

10. Summers, *George Herbert*, 189.

Thine clad with simplenesse, and sad events;
    The other fine,
  Full of glorie and gay weeds,
    Brave language, braver deeds.

(9–14)

The adjectives "fine," "gay" and "brave" evoke (with a touch of irony) the splendid, showy world of "The Quip"; God's "Regiment" stands apart in its sobriety. "*But thou shalt answer, Lord, for me*" resembles the scriptural verses that, as we shall see, Herbert opposes to the pretensions of human wit in a variety of adversary situations. Its power resides not in any bravery of language but in its very "simplenesse."

Herbert has borrowed from the Book of Psalms not only his refrain but the poem's scenario as well. He dramatizes, in contemporary dress, one of the most familiar of psalm situations: the believer trusting in God in the face of a hostile world. "Deliver mee from mine enemies" (59:1) the psalmist cries: "Mine enemies revile me all the day long" (102:8); "For loe, they lie waiting for my soule: . . . and swords are in their lips" (59:3, 7); "With the flatterers were busie mockers. . . . They gaped on mee with their mouthes, and said, fie on thee, fie on thee" (35:16, 21). In the Psalms the victim is often reduced to a painful silence by his adversaries; "I became even as a man that heareth not: and in whose mouth are no reproofes" (38:14) comes just before the verse that Herbert chose as his refrain. But even in his suffering, the psalmist typically expresses a resolute confidence in God: "Whensover I call upon thee, then shall mine enemies be put to flight" (56:9).[11]

What we have in "The Quip" is not simply a "literary" echo of the Psalms. The rhetorical strategy of the poem reflects an actual situation from life: the believer in distress repeating verses from the Psalms in order to invoke

----

11. E.g., Pss. 35, 54, 56, 59, 140, etc. In chap. 5 I will consider this aspect of the psalm complaints in some detail.

their saving power. We may be certain that Herbert and his readers turned to the Bible in precisely this way. To do so is to follow the example of Christ, who answers the temptations of Satan with Scripture: "It is written, Man shall not live by bread alone, but by every word that proceedeth out of the mouth of God" (Matt. 4:4; cf. 4:7, 4:10). Indeed one of the arguments advanced in this period for the vernacular translation of the Scriptures is that "the people should not be deprived of those arms by which they are to be protected against Satan." As William Whitaker writes in his *Disputation on Holy Scripture:*

> If Christ defended himself against Satan with the scriptures, how much more needful are the scriptures to us against the same enemy! And it was for this end that Christ used the weapons of scripture against Satan, that he might afford us an example; for he could have repelled Satan with a single word. We therefore ought to resist Satan in the same manner.[12]

The band of mockers in "The Quip" are hardly satanical, but they do have the power to perturb. At the very least, they are old remembered temptations that still jangle from time to time. When he quotes Scripture at them, the victim in Herbert's poem speaks softly but carries a big stick. Turning his back on the world, he appeals to God: *"Thou shalt answer."* There is something here of the little boy asking his father to help in confronting the bullies, as in "Assurance," where he threatens: "But I will to my Father, / Who heard thee say it" (19–20). This is a situation met with frequently in the Bible: the one against the many, the boy with his slingshot against the giant with sword, spear and shield. However vulnerable he may appear, the believer comes "in the Name of the LORD of hostes" (as David says, unmoved by Goliath's taunts, 1 Sam. 17:45), and always has the advantage.

12. William Whitaker, *A Disputation on Holy Scripture* [1588], trans. William Fitzgerald, Parker Society (Cambridge, 1849), 237.

In the Book of Psalms we find the notion that God can silence the persecutors by directly addressing their victim: "Stop the way against them that persecute me: say unto my soule, I am thy salvation" (35:3). But that passage, like many others in the Psalms, goes on to say, "Let them be confounded, and put to shame that seeke after my soule" (35:4). The motif of vengeance, so prominent in the Psalms, is conspicuously missing from *The Temple*; Herbert asks God not to punish his persecutors but rather to love him. "I am thine," the declaration of love he hopes for, gives the poem its final turn, its Herbertian signature: though he speaks as a dependent, he dreams of being answered as a beloved. In God's own good time, that declaration of love will furnish the final irrefutable reply: "And then they have their answer home."

Meanwhile the psalm verse constitutes a firm line of defense. It stands emphatically apart from the taunting voices of the world, refusing to engage them on their own terms but appealing instead to a different order of reality. Herbert's quotation from Psalm 38 conveys an unwavering assurance: not self-confidence, but trust in God. Herbert can afford to be more brief than his assailants; he can repeat himself; and he can speak without a hint of bluster or arrogance. The very modesty of his address reveals the power of the Word.

If the figure of Wit is given prominence in "The Quip" by its position as the last of the mockers, in "The Posie" wit and its progeny are the sole antagonists:

> Let wits contest,
> And with their words and posies windows fill:
> *Lesse then the least*
> *Of all thy mercies,* is my posie still.
>
> This on my ring,
> This by my picture, in my book I write:
> Whether I sing,
> Or say, or dictate, this is my delight.

> Invention rest,
> Comparisons go play, wit use thy will:
> *Lesse then the least*
> *Of all Gods mercies,* is my posie still.

Herbert is not under attack in "The Posie." He too has ring, picture and book; he too has a verse to inscribe on them. Still, there is a difference: his posy is "not witty, . . . but Holy," as we are told elsewhere that a sermon should be.[13] And here too Herbert's answer to the world is a verse of Scripture.

Herbert's "posie" comes from an Old Testament passage where Jacob, afraid of his impending reunion with Esau, beseeches God's aid; the episode occurs just before he wrestles with an angel and is confirmed in his mission:

> And Jacob said, O God . . . I am not worthy of the least of all the mercies, and of all the trueth, which thou hast shewed unto thy servant: for with my staffe I passed over this Jordan, and now I am become two bands.
>
> (Gen. 32:9–10)

One can understand why this verse should have been of such consequence to Herbert. Here several of his recurrent themes come together: crossing the Jordan as a symbol of redemption, the servant's loving relationship to his master, thankfulness for God's abundant blessings, and most important, the sense of man's utter unworthiness and dependence on God.[14] We hear about this verse elsewhere. Ferrar in the preface to *The Temple* calls it Herbert's "own Motto, with which he used to conclude all things that might seem to tend any way to his own honour," and Walton (who may be simply embroidering on Ferrar's words) tells us that Herbert spoke the verse on his deathbed, when he delivered the "little Book" of his poems for Ferrar's approval: if the volume was found to

---

13. *A Priest to the Temple, Works,* 233.
14. Tuve, *A Reading,* 182–203. Tuve finds in the Jordan symbol a link between Herbert's poetic theory and his search for humility.

be of no use to others, he instructed Mr. Duncon, "let him burn it: for *I and it, are less than the least of God's mercies.*"[15]

A posy is a brief motto or line of verse inscribed on a ring or windowpane; in "Miserie" Herbert writes that "at first Man was . . . A ring, whose posie was, *My pleasure*" (67–69). G. H. Palmer provides some examples garnered from "old authors," including "Let us be one till we are none," "I would be glad if you I had," "Not too fast, but to last," "Once mine, always thine," "Thy death is mine, my life is thine."[16] Herbert's "posie" conflates "I am not worthy of the least . . ." with Paul's "lesse then the least of all Saints" (Eph. 3:8), elision and alliteration making the verse more compact and epigrammatic, that is, more like the typical posy. All the same, it is distinguished from the facile jingles cited by Palmer, where the outward form controls the meaning, by its unrhymed prose and slight metrical irregularity (no workman's tool hath touched the same) as well as by its pious sentiment.

In "The Posie," as in "The Quip," the biblical verse is presented as a self-evident truth, and there is no clash between the antagonists. Arnold Stein notices that a "strange force is developed by the poem's lack of a serious argument."[17] That force, I would suggest, depends precisely on the special weight that Herbert grants the biblical words. The lack of an argument asserts the authority of Scripture as beyond "contesting."

"The Quip" and "The Posie" reflect the concerns of the courtier, and "Divinitie," which we are about to consider, those of the cleric. Given the differences between these two worlds—the antipodes of Herbert's adult life—one is

15. "The Printers to the Reader," *Works*, 4–5; Walton, *Life*, 314 (italics reversed). Cf. chap. 4, n.14, on Walton's way of inventing speeches for Herbert.

16. George Herbert Palmer, ed., *The English Works of George Herbert*, 3 vols., 2d ed. (Boston, 1907), III, 28.

17. Stein, *Herbert's Lyrics*, 147.

struck by the similarity that Herbert discovers. The bustling exegetes of "Divinitie," like their secular brethren, alas, "cut and carve" with "the edge of wit" (7). Herbert addresses them with three scriptural injunctions that are among Jesus' most familiar words:

> *Love God, and love your neighbour. Watch and pray.*
> *Do as ye would be done unto.*
>
> (17–18)

This is a good Protestant answer: all we need to know is found in Scripture, and it is couched in language that any man, with the help of faith, can understand. Herbert underscores the directness of Jesus' words by the "handsome irony" (as Ryley calls it)[18] of the lines that follow: "O dark instructions; ev'n as dark as day! / Who can these Gordian knots undo?"

Each of the three injunctions is abridged in such a way as to point up its simple truth. *"Watch and pray"* is taken from Jesus' warnings to his disciples: "Watch and pray, that yee enter not into temptation: The spirit indeed is willing, but the flesh is weake" (Matt. 26:41); "Take ye heed, watch and pray: for ye know not when the time is [of the Second Coming]" (Mark 13:33). Quoted in this fashion, the phrase becomes a Christian rallying cry, like "Be strong, and of a good courage" in the Old Testament (Deut. 31:6, Josh. 1:6, etc.). The other two statements come from passages where Jesus sums up in a few words the substance of Old Testament Law. Herbert carries the process of condensation one step further, distilling Jesus' summaries in aphoristic form. *"Love God, and love your neighbour"* gives us the essence of Jesus' reply to the Pharisee lawyer: "Thou shalt love the Lord thy God with all thy heart, and with all thy soule, and with all thy minde. This is the first and great Commandement. And the second is like unto it, Thou shalt love thy neighbour

18. Ryley, "Herbert's Temple," 259.

as thy selfe. On these two Commandements hang all the Law and the Prophets" (Matt. 22:37–40, citing Deut. 6:5 and Lev. 19:18). *"Do as ye would be done unto"* makes an aphorism of a verse from the Sermon on the Mount: "Therefore all things whatsoever ye would that men should doe to you, doe ye even so to them: for this is the Law and the Prophets" (Matt. 7:12).

Many biblical maxims have been filed down in this fashion by popular usage: "Pride goeth before destruction: and an hautie spirit before a fall" (Prov. 16:18) yielded "Pride goeth before a fall"; "A mans heart deviseth his way: but the LORD directeth his steps" (Prov. 16:9) became "Man proposes, but God disposes"; "The love of money is the root of all evill" (1 Tim. 6:10) was reduced to "Money is the root of all evil."[19] Thus, in "Lent," *"Be holy ev'n as he"* (35) is abridged from Lev. 19:2: "Ye shalbe holy: for I the LORD your God am holy," and Matt. 5:48: "Be yee therefore perfect, even as your father, which is in heaven, is perfect." The purpose of such abridgments is to produce a form that can be more easily held in the memory, taken into one's life and used.[20]

But in "Divinitie" Herbert has an additional motive. He deliberately reduces Christianity to its first elements here—*love, watch, pray, do*—in order to mock the intellectual pride of the divines. Indeed the very impulse toward simplification is significant: the truth, we are made to see, is not diminished in the process, for in its very essence it is "cleare as heav'n," "not obscure" (14, 24). The Bible, as the Reformers argued, should be understood in its natural sense. Thus the simple clarity of these two lines is an integral part of their meaning. Finally, however, they are set apart not only by their style. What gives them their immense authority is that they are Jesus' own words, "the doctrine, which he taught" (13). They summon us

19. Cf. Archer Taylor, *The Proverb* (Cambridge, Mass., 1931; facs. rpt. 1962), 55.
20. See my discussion of proverbial wisdom in chap. 4.

with their imperatives to live a holy life, which Herbert
believes is the first step to understanding Scripture.

Herbert speaks as a poet rather than as a courtier or a
cleric in "Jordan, I" and "The Forerunners," but the
terms of the conflict remain the same: human wit opposed to the authority of Scripture. In "Jordan, I" the
opposition is externalized and the tone assured. Herbert
takes the offensive against a group of poets who are concerned with "fictions" rather than "truth"; "enchanted
groves," "sudden arbours" and "purling streams" give us
some notion of their style. For two stanzas he mocks
them roundly, pressing question upon question in an aggressive display of scorn. But then, in the final stanza, he
suddenly grows generous and expansive, proposing a
pact of mutual coexistence:

> Shepherds are honest people; let them sing:
> Riddle who list, for me, and pull for Prime:
> I envie no mans nightingale or spring;
> Nor let them punish me with losse of rime,
> Who plainly say, *My God, My King.*
>
> (11–15)

After the disdainful outburst about fictions and false hair,
one hardly expects to hear that "shepherds are honest
people"; much less the concessive, "let them sing"; and
least of all a biblical declaration of faith.

The final phrase, set off from the rest of the poem by
italics, echoes a formula of address that occurs in the
Psalter variously as "my King and my God" (Pss. 5:2,
84:3), "my God and king" (68:24) and "O God, my King"
(145:1). Herbert uses the formula again in "The Elixir" as
well as in "Antiphon, I," an imitation of a biblical hymn,
where it unmistakably points to the Psalms: "Let all the
world in ev'ry corner sing, / *My God and King.*" "Antiphon, I" comes just a few pages before "Jordan, I," alert-
ing us to the provenance of the phrase.

Nothing in "Jordan, I," aside from the allusive title,
prepares us for the biblical turn at the end. Coburn Freer

writes that "one difficulty in the rhetoric of the poem is that the speaker's own devotion consists of only one line; the rest is all attack and counterattack."[21] But that, I think, is precisely Herbert's intention. In poems like "The Pearl" and "The Collar," Herbert builds imbalanced structures, where the argument pivots on a couplet, a phrase, or even a single word at the very end, to mirror the disproportion of the opposing forces.[22] In a sense, such poems may be classified with his pattern poems, where the outward form literally enacts the meaning. In "Jordan, I," the very shape of the poem makes his point: God's Word more than balances all the empty wordiness of the "painted" poets. "Let them sing" has the force of "Let wits contest" in "The Posie." Noblesse oblige: the reason Herbert can afford to be so grandly concessive is that he speaks out of a conviction of superior strength.

In "The Quip," "The Posie," "Divinitie" and "Jordan, I," the Word of God easily carries its own weight against the pretensions of human speech; there is no struggle, and the emotions of the speaker are not engaged. The voices of the world are heard or imagined with varying degrees of detachment, but always from a position of advantage. In "The Forerunners," however, the situation is painfully different. The "lovely enchanting language" of the world is abandoning the speaker, much to his distress, and as "winter" approaches, he is left with only a verse of Scripture in his heart:

> The harbingers are come. See, see their mark;
> White is their colour, and behold my head.
> But must they have my brain? must they dispark
> Those sparkling notions, which therein were bred?
>   Must dulnesse turn me to a clod?
> Yet they have left me, *Thou art still my God.*

21. Coburn Freer, *Music for a King: George Herbert's Style and the Metrical Psalms* (Baltimore, 1972), 241.

22. See also "The Thanksgiving," "Redemption," "Affliction, I," "The Quidditie," "Deniall" and "The Crosse."

Good men ye be, to leave me my best room,
Ev'n all my heart, and what is lodged there:
I passe not, I, what of the rest become,
So *Thou art still my God*, be out of fear.

(1–10)

Here the Bible verse is not a stick to brandish at the world, but the last comfort of a suffering man, who clings to it with a desperate pathos.

Thou art . . . my God, like *Thou shalt answer, Lord, for me* and *My God, My King*, is a formula of trust and allegiance from the Psalms. Herbert has added "still," meaning "always, now as before" (as in *"Lesse then the least / Of all Gods mercies*, is my posie still"), partly to fill out the pentameter line, but also because the adverb gives emphasis to his avowal of faith. In a number of psalm complaints, the speaker, beset by his enemies, declares *Thou art my God* as an expression of confidence that God will save him.[23] The following passage comes from Psalm 31, a psalm Herbert often quotes:[24]

> I became a reproofe among all mine enemies, but specially among my neighbours: . . . .
> For I have heard the blasphemie of the multitude: and feare is on every side, while they conspire together against me, and take their counsaile to take away my life.
> But my hope hath beene in thee, O Lorde: I have said, Thou art my God.

(Ps. 31.13, 15–16)

---

23. Pss. 22:6–10, 140:4–6, 143:10. *Thou art my God* also occurs as an expression of thanksgiving for God's mercy (e.g., Pss. 63:1, 118:28) and as a declaration of covenantal loyalty (Hos. 2:23; cf. Zech. 13:9).

24. In addition to "The Forerunners," Herbert recalls Psalm 31 in "Longing," 21 (31:2: "Bow downe thine eare"); "Assurance," 35 (31:3: "bee thou my strong rocke, and the house of defence"); "Affliction, I," 65, and "Affliction, IV," 1–3 (31:14: "I am cleane forgotten, . . . I am become like a broken vessell"). Amy M. Charles notes, in *A Life of George Herbert* (Ithaca, 1977), 121, that Ps. 31 was one of two psalms Herbert was required to recite privately each day as canon of Lincoln Cathedral and prebendary of Leighton Ecclesia (the other being Ps. 32, one of the familiar Penitential Psalms); this may suggest why he draws upon it so frequently.

Calvin attests to the power of this verse in his commentary on Psalm 31:

> And surely this is the very true tryall of fayth, that though never so hideous waves rise ageinst us, and though never so sore assaultes shake us: yit we hold stil this stedfast ground that we are under gods tuition, and may freely say unto him, "Thou art our God."[25]

Calvin makes these words into a rock-and-tower for the believer: the very act of pronouncing "Thou art my God" confirms his faith.

In this act Herbert finds whatever consolation is possible for him. Finally, he gives up the sensual music he has cared for, and to all appearances still cares for—that is no country for old men—insisting he can bear his loss so long as the biblical verse remains safe in his heart:

> Yet if you go, I passe not; take your way:
> For, *Thou art still my God,* is all that ye
> Perhaps with more embellishment can say.
>
> (31–33)

All his poems, however "embellished," cannot say more than what is embodied in that stark biblical verse. The monosyllabic austerity of *Thou art still my God* stands over against a tempting sweetness of phrase ("sugar-cane, / Hony of roses," 19–20), representing the achieved simplicity of the mature artist, the simplicity of the Christian. It is as if, in his experience as poet, he had traversed the stages of sacred history, from the showy splendors of the ancient Temple, "all embellished / With flowers and carvings,"[26] to the bare room of the heart. The poem conveys very movingly the pain that is a necessary part of such growth. Finally, all that sustains the speaker is his will to believe in the power of the biblical verse.

In the poems I have just discussed, God's Word, im-

25. Calvin, *Psalmes,* pt. 1, fol. 114ᵥ, substituting quotation marks for the square brackets in the original.
26. "Sion," 4–5.

measurably more powerful than any human word, calls
into question the empty language of gallants, theologians
and poets, and we are made to acknowledge that "thy
word is all." For Herbert the implications of this truth are,
in the first instance, not "humiliating" but healing.[27] If
God's Word checks the pretensions of the prideful self, in
the very same poems it mends the eyes and salves the
spirit; it rescues, protects and sustains the believer in his
need. And the Word of God goes forth to do its work out
of the mouths of men: it is a human being, after all, who
invokes the Word and activates its more-than-human
powers.

Herbert gives man a larger role still in a group of
poems about "spelling the word" in the literal sense of
reading the Scriptures. In these poems, to which I now
turn, he is writing about not the authority of the Word
but rather the forms of human response.

ENTERING INTO THE TEXT: "MY WORDS"

The Book that holds such authority for Herbert and his
contemporaries is not always an open book. Although in
all essentials the Scriptures are "cleare as heav'n" ("Divinitie," 14), many passages are difficult—and not only
for the ordinary reader. Indeed Herbert raises this point
in his critical notes on Valdesso:

> The Authour doth still discover too slight a regard of the
> Scripture, as if it were but childrens meat, whereas there is
> not onely milke there, *but strong meat also. Heb.* 5.14. *Things
> hard to bee understood.* 2 *Pet.* 3.16. *Things needing great Consid-
> eration. Mat.* 24.15.[28]

The difficulty is compounded by man's sinfulness, which
impairs his understanding. Sin defiles more than the

---

27. "The Flower," 21. Fish, *Self-Consuming Artifacts*, 156: "Herbert's
poems characteristically ask us to experience the full force of this admis-
sion in all its humiliating implications."
28. "Briefe Notes on Valdesso's *Considerations*," *Works*, 317.

body: "It blots thy lesson written in thy soul; / The holy lines cannot be understood" ("The Church-porch," 9–10). Speaking as a churchman, Herbert feels his own inadequacy with particular keenness: "Lord, how can man preach thy eternall word? / He is a brittle crazie glasse" ("The Windows," 1–2); "I am both foul and brittle; much unfit / To deal in holy Writ" ("The Priesthood," 11–12).

Still, for all his anxieties, Herbert believes that the Bible will yield its truths to the reader who approaches it in the right way. In *A Priest to the Temple,* he enumerates the steps by which the parson should enter into the text. The first of these is "a holy Life," for the Scriptures "are not understood but with the same Spirit that writ them." Next, Herbert recommends prayer: the parson always begins "with some short inward ejaculation, as, *Lord, open mine eyes, that I may see the wondrous things of thy Law. &c.*" Only after this preacherly advice does he turn to what are today considered the standard professional procedures. The "third means" to understanding is a "diligent Collation of Scripture with Scripture," referred to in "The H. Scriptures, II." Since all the books of the Bible were "penn'd by one and the self-same Spirit," Herbert reasons, "an industrious, and judicious comparing of place with place must be a singular help for the right understanding of the Scriptures."[29] Finally, he advises the parson to consult the "Commenters and Fathers, who have handled the places controverted," suggesting that he have "one Comment at least upon every book of Scripture." In Herbert's view neither man's "brittleness" nor the inherent difficulty of Scripture absolve him from the necessity of confronting the text, for in this, as in all else, he can rely on the help of God to eke out his poor resources; indeed, "he doth not so study others, as to neglect the grace of God in himself, and what the Holy Spirit teacheth him." The chapter ends on a confident

29. See chap. 2 on collation.

note: "ploughing with this, and his own meditations, he enters into the secrets of God treasured in the holy Scripture."[30]

Believing that what he finds in the Bible intensely concerns him, Herbert brings to his study of the text that minute attention with which we examine ourselves in the mirror, that absorption with which we read whatever is written about us: it is his mirror, his story. One imagines Herbert reading the Bible with the same passionate involvement that Augustine recounts, the same warmth of feeling and readiness to be moved:

> What cries I sent up unto thee, my God, whenas I read the Psalms of David; . . . Oh, how was I inflamed towards thee by them! . . . I quaked for fear, and boiled again with hope and with rejoicing in thy mercy, O Father.[31]

Herbert's faith enables him to enter into the text, to witness, as it were, the events of biblical history:

> Faith makes me any thing, or all
> That I beleeve is in the sacred storie:
> And where sinne placeth me in Adams fall,
> Faith sets me higher in his glorie.
>
> If I go lower in the book,
> What can be lower then the common manger?
> Faith puts me there with him, who sweetly took
> Our flesh and frailtie, death and danger.
>   ("Faith," 17–24)

Present at the Creation, he overhears a thoughtful Creator deliberating as he pours blessings on man ("The Pulley"); like the shepherds he offers a song for Christ's Nativity ("Christmas"); he arrives just in time to hear Christ's last words from the cross—addressed to him ("Redemption"). In the second part of "Easter," his faith makes him an active participant. Herbert begins by describing how he

30. *A Priest to the Temple, Works,* 228–29.
31. Augustine, *The Confessions,* trans. William Watts [1631], Loeb Classical Library, 2 vols. (London, 1912), II, 17, 19 (bk. IX, chap. 4).

prepared his church for Easter morning; as he writes in *A Priest to the Temple,* the parson's church should be "at great festivalls strawed, and stuck with boughs":[32]

> I got me flowers to straw thy way;
> I got me boughs off many a tree.
>
> (19–20)

At the same time, we discover, he is echoing the gospel account of Jesus' entry into Jerusalem: "And a very great multitude spread their garments in the way, others cut downe *branches* from the *trees,* and *strawed* them in the *way*" (Matt. 21:8, my italics). We may think of Herbert as painting himself into the biblical scene, much as Rembrandt, for example, does in the *Elevation* and the *Descent from the Cross* (1633).

Herbert's poems, to put it another way, are constructed in the space between the Bible and the believer. The poems on Old Testament subjects—"Sion," "Aaron," "The Bunch of Grapes" and some others—are a special case by virtue of their concern with typology.[33] The four poems in which Herbert takes his title from the New Testament, three from the Epistles and one from the Gospels, reveal more immediately, each in its own way, his recognition that the text "means" him.[34] These poems give us not just "doctrine" but "doctrine and life."

Writing about Scripture, Herbert sets before us the mind and heart of the Christian who reads and interprets. Precisely where we might expect to find the self humbled

---

32. *A Priest to the Temple, Works,* 246.
33. See chap. 3 on typology in *The Temple.*
34. The only explicitly biblical poem where Herbert does not paint himself, so to speak, in the corner of the canvas is "Marie Magdalene," which is based on Luke 7:36–50. The application of the text is phrased in the plural here ("Though we could dive / In tears like seas, our sinnes are pil'd / Deeper then they, in words, and works, and thoughts," 10–12) and, for all its earnestness, lacks the stamp of lively *personal* involvement that otherwise distinguishes Herbert's use of biblical materials.

and subordinated, we find it instead vigorously at work and conscious of its own motions in bringing the text to life. Herbert paraphrases or adapts the text to suit his purpose—much more freely than in the poems just discussed—and clearly enjoys taking such liberties with the sacred Word. The delighted play of the mind, so characteristic of *The Temple*, belies Stanley Fish's picture of Herbert, martyrlike, building his poetry into a pyre of self-immolation. In Herbert's poetry the self is not effaced but improved. The poems we shall now be considering are by no means "self-consuming"; one might even call them self-absorbed, with the proviso that the self is always seen in its relation to God.

In his choice and handling of texts, Herbert follows his own advice about preaching, that the proper "character" of the sermon may be attained

> first, by choosing texts of Devotion, not Controversie, moving and ravishing texts, whereof the Scriptures are full. Secondly, by dipping, and seasoning all our words and sentences in our hearts, before they come into our mouths, truly affecting, and cordially expressing all that we say; so that the auditors may plainly perceive that every word is hart-deep.[35]

The New Testament poems fit this description particularly well. They are all based on "moving and ravishing texts": the Holy Spirit grieves for us, our life is hid in Christ, we may be a sweet savor to God, we may purchase the kingdom of heaven. It is important to notice, however, that these poems about texts do not follow Herbert's precepts for "handling" a text:

> The Parsons Method in handling of a text consists of two parts; first, a plain and evident declaration of the meaning of the text; and secondly, some choyce Observations drawn out of the whole text, as it lyes entire, and unbroken in the Scripture it self.[36]

---

35. *A Priest to the Temple, Works*, 233.
36. Ibid., 234–35.

Now of course Herbert's poems about biblical verses are poems and not sermons, but these poems make a point of being unsermonlike. What they present is not "a plain and evident declaration of the meaning of the text," but rather the believer in the act of embracing it.

Herbert characteristically enters the text by way of the personal pronoun, as in "The Call," where he answers Jesus' challenge—"I am the Way, the Trueth, and the Life: no man commeth unto the Father but by mee" (John 14:6)—by extending an invitation: "Come, my Way, my Truth, my Life." In the Gospels it is Jesus who commands, "Come unto me" (Matt. 11:28), "Come and follow me" (19:21), "Follow mee" (4:19, 9:9, etc.). By addressing Jesus with his own imperative—"Come"—and by changing "the way" into "my Way," he is doing what is required of the reader of the Bible: taking it personally. Reading the text in the right way means reading oneself into the text.

This is precisely what happens in "Ephes. 4.30." In Paul's Epistle the Ephesians are called upon to "put off . . . the olde man" and "put on [the] new man": to avoid bitterness and malice, and renewed in spirit, to become tenderhearted, forgiving and kind (Eph. 4:22–32); the entire passage (one would never guess it from Herbert's poem) is filled with a sense of energetic purpose. Paul's admonition "And grieve not the holy Spirit of God, whereby yee are sealed unto the day of redemption" (4:30) is addressed in the plural and given no particular emphasis in its context, but Herbert fastens upon it, taking it to heart: "Grieved for me?" That marvelous "me?" is the kind of response, one imagines, that Paul would have wished to elicit from those who read his Epistles. It is, in fact, precisely the kind of response that Calvin thought appropriate. The metaphor of the Holy Spirit grieving, Calvin writes, is intended

> too put us too shame, and too make the heare too stand up
> upon our heads. Behold (sayeth Saint Paule), Gods spirit

hath chozen his dwelling place in us, (according as it is sayd
in another place, that not only our soules, but also our
bodyes are the temples of the holy Ghoste) and he is glad too
bee in us, and too abyde there, and too make it his continuall
home: nowe then if wee fall too spyting of him, as though we
mynded to chace him and banish him from us, is it not too
divelish a dealing?[37]

Herbert, reading Paul's words, is excited by the notion
that God grieves for him, "worm" though he is:

And art thou grieved, sweet and sacred Dove,
      When I am sowre,
      And crosse thy love?
Grieved for me? the God of strength and power
      Griev'd for a worm, which when I tread,
      I passe away and leave it dead?

                                  (1–6)

The opening "And" (no other poem begins in this way)
functions logically to connect Herbert's questions with
Paul's verse quoted in the subtitle; it prompts us to go
back and look at the verse again, and thus has the effect
of placing us, for a moment, with Herbert in the act of
reading Scripture. But what for us may be just a sequence
of words is for Herbert a source of astonishment: "Can it
really be that God is grieved by my 'sowre' behavior?"

The three questions of the first stanza, with their insistent repetition of "grieve," convey his sense of baffled
wonder. Paul's figure for God's loving attention gives him
a new dignity in his own eyes, a dignity he did not know
he had, and a concomitant obligation. Understanding the
biblical verse in its most radical sense—"You must change
your life"—he sentences himself to endless grief, a tear
for a tear. The poem seems to modern taste an extrava-
gant lament like "Grief," part of that "literature of tears"
which, as Louis Martz says, "flooded Europe during the

37. *The Sermons of M. John Calvin upon the Epistle of S. Paule too the
Ephesians*, trans. Arthur Golding (London, 1577), fol. 231.

sixteenth and seventeenth centuries."[38] But in starting
from the verse in Ephesians, Herbert has given the subject his own distinctive emphasis: his poem is not simply
about tears but about man's need to answer God's love,
however inadequate his response may be.

If "Ephes. 4.30" is meant to sound like a spontaneous
cry of the heart, "Coloss. 3.3" is a kind of verbal mon-
strance, carefully fashioned to enshrine Paul's teaching.
Herbert's text is taken from the Epistle for Easter Day,
which reads in part:

> If yee then bee risen with Christ, seeke those things which
> are above, where Christ sitteth on the right hand of God:
> Set your affection on things above, not on things on the
> earth.
> For yee are dead, and your life is hid with Christ in God.
> When Christ, who is our life, shall appeare, then shall yee
> also appeare with him in glorie.

(Col. 3:1–4)

Both in the subtitle and in the italicized verse that is set
obliquely in the poem, Herbert departs from the text in
order to enter it more fully. In the subtitle Herbert tran-
scribes the Apostle's "your" as "our" (cf. Col. 3:4): *"Our
life is hid with Christ in God."* And then, in the first line, he
changes the pronoun again, this time to "my": *"My Life Is
Hid In Him, That Is My Treasure"*:[39]

> *My* words & thoughts do both express this notion,
> That *Life* hath with the sun a double motion.
> The first *Is* straight, and our diurnall friend,

38. Martz, *Poetry of Meditation*, 199. On Herbert's complex relation
to this tradition, see Richard Strier, "Herbert and Tears," *ELH* 46 (1979):
221–47.

39. According to Aubrey he had *"My life is hid with Christ in God"*
painted "at his Wive's Seate" in church (*Aubrey's Brief Lives*, ed. Oliver
Lawson Dick [London, 1949], 137). It would be interesting to know that
Herbert took this same liberty with a text painted in his church, but
Aubrey's evidence, like Walton's, is not to be trusted; he is aware that
Herbert "hath verses on this Text in his Poëms," and he may have cited
the verse in this form precisely because of his memory of "Coloss. 3.3."

The other *Hid* and doth obliquely bend.
One life is wrapt *In* flesh, and tends to earth:
The other winds towards *Him*, whose happie birth
Taught me to live here so, *That* still one eye
Should aim and shoot at that which *Is* on high:
Quitting   with   daily   labour   all *My* pleasure,
To   gain   at   harvest   an   eternall *Treasure.*

Herbert might have left the Apostle's "your"—rhythmic considerations play no part here. He might also have used "our," as he does in the poem's subtitle, a possibility he may have actually entertained: the plural "our" in line 3, which does not agree with the singular pronouns in lines 1, 7 and 9, may be a remnant of an earlier stage of the poem. Instead, he responds to Paul's text by rephrasing it in the first person singular. This is the most obvious expression of a process by which the believer makes the biblical text his own.

In the Epistle this verse is surrounded by the imperatives of the new life—"Set your affection on things above," "Mortifie therefore your members which are upon the earth"—and addressed to those who have "put off the old man with his deedes" and have "put on the new man" (Col. 3:2, 5, 9–10). Herbert's speaker acknowledges Paul's challenge. Christ's "happie birth" does not absolve him of moral effort; rather, it teaches him to "aim and shoot . . . on high," "quitting" his earthly pleasure "with daily labour." By altering the biblical text, substituting "my" for Paul's "your," he is responding directly to the Apostle's exhortation, saying "Amen."

Hence I cannot agree with Stanley Fish's reading of the poem as "asserting simultaneously the loss of the self and the finding of its greater glory in a union with divinity." While it is true that the reader is "involved in a double motion," it does not follow that his "attention is gradually drawn away from the first-person voice" or that "in the end the hidden word is triumphant and the personal pronoun is dismissed along with all its pleasure." Fish's quasi-mystical interpretation—"the poet loses himself," "the speaker's voice becomes indistinguishable from that of God's"—depends on his assumption that the first word of the poem, "*My*," "belongs not to the speaker's words and thoughts, as the line apparently asserts, but to the (literally) revealed word"; in his reading, "the poem is acknowledged to be God's from the very beginning."[40] In fact, as we have seen, "*My*" does not belong to the revealed word at all, but rather to Herbert's deliberate restatement of it.

Now, there is nothing sinful about the personal pronoun. To be sure, the prideful self, which aggressively or ingenuously sets itself in opposition to God, is consistently rebuked, as we have just seen. But Herbert never abandons his belief that man is a vessel "of lowly matter for high uses meet"[41] which, when filled with God's presence, may become a temple. When the believer's "I" serves as a vessel for God—or for God's Word—it need not be suppressed, for it is fulfilling its true function. In "Coloss. 3.3" Herbert does not "lose himself" in God's words but, quite the contrary, finds the true meaning of those words—and the hidden meaning of his life as well—when he rephrases them as a first-person statement. Nor is there anything remotely prideful about such an action: it is, indeed, a model for man's proper response to Scripture.

The personal pronoun is conspicuous again in "The Odour," where the phrase *My Master* is savored for its sweetness. That phrase, according to Nicholas Ferrar, was often on Herbert's lips:

> To testifie his independencie upon all others, and to quicken his diligence in this kinde, he used in his ordinarie

40. Fish, *Self-Consuming Artifacts*, 206, 203–4, 205.
41. "The Priesthood," 35.

speech, when he made mention of the blessed name of our Lord and Saviour Jesus Christ, to adde, *My Master.*[42]

In the Gospels Christ is called (and calls himself) "Master"—"My Master" is the literal translation of Mary Magdalene's *"Rabboni"* (John 20:16)—and many of the parables and sayings are concerned with the proper relations of master and servant.[43] At one level "The Odour" may be construed as a personal response to the texts about masters and the Master.

The main action of the poem is to connect these passages with the text of the title. Herbert compares the sound of *My Master,* and by extension the joy of serving Christ, to an "odour," an "orientall fragrancie."[44] Images of fragrant sweetness suffuse the poem, calling to mind the Song of Songs: "Because of the savour of thy good ointments, thy name is as ointment powred forth" (1:3; cf. 4:10–16, 5:13). But Herbert's reference to Corinthians is at once more complex and more playful. In 2 Cor. 2:15— "For wee are unto God, a sweet savour of Christ"—Paul compares those who preach the gospel, spreading the "savour" of the knowledge of God, to sacrificial incense. The expression "sweet savour" (Heb. *reaḥ niḥoaḥ*) is a technical term that occurs frequently in the books of Leviticus and Numbers: "a burnt sacrifice, an offering made by fire, of a sweet savour unto the LORD" (Lev. 1:9). This is an image of divine approbation; "And the LORD

---

42. "The Printers to the Reader," *Works,* 4. Herbert uses *master* in this sense also in "Affliction, I," 64; "Love unknown," 62; "The Church-porch," 443; and "To all Angels and Saints," 30.

43. E.g., Matt. 22:36, 23:8, John 13:13; Matt. 10:24–25, 24:45–51, 25:14–30, Luke 17:7–10.

44. Garret Keizer, in "Fragrance, 'Marie Magdalene,' and Herbert's *The Temple,*" *George Herbert Journal* 4 (1980): 29–50, notes that "the human ability to please God is often expressed in the Bible through an image of fragrance," citing in addition Lev. 26:31, Ps. 141:2, Amos 5:21, Luke 7:38, John 12:3 and Rev. 5:8 (p. 31). See also Keizer's remarks on "the ubiquitous word 'sweet,'" "the idea of a fragrant worship" and "the human capacity for action" (pp. 32, 38).

smelled a sweete savour" (Gen. 8:21), for example, brings to a happy ending the episode of the Deluge. In the New Testament, the image comes to typify Christ's free gift of himself: "And walke in love, as Christ also hath loved us, and hath given himselfe for us, an offering and a sacrifice to God for a sweet smelling savour" (Eph. 5:2). Behind each of these biblical texts is the ancient image of God with flaring nostrils.

Herbert responds to this verse by turning it on its head—or rather, on its nose. In the first two stanzas, he boldly reverses the biblical figure so that it is he, not God, who is breathing incense; these lines plainly say, "For Christ is unto me a sweet savour":

How sweetly doth *My Master* sound! *My Master!*
As Amber-greese leaves a rich sent
Unto the taster:
So do these words a sweet content,
An orientall fragrancie, *My Master.*

With these all day I do perfume my minde,
My minde ev'n thrust into them both:
That I might finde
What cordials make this curious broth,
This broth of smells, that feeds and fats my minde.

(1–10)

Although Herbert uses a phrase that belongs to God, we are not troubled by any suggestion of blasphemy; this is, rather, an instance of "lover's license."[45]

Having declared his heart, Herbert invites Christ to enjoy his own "spicinesse" in the third stanza, invoking the

45. Herbert appropriates God's words in a similar fashion at the end of "The Quidditie," where the speaker defines poetry as "that which while I use / I am with thee" (11–12). In the Old Testament, God often comforts man with these words, saying, for example, to Isaac, "Feare not, for I am with thee, and will blesse thee" (Gen. 26:24; cf. Isa. 41:10, 43:5; Jer. 1:8, 1:19), and man echoes God's phrase as a confession of faith: "I will feare no evill: for thou art with me" (Ps. 23:4). In the New Testament, the risen Christ repeats this expression to his disciples (Matt. 28:20) and to Paul (Acts 18:10).

verse for the first time in its true sense. Even here one feels
a certain playful audacity. His tone is properly deferential
("O that to thee / *My servant* were a little so, / As flesh may
be," 11–13), but the arguments he advances are, after all,
mutual self-interest and his own "employment":

> This breathing would with gains by sweetning me
> (As sweet things traffick when they meet)
> Return to thee.
> And so this new commerce and sweet
> Should all my life employ and busie me.
>
> (26–30)

There is no question of reciprocity—Christ is Master, and
he is servant—but a poor lover may permit himself such
liberties when he knows that he is loved. One cannot
help noticing the delight with which Herbert adapts the
verse from Corinthians to his bantering expression of
love. This is one example of his freedom in the handling
of biblical texts—a subject to which we will return later in
some detail.[46]

"The Pearl. Matth. 13.45" is distinguished from the
three poems we have just looked at in that the speaker is
not just a representative Christian but Herbert himself,
the learned and courtly scion of a great family. The title of
the poem refers to one of the most familiar of the parables
about the Kingdom of Heaven: "Againe, the kingdome of
heaven is like unto a marchant man, seeking goodly
pearles: Who when hee had found one pearle of great
price, he went and solde all that he had, and bought it."
Calvin explains "the simple meaning of the wordes": "the
Gospel hath not the honour due to it, except we preferre
it above all the riches, delightes, honours and commodities of the world."[47]

---

46. See my discussion of Herbert's "transformations" in chap. 2.
47. *A harmonie upon the Three Evangelistes, Matthewe, Marke, and Luke,
with the Commentarie of M. John Calvine,* trans. E. P. [Eusebius Paget],
(London, 1584), fol. 365.

Herbert, reading "marchant," says "me" again. The story he tells here is clearly his own, but it is refracted through a vocabulary of profit and loss—"stock and surplus," "quick returns," "projects of unbridled store," "main sale," "commodities," "rate and price"—that gives us the very jargon of the merchant. An experienced man of the world who knows how to value his assets, he tallies up a businesslike inventory of "all that he had" and frankly weighs it in the balance against God's love. "The Pearl," then, is a poem of the divided self, in which the speaker is faced with a choice between God and the world.[48]

The merchant of the parable chooses without hesitation—or so it appears; the parable, like most biblical narrative, moves swiftly to the point of the action, leaving a great deal to the imagination of the reader.[49] The brisk verbal sequence *found-sold-bought,* which has the ring of *veni vidi vici,* makes the choice seem almost too easy. "The Pearl" enlarges upon these few lines of Scripture as retellings of biblical stories typically do, fleshing out the bare action with a complexity of motives, of inner tensions. Herbert's speaker admits that he is often troubled by the seeming disproportion of the alternatives that face him: "my senses live, / And grumble oft, that they have more in me / Then he that curbs them, being but one to five" (27–29). But he too finally knows the value of "one"—or rather, "One." The shapes of Herbert's stanzas make that point graphically. We have already noted, in the discussion of "Jordan, I," how Herbert invents a

48. Herbert presents that choice, as Tuve notices ("*Caritas,*" 320 n. 16), in terms that resemble 1 John 2:15–16: "Love not the world, neither the things that are in the world. . . . For all that is in the world, the lust of the flesh, the lust of the eyes, and the pride of life, is not of the Father, but is of the world."

49. On biblical narrative see especially Erich Auerbach, *Mimesis: The Representation of Reality in Western Literature,* trans. Willard Trask (1953; rpt. New York, 1957), 1–19, and Robert Alter, *The Art of Biblical Narrative* (New York, 1981).

variety of forms to convey the tension of opposing forces. But nowhere else in *The Temple* do we find such an extreme disproportion. Ten packed pentameter lines, piling example upon example, are offset by a two-foot bob: "Yet I love thee." The value of the speaker's entire inventory is outweighed each time in that terse refrain.

In the poem, as in the parable, the best that the world has to offer cannot match the worth of the "pearl"—and the merchant himself knows it. The ironic contrast of "I know all these" and "my groveling wit" in the final stanza is one measure of the speaker's self-understanding, not the poet's judgment on his ignorance: he himself is acknowledging, "with open eyes," his dependence on God. Nor is there any evidence in the poem that this wisdom is thrust upon him against his will. Fish suggests that the speaker's piety is "a thinly disguised form of pride," and that his refrain is "self-congratulatory": " 'Yet *I* love thee.' "[50] Rosemond Tuve, more justly, reads this line as a disclosure of motive: " 'Yet I *love* thee' ";[51] the most obvious and natural reading, logically and metrically, is "Yet I love *thee*."

In "The Pearl" Herbert is concerned with understanding both Jesus' parable and his own life. Why should a man be moved to give up "all that he had" for a single "pearl," no matter how valuable? Might not such an action seem foolish, perhaps even at times in his own eyes? "Such are thy secrets," Herbert writes in "The H. Scriptures, II" (9–10), "which my life makes good, / And com-

50. Fish, *Self-Consuming Artifacts*, 178. The speaker, in Fish's view, is also guilty of misreading Scripture: "And, worst of all, he misinterprets the parable of the Pearl, making himself the purchaser of the kingdom of heaven and forgetting that the great price and rate has been paid not by him, but by Christ. (It is we who have been bought and he is the buyer.)" Misled perhaps by the word "price," Fish confuses Paul's figure of the Redemption ("yee are bought with a price," 1 Cor. 6:20, 7:23) with Christ's teaching about the kingdom of heaven. The opening words of the parable make its subject clear.
51. Tuve, "*Caritas*," 320.

ments on thee." "The Pearl" illustrates the notion that a human life may comment on a text, helping (in Calvin's words) to expound its inward meanings. Approaching the parable through the "commentary" of his own experience, Herbert shows what Jesus' poetic fiction means in specific human terms: what choices are implied, what kinds of sacrifice. At the same time, the parable helps the speaker to fathom the mysterious impulses that have governed him and made his life what it is. "Thy words do finde me out, & parallels bring, / And in another make me understood" ("The H. Scriptures, II," 11–12): "another" here is Jesus' figure of the "marchant man," who in giving up everything for a treasure of surpassing value provides a precedent, a sanction, for the believer. By enlarging upon the situation of the merchant in terms that we recognize as autobiographical, Herbert shows again how "thy words" and "my life" explain each other, how "doctrine" and "life" are one.

I would like to summarize what I have been saying about scriptural authority and the Christian's response by looking at the ending of "The Crosse," perhaps Herbert's most painful poem. As Helen Vendler shows, the resolution of the poem begins in the penultimate stanza, where Herbert turns from baiting God to confront his own temperamental disability, that carping nature that always feels most keenly its own deprivations:[52]

> To have my aim, and yet to be
> Further from it then when I bent my bow;
> To make my hopes my torture, and the fee
>   Of all my woes another wo,
> Is in the midst of delicates to need,
> And ev'n in Paradise to be a weed.

$$(25–30)$$

But the poem does not end with this insight, enlightening though it is. Self-knowledge is not enough to free him

52. Vendler, *Poetry of Herbert*, 266–67.

from the burden of self, though it prepares him to accept
the relief that awaits his turn of the head:

> Ah my deare Father, ease my smart!
> These contrarieties crush me: these crosse actions
> Doe winde a rope about, and cut my heart:
> And yet since these thy contradictions
> Are properly a crosse felt by thy Sonne,
> With but foure words, my words, *Thy will be done.*
>
> (31–36)

"*Thy will be done,*" that somber, resonant phrase, has the
effect of resolving the "contrarieties" and "contradictions" that the speaker suffers by setting them in the context of Christ's Passion. This resolution comes as no surprise to the reader, even aside from the poem's title, since
Christ's prayer in Gethsemane—"O my father, if this cup
may not passe away from me, except I drinke it, thy will
be done" (Matt. 26:42)—lies behind the stanza from first
to last, and much of the language of the stanza alludes to
the crucifixion. In pronouncing "*Thy will be done,*" as in
repeating "*Thou shalt answer, Lord, for me,*" or "*Thou art
still my God,*" the speaker finds if not the healing he
seeks, then at least the promise of relief. When Vendler
writes that "the last lines of *The Crosse* . . . come suddenly, almost too suddenly to erase the earlier bitterness,"[53] she does not acknowledge the authority that the
biblical verse holds for Herbert. The seeming disproportion is deliberate: four words of Scripture, Christ's words,
more than balance all the stanzas of complaint.

On the other hand, one cannot ignore the way in
which the phrase "my words" is placed just before the
words of Christ. That insertion, or rather assertion, is
entirely characteristic of Herbert, and it seems to me crucial to the sense and movement of the line. Fish's view
that the speaker "finds himself by totally losing himself," that the poem ends with "the disappearance . . .

53. Ibid., 267. Cf. Freer on "Jordan, I," *Music for a King*, 241.

of the first-person voice,"[54] denies the poignant force of those two words, "my words." I resist the implications that Fish draws from this and other poems: "the pressure exerted by the insight 'Thy word is all' is relentless and in the end it leaves him no room at all."[55] For in the last line of "The Crosse" Herbert does not present God's doctrine in all its absoluteness, all its exacting authority; he presents a human being speaking God's Word, bringing it to life by living it. The man who pronounces "*Thy will be done*" has a "glorious and transcendent place": he is a window in God's temple, with Christ's life shining through him.[56]

At this point we may pause to note one of the major problems of recent Herbert criticism: what value Herbert places on the self in his poetry. Fish sees the self as reduced to nothing before God; Vendler conceives of a God reinvented in the image of the self. Fish speaks of Herbert's poems as characteristically "self-consuming," whereas Vendler writes that the "self-abasement" of the "early poems" is replaced by "self-acceptance" in "all the greatest of [the] late poems."[57] It is not surprising that these views are so opposed, for each tells, I think, only one side of the story; neither sees the relations of man and God in *The Temple* with the full depth and complexity of Herbert's vision.

In "The Crosse" Herbert shows how that clamorous unhappy creature, a human being, can move toward resolving the "contrarieties" that beset him. Herbert believes that man, trusting only to his own resources, cannot take a single step in the direction of the good. But neither will God do man's work. With God's help it is man who stirs, who grows, who "aims at thee,"[58] Herbert

54. Fish, *Self-Consuming Artifacts*, 188–89.
55. Ibid., 191.
56. "The Windows," 4–5, 7.
57. Fish, *Self-Consuming Artifacts*, 223; Vendler, *Poetry of Herbert*, 231ff., 161.
58. "Longing," 38.

writes, in poems that make plain the value and significance of human experience. What we find at the heart of Herbert's poetry is not the specter of God cornering the sinner into submission, nor, alternatively, that contemporary vision of the spirit freeing itself to untrammeled self-realization, but rather the image of the believer confronting, assimilating, and speaking the Word of God in his human and fallible existence. When "thy words" are made "my words," as so often in *The Temple*, when they are taken off the printed page and admitted to the heart, they do not obliterate the self but rather free it to fulfill its high purpose—as God's own creature.

· 2 ·

The Rhetoric of Allusion

CONSTELLATIONS: "SO IN ONE WORD"

The Bible is a "book of starres" in "The H. Scriptures, II,"
and Herbert a stargazer of no mean ambition. He yearns
to understand each shining verse and beyond that the
large formations that light up its sky:

> Oh that I knew how all thy lights combine,
>   And the configurations of their glorie!
>   Seeing not onely how each verse doth shine,
> But all the constellations of the storie.
>
> (1–4)

This is not a simple undertaking. To read the Bible as
Herbert wishes to read it requires more than wishing.
Only a trained observer can look up at that sky and see
not a bewilderment of stars but, in Herbert's image, "constellations."

The sacred text that we call "the Bible" (from the Greek
ta biblia, "the books," significantly a plural noun) is an
anthology of sixty-six books, composed over more than a
millenium. Against the centrifugal force of so many books,
so many centuries, stands the presumption of its essential
unity. The Bible asks to be read as a single work. Its diverse
parts are held together by one great theme—the relations
of God and man. And its very words call out for connection. The later books of the Old Testament allude to the
earlier ones, and the New Testament authors frequently
recall the Old; hence many words have a range of meanings acquired in the course of centuries and extending over

46

both Testaments. Some carry over their meanings intact from the one to the other, or accumulate new meanings that conspicuously enlarge the old; in some cases the new meaning is opposed to the old with the full force of the difference between the two Testaments.

From the language of the Bible, with its networks of inner correspondences, Herbert has fashioned his poems. A single word of Scripture may summon to mind a number of related passages, each with its own train of associations, its nuances and implications. The concision and resonance of Herbert's poetry owes a great deal to the specific density of his biblical vocabulary. I can best illustrate this point by looking closely at a number of "constellations" that appear in his poems.

Dust, which occurs so often in *The Temple,* naturally calls to mind the biblical account of man's creation and fall.[1] Dust is man's once and future state: "And the LORD God formed man of the dust of the ground"; "for dust thou art, and unto dust shalt thou returne" (Gen. 2:7, 3:19). Even within the pages of the Old Testament *dust* becomes a literary topos. Abraham, excusing his boldness, alludes to Genesis: "Behold now, I have taken upon me to speake unto the LORD, which am but dust and ashes" (Gen. 18:27). So too does Job, demanding justice: "Remember, I beseech thee, that thou hast made me as the clay, and wilt thou bring me into dust againe?" (10:9), and the psalmist, bargaining for his life: "Shall the dust give thankes unto thee?" (Ps. 30:10).

Dust, then, speaks of man as God's creature, of his helplessness, his unworthiness, his mortality. Herbert believes that to be a man is to be "guiltie of dust" ("Love,

---

1. Cf. Mario A. Di Cesare and Rigo Magnani, *A Concordance to the Complete Writings of George Herbert* (Ithaca, 1977). *Dust* occurs thirty-five times (and *dustie* once) in *The Temple* and only three times in *A Priest to the Temple*—an odd proportion, suggesting that for Herbert *dust* is a "poetic" word. (Two of the three uses in *A Priest to the Temple* are intended literally and have no biblical overtones.)

III," 2). When he calls himself *dust* in a petition to God, he is, in a word, pleading guilty and begging for mercy:

> But I am frailtie, and already dust;
> > O do not grinde me!
> > > ("Sighs and Grones," 17–18)

> > Put me not to shame,
> > Because I am
> Thy clay that weeps, thy dust that calls.
> > > ("Complaining," 3–5)

The image of dust focuses for him the pathos of mortality, and the outrageousness of God's testing, or worse, ignoring him:

> Wilt thou meet arms with man, that thou dost stretch
> > A crumme of dust from heav'n to hell?
> > > ("The Temper, I," 13–14)

> > O that thou shouldst give dust a tongue
> > > To crie to thee,
> And then not heare it crying!
> > > ("Deniall," 16–18)

Herbert sets the dust in motion, visualizing its physical properties, in order to express what it feels like to be totally dependent on God. Man may "fall with dust" ("The Temper, I," 25), yet dust can be blown about, dust can rise:

> > Behold, thy dust doth stirre,
> > It moves, it creeps, it aims at thee:
> > > Wilt thou deferre
> > > To succour me,
> > Thy pile of dust, wherein each crumme
> > > Sayes, Come?
> > > > ("Longing," 37–42)

In the very boldness of his address, we hear the voice of Job and the psalmist.

While dust as a symbol of the human condition occurs only in the Old Testament,[2] *rest* is a word that grows

---

2. In the New Testament *dust* appears in the expressions "to shake off the dust of the feet," (Matt. 10:14), "to throw dust into the air" (Acts 22:23), and "to cast dust on the head" (Rev. 18:19).

steadily in resonance from the Old Testament to the New. *Rest* is the gift of God the Creator: God himself "rested on the seventh day from all his worke" (Heb. *vayishbot*, Gen. 2:2), and he blessed and sanctified the Sabbath for man and beast: "Sixe dayes thou shalt doe thy worke, and on the seventh day thou shalt rest" (Ex. 23:12). The *rest* of the Sabbath day commemorates not only the work of Creation but also the liberation from slavery in Egypt (Ex. 20:8–11, Deut. 5:12–15). In the Deuteronomic history, *rest* symbolizes the end of wandering, settlement in the promised land, and respite from war: the Lord "giveth you rest from all your enemies round about, so that ye dwell in safety" (Heb. verbal root, *nwḥ*, Deut. 12:10). This sense is implicit in Solomon's words at the dedication of the Temple: "Blessed be the LORD, that hath given rest unto his people Israel" (Heb. *menuḥah*, verbal root *nwḥ*, 1 Kings 8:56), or in the psalmist's "Turne againe then unto thy rest, O my soule" (Ps. 116:7). Jesus' invitation, "Come unto me all yee that labour, and are heavy laden, and I will give you rest" (Gk. *anapauo*, Matt. 11:28), or Paul's assurance, "For we which have beleeved do enter into rest" (Gk. *katapausis*, Heb. 4:3; cf. Ps. 95:11) presuppose these Old Testament accretions of meaning. Herbert uses the word with its full symbolic weight. Knowing the biblical sources, we can see why *rest* is paired with "thy way" in "The H. Communion" (9) and with "life" in "Aaron" (4); why the pun on *rest* is crucial to the resolution of "The Pulley" (10, 16) and "The Answer" (14); why "Evensong" ends "in this love, more then in bed, I rest"; and why "Trinitie Sunday" culminates in the prayer, "That I may runne, rise, rest with thee."

Because the second half of the Bible is devoted to the systematic reinterpretation of the first, many words are significantly altered when they cross the great divide between the two Testaments. "Search the Scriptures," Jesus instructs his disciples; "they . . . testifie of me" (John 5:39). *Lamb* is an Old Testament word that takes on a new

dimension of meaning when it testifies of Christ. John's
"Lambe of God" (1:29) looks back to Gen. 22:8: "God will
provide himselfe a lambe." Peter's image of Christ as "a
Lambe without blemish and without spot" (Gk. *amnos*,
1 Pet. 1:19) recalls ancient commandments about animal
sacrifice in Exodus, Leviticus and Numbers (Heb. *seh*,
keves). Paul is thinking specifically of the commandments
about the paschal lamb when he writes that "Christ our
Passeover is sacrificed for us" (Gk. *pascha*, 1 Cor. 5:7; Heb.
pesaḥ, Ex. 12:21). Finally, Isaiah's description of the Suffering Servant—"he is brought as a lambe to the slaughter, . . . so he openeth not his mouth" (Heb. *seh*, Isa.
53:7) is understood in Acts 8:32 as a prophecy of Christ.
The author of Acts records the genuine puzzlement with
which the Ethiopian eunuch, encountering that passage
for the first time, turns to Philip: "I pray thee, of whom
speaketh the Prophet this?" (Acts 8:34). Only before the
symbol becomes firmly established is it possible to ask
such a question. For Herbert, as for us, the Old Testament images of lamb are interpreted and indissolubly
connected by their application in the New Testament to
the person of Christ. When Herbert calls Christ "the
meek / And readie Paschal Lambe" in "The Sacrifice" (58–
59) he puts us in touch with a system of established correspondences, and we do not even pause to reflect that the
phrase combines prescriptions for ritual sacrifice with images of mute suffering.

Sometimes there is considerable tension between old
and new meanings, as in the case of *thorn*. Tracing out the
history of such a word in the Bible, one reads in brief the
history of man. In the Old Testament, thorns are a sign of
God's anger. After the Fall, God pronounces the sentence, "Cursed is the ground for thy sake: in sorow shalt
thou eate of it all the dayes of thy life. Thornes also and
thistles shall it bring forth to thee" (Heb. *qoṣ*, Gen. 3:17–
18). In Isaiah's parable, God plants his vineyard "with the
choicest vine," but when it brings forth only wild grapes,

he threatens to lay it waste: "there shall come up briars and thornes" (Heb. *shayit,* Isa. 5:2, 6). Although the New Testament echoes some of these negative senses of the word—Jesus' "Doe men gather grapes of thornes?" (Gk. *akantha,* Matt. 7:16) or Paul's "thorne in the flesh" (Gk. *skolops,* 2 Cor. 12:7)—the very word is transfigured when the "crowne of thornes" (Gk. *akantha*) that the Roman soldiers offer in mockery (Matt. 27:29) becomes, in God's mysterious providence, a symbol of Christ's glory.

Herbert likes to bring into play the full richness of such a word's repertory. When he writes in "Love unknown," *"The Thorns did quicken, what was grown too dull"* (66), he is thinking of Adam, Isaiah and Paul all at once. Or when in "The Collar" the speaker complains, "Have I no harvest but a thorn / To let me bloud . . .?" (7–8), the very question catches him up because of the implied Christian sense of *thorn* (and of *harvest* and *blood* as well). In "The Sacrifice," Herbert exploits the tension between the various senses of *thorn,* revealing at the same time their essential relation:

> Then on my head a crown of thorns I wear:
> For these are all the grapes *Sion* doth bear,
> Though I my vine planted and watred there:
> > Was ever grief like mine?
>
> So sits the earths great curse in *Adams* fall
> Upon my head: so I remove it all
> From th' earth unto my brows, and bear the thrall:
> > Was ever grief like mine?
> > > (161–168)

To one who believes in the unity of Scripture, it is not by chance that Adam's and Isaiah's curse become Christ's crown. As Tuve puts it, "The 'thorns' of all three situations have become the very principle of all mortal imperfection brought on the world of nature by the Fall."[3]

Herbert is intrigued that a single word can mean so much. "How neatly," he might say, to paraphrase "The

3. Tuve, *A Reading,* 62.

Sonne," "doe we give one onely name" to human failure and the sorrow of God! That we do so is one of the distinctions of the English language, like the pun on *sun/son* that is celebrated in that poem: "So in one word" (11) we convey a world. *Thorn*, like *rest* and *lamb*, is represented by a number of different terms in Hebrew and Greek, each with its own semantic field. The English translation of the Bible performs an exegetical function in bringing these together under a single "name," making their relation felt even more strongly than in the original.

A good part of Herbert's lexicon has the evocative power of *dust, rest, lamb* or *thorn*. Words associated with major biblical episodes like the Fall (*garden, fruit, cunning, shame*) or the Exodus (*manna, rock, thunder, law*) come to mind first; for Herbert these are, to borrow a phrase, "bright spark[s], shot from a brighter place." But there are many other words—*house, furniture, father, child, master, servant, steward, shepherd, light, water, tree, bread, corn, wine, harvest*, to name just a few—whose biblical provenance "impute[s] a lustre, and allow[s] them bright." Some, like *wrastling, Pharaohs wheels* or *sling*, reflect light from a single, clearly defined source. More often a word of Scripture is a "hive of beams," making *The Temple* luminous. Poetry of this sort inevitably demands a great deal of its readers. To change the metaphor, I am reminded of the way in which composers in Herbert's day often wrote out just the melodic line, with a few brief notations—a kind of musical shorthand—to indicate how the melody was meant to be harmonized. The skilled reader of *The Temple* will not be content with hearing the thin voice of melody, but will attempt to render Herbert's score in all its intended richness, participating in the process of making his "musick shine."[4]

---

4. *Wrastling* ("The Crosse," 8): Gen. 32:24; *Pharaohs wheels* ("Praise, III," 17): Ex. 14:25; *sling* ("The Church-porch," 352): 1 Sam. 17:50. "Bright spark," "hive of beams": "The Starre" (1, 31); "impute a lustre": "Faith" (35); "musick shine": "Christmas" (34).

COLLATION: "THIS VERSE MARKS THAT"

The reader of the Bible who wants a star chart begins by drawing a line between points of light. The Bible actively invites such an approach: "This verse marks that, and both do make a motion / Unto a third, that ten leaves off doth lie." The "immediate context" of any verse, as Northrop Frye puts it, is "as likely to be three hundred pages off as to be the next or the preceding sentence. Ideally, every sentence is the key to the whole Bible."[5] One means to understanding the text is "a diligent Collation of Scripture with Scripture," as Herbert writes in "The Parsons Knowledg":

> For all Truth being consonant to it self, and all being penn'd by one and the self-same Spirit, it cannot be, but that an industrious, and judicious comparing of place with place must be a singular help for the right understanding of the Scriptures.[6]

Bringing together passages that "mark" one another, the reader learns to divine their true intent. An example momentous for the history of the Reformation is Luther's connection (based on Paul's) between the familiar Old Testament concept of the "justice" of God and Habakkuk's "The just shall live by faith" (Rom. 1:17; cf. Hab. 2:4).[7]

Herbert's remarks about the collation of texts reveal how he himself read Scripture; what is more, they offer a glimpse, I believe, of how he went about writing his poems. Barbara Lewalski observes that imaginative writers in the seventeenth century were interested in

5. Frye, *Great Code*, 208.

6. *A Priest to the Temple, Works*, 229.

7. Cf. Wayne A. Meeks, ed., *The Writings of St. Paul* (New York, 1972), 69 nn. 8–9; Roland H. Bainton, *Here I Stand: A Life of Martin Luther* (Nashville, 1950), 65. The point of connection that is apparent in the underlying Hebrew (*ṣedaqah/ ṣaddiq*), in Paul's Greek (*dikaiosune/dikaios*) and in Luther's Latin (*justitia/justus*) is obscured in the AV, which translates *righteousnesse/just*.

"exploring the tensions arising from the various connotations carried by a given metaphor in different scripture texts" and fusing "these figures into complex networks and interconnected webs of reference."[8] In this sense collation is a creative activity, one form of that charged discovery of connections that we value in the making of metaphors. In what follows I wish to show how the collation of texts has informed, and perhaps inspired, Herbert's process of poetic composition.

Many a poem in *The Temple* has been constituted by the collation of two or more biblical passages. Herbert often chooses texts that "mark" one another by some common word, as in "Sepulchre," which is built upon a catena of verses about *stone* and *rock*. In composing the poem, Herbert moves freely through the terrain of the Bible, discovering stones in all its strata and bringing them together in one structure in order that we may perceive their essential interrelation. His method here is like that of the New Testament authors seeking proof texts in the Old. The first Epistle of Peter, for example, locates a number of passages involving the word *stone* and draws as it were a line between them so that a picture, till then invisible, is seen to emerge:

> To whom comming as unto a living *Stone* [cf. Gen. 49:24], disallowed in deed of men, but chosen of God, and precious,
> Ye also as lively *stones* [cf. Matt. 3:9], are built up a spirituall house, an holy Priesthood to offer up spirituall sacrifice, acceptable to God by Jesus Christ.
> Wherefore it is contened in the Scripture, Beholde, I lay in Sion a chiefe *corner stone*, elect, precious, and he that beleeveth on him, shall not be confounded [Isa. 28:16].
> Unto you therfore which beleeve hee is precious; but unto them which be disobedient, the *stone* which the builders disallowed, the same is made the head of the corner [Ps. 118:22],
> And a *Stone of stumbling*, and a *Rocke of offence*, even to them which stumble at the word [Isa. 8:14].
> (1 Peter 2:4–8, my italics)

8. Lewalski, *Protestant Poetics*, 86–87.

This way of thinking is fundamental to Christianity: in reading the New Testament as the continuation and fulfillment of the Old, the Christian must continually make such connections.

The reader of the Bible in Herbert's day was encouraged to collate passages by the apparatus printed in the margin. In the AV that apparatus includes not only the literal Hebrew meanings of certain words, and some parallel or alternative readings, but also references to constellations of related passages (marked, appropriately enough, by an asterisk, a little star). The reader who looks up 1 Peter 2:4–8, for example, will find noted in the margin the passages from Isaiah and the Psalms that Peter cites, as well as Matt. 21:42 and Acts 4:12 [4:11], which allude to the "corner stone" of Psalm 118. The serious student of the Bible could also consult a concordance, as Herbert is likely to have done when composing sermons. Bound up with some editions of the Geneva Bible are "Two right profitable and fruitfull Concordances," the first elucidating foreign words, the second "comprehending all such other principall wordes and matters, as concerne the sense and meaning of the Scriptures." Among the headings for *rock* and *stone* in the second table, we find the elements of Herbert's "Sepulchre":

Water out of the *Rocke* in Horeb. Exo. 17.6. Nom. 20.8, to 12.

Christ the *Rocke* of offence to some. 1 Pet. 2.8. Rom. 9.33. the spiritual *Rocke* which the Jewes dranke of by faith. 1 Cor. 10.4.

The *Rocke*, whereupon Christ buylded his Church, himself being the head stone. Matth. 16.18. & 21.42.

Christ the refused head corner *Stone* conjoyning Jewes and Gentiles. Mat. 21.40 [42]. 1 Pet. 2.7. Eph. 2.20.

The Jewes woulde have *Stoned* Christ, & why. Joh. 10.30, 31, 33.

God will give unto the faithfull a heart of flesh, for a *Stonie*
heart. Jere. 32.39. Ezek. 36.27 [26].[9]

"Sepulchre" begins with the stone of Christ's tomb. In
the first stanza, the speaker is imagined at the tomb, expressing his dismay:

> O blessed bodie! Whither art thou thrown?
> No lodging for thee, but a cold hard stone?
> So many hearts on earth, and yet not one
> Receive thee?
> Sure there is room within our hearts good store;
> For they can lodge transgressions by the score:
> Thousands of toyes dwell there, yet out of doore
> They leave thee.
>
> (1–8)

Herbert has rewritten this part of the Gospel story to en-
hance its pathos. This sepulcher is not the newly prepared
tomb, "hewen out of a rocke" (Mark 15:46), where the
good Joseph of Arimathaea lovingly laid Christ's body
after wrapping it in fine linen. It is, rather, a miserable
manger of a place where that body is "thrown" because
there is no room for it in any human inn. The adjectives
"cold" and "hard"— the physical characteristics of stone—
literally describe the sepulcher, though the phrase "so
many hearts" that follows immediately makes clear where
Herbert's gaze is directed. If the stone is "cold" and
"hard," then the hearts that have abandoned Christ to
such a place are colder and harder still.

In stanza 2 Herbert brings together images of stone that
suggest, on the one hand, divine protection and nurture
and, on the other, man's unbridled viciousness:

9. "Two right profitable and fruitfull Concordances, . . . Collected
by R. F. H." [Robert F. Herrey], *The Bible* [Geneva] (1560; rpt. London,
1583), sigs. K.[vii], L.iii$_v$–L.iiii. Herrey's explanatory preface to these
tables is dated 1578.

> But that which shews them large, shews them unfit.
> What ever sinne did this pure rock commit,
> Which holds thee now? Who hath indited it
>   Of murder?
> Where our hard hearts have took up stones to brain thee,
> And missing this, most falsly did arraigne thee;
> Onely these stones in quiet entertain thee,
>   And order.
>   (9–16)

"This pure rock" in line 10 and "these stones" in line 15 refer to the sepulcher, though again (as in "cold hard stone") Herbert implies more than he says directly. Both the adjective "pure" (used in the sense of "innocent" rather than "unalloyed") and the verbs of action ("commit," "entertain") point beyond the actual sepulcher to Christ and the living stones of his Church.[10] In the Old Testament God is often called a "Rocke" (Deut. 32:31, 1 Sam. 2:2, Ps. 31:3, etc.); in the New Testament Christ is the "Rocke" that provides "spirituall drink" to man (1 Cor. 10:4, cf. Num. 20:11), the "living Stone" (1 Pet. 2:4) and the "chiefe corner stone" (1 Pet. 2:6) of the church he built upon a "rocke" (Matt. 16:18). "These stones" in line 15 recalls Peter's image of believers as "lively stones" that are "built up a spirituall house" (1 Pet. 2:5). Against these positive associations for *rock* and *stone* Herbert sets the obduracy of man. In "our hard

---

10. Cf. Fish, *Self-Consuming Artifacts*, 171. Strier, *Love Known*, 14 n. 24, argues that there are no "clues" in the context to activate the allusion to Christ as Rock, remarking on the "literal meaning and straightforward syntax" of lines 10–12. But even when Herbert writes in a seemingly "literal" and "straightforward" manner, he is always aware of the symbolic penumbra of the words he is using, particularly when those words, like *rock* and *stone*, have a long biblical history. In this case, besides, as I have indicated, I think there are "clues" in the adjective and verb of line 10, as well as in the network of related allusions to *rock*. Strier (p. 15) also questions the relevance of 2 Cor. 3:2–3 cited by Fish, since Herbert is using the image of the epistle in the heart without Paul's polemical intent. But Herbert often appropriates biblical images for his own purposes—just as the New Testament authors do in adapting images from the Old.

hearts" he alludes to Ezekiel's image of the "stonie heart" (36:26), making explicit what he hinted at in stanza 1. Jesus frequently "grieved for the hardnesse" of men's hearts (Mark 3:5), a hardness he literally experienced when they "tooke up stones againe to stone him" (John 10:31).

But the very hardness of man's heart paradoxically offers God an occasion for action. "A HEART alone / Is such a stone, / As nothing but / Thy pow'r doth cut" ("The Altar," 5–8), Herbert writes; "O smooth my rugged heart, and there / Engrave thy rev'rend Law and fear" ("Nature," 13–14); "And though my hard heart scarce to thee can grone, / Remember that thou once didst write in stone" ("The Sinner," 13–14). In these poems, as in "Sepulchre," Herbert is thinking of the image of the Law "written with the finger of God" in "tables of stone" (Ex. 31:18), which the prophets dreamed would one day be inscribed in the heart:

> After those dayes, saith the LORD, I will put my law in their inward parts, and write it in their hearts, and wil be their God, and they shall be my people,
>
> (Jer. 31:33)

and which Paul sees as fulfilled in Christ:

> Forasmuch as yee are manifestly declared to be the Epistle of Christ ministred by us, written not with inke, but with the spirit of the living God, not in tables of stone, but in fleshy tables of the heart.
>
> (2 Cor. 3:3)

The final stanza moves from this vision of redemption to a despairing sense of man's unfitness, and thence to the realization that Christ's love has made it possible after all—a love that is the greater as it is measured against the hardness of man:

> And as of old the Law by heav'nly art
> Was writ in stone; so thou, which also art
> The letter of the word, find'st no fit heart
>   To hold thee.

Yet do we still persist as we began,
And so should perish, but that nothing can,
Though it be cold, hard, foul, from loving man
                    Withhold thee.

                                                    (17–24)

This stanza reaches out to other poems in the volume: to
the "heavie" stones of the Hebrew Temple in "Sion" and
the stony heart of "The Altar," "Nature" and "The Sinner." The "lights" of *The Temple* "combine," it appears, in
much the same way as the lights of the Bible. Reading
"Sepulchre" in its full associative context, we can see
more clearly how it develops two of the principal themes
of *The Temple:* a dwelling place for God, the law inscribed
in the heart.

Herbert's poem ranges from the sepulcher of Christ to
the sinful impulses of man, to Christ's bounty, the true
Church, and the Law inscribed in the heart—yet remarkably, it does not strike us as a succession of dizzying
leaps. The movement from *stone* to *stone* is made possible
by Herbert's belief in the unity of the Bible. Modern critical study of the Bible has taught us that even the smallest
units of the text may be the product of many hands; contemplating the heterogeneity of the Bible rather than its
unity, we are less inclined today, perhaps, to make such
connections. But we must remind ourselves that Herbert
read the Bible differently, never doubting that it was
"penn'd by one and the self-same Spirit." Upon this rock
Herbert has built his poem—and in a larger sense, his
Temple.

If "Sepulchre" depends upon a chain of allusions about
stone, "A true Hymne" turns on the play between two
texts about *love*. This has not been remarked, though each
of the texts has been identified.[11] Herbert writes in the
third stanza that God, who demands that we serve him

---

11. Summers, *George Herbert*, 223 n. 34, notes the allusion to Luke
10:27; Tuve, "*Caritas*," 308, cites 1 John 4:19.

with every fiber of our being, has cause to grumble if we offer up uninspired doggerel in which "the words onely ryme." The stanza itself, as Stein notes, is a perfect illustration of what Herbert has in mind:[12]

> He who craves all the minde,
> And all the soul, and strength, and time,
> If the words onely ryme,
> Justly complains, that somewhat is behinde
> To make his verse, or write a hymne in kinde.
>
> (11–15)

The reader will recognize in the first two lines a somewhat garbled paraphrase of Jesus' summary of Old Testament law: "Thou shalt love the Lord thy God with all thy heart, and with all thy soule, and with all thy strength, and with all thy minde" (Luke 10:27).[13] That this paraphrase of the commandment to love God says nothing about *love* we may realize only in retrospect, when we have read the last line of the poem. Meanwhile line 12 should give us pause. "All the minde, / And all the soul, and strength, and . . ." requires "heart" to complete the sequence; instead, in the crowning position we find the prosaic "time." The anticlimax is deliberate, as the next line reveals: "time" has been chosen only because "the words . . . ryme." At the end of "Home," stirred by love and longing, Herbert says *"Come"* where the "ryme and reason" demand *"Stay"*; here he mimics the poetaster who is the slave of his form.

In the fourth stanza, where "heart" and "love" occur twice, we learn that Herbert's *Poetics* is of a piece with his *Ars Amatoria*. Only if the poet's "heart" is "moved," will God infuse his meager lines with spirit:

---

12. Stein, *Herbert's Lyrics,* 7.
13. Cf. Matt. 22:37, Mark 12:30. Deut. 6:5, the source of the commandment, has "heart," "soule" and "might." Mark and Luke translate "might" (which Matthew omits) as "strength," and all three Gospels add a new term, "minde." Herbert paraphrases this commandment also in "Divinitie" (17) and "The Holdfast" (1–2).

> Whereas if th' heart be moved,
> Although the verse be somewhat scant,
> God doth supplie the want.
>
> (16–18)

This could be taken as a definition of poetic inspiration. But because the definition is somewhat scant—what is it, after all, that "moves" the heart?—Herbert offers an analogy to art from life:

> As when th' heart sayes (sighing to be approved)
> O, *could I love!* and stops: God writeth, *Loved*.
>
> (19–20)

The last three words are a characteristic piece of Herbertian wit. Vendler notes that we expect *"Thou dost love"* and are brought up short by *"Loved."*[14] "God writeth" deserves comment as well: the "logical" verb would be "answers." God is said to "write" here because it is his Writ that supplies the last word of the poem: *"Loved."* The Old Testament commands: "Thou shalt love the LORD thy God" (Deut. 6:5); the New Testament explains: "We love him: because hee first loved us" (1 John 4:19). These familiar passages, related to each other paradigmatically as Old and New, law and grace, stand behind the final stanzas, though the first is mangled in paraphrase and the second marked by only a single word. Herbert glosses one biblical text about love with another that illuminates it, telling us what God demands of us and, at the same time, how he makes its attainment possible. With one word of Scripture—*loved*—he says how the Christian is enabled to love God, unfit though he may be, and how the poet is inspired to write a true poem.

Collation involves the comparison not only of similar but also of dissimilar passages. William Whitaker, in his *Disputation on Holy Scripture*, demonstrates how either type of collation may be useful in elucidating difficult questions

14. Vendler, *Poetry of Herbert*, 27–28.

of interpretation, choosing as an illustration a text about which all parties were in violent disagreement: "Except yee eate the flesh of the sonne of man, and drinke his blood, yee have no life in you" (John 6:53). Turning first to a "like place," "Whosoever drinketh of the water that I shall give him, shall never thirst" (John 4:14), Whitaker reasons, "This water is spiritual, and the mode of drinking it is spiritual," and "to eat and to drink are similar kinds of expression," thus "the flesh of Christ must be eaten, and his blood drunk, only in a spiritual manner." Next he compares the verse with an "unlike place," the sixth commandment, "Thou shalt not kill" (Ex. 20:13), arguing that "if it be a crime, yea, an enormity, to slay a man, it is certainly a far deeper crime to eat and devour a man." Hence, Whitaker concludes, "these words must be understood and explained figuratively."[15] Whitaker's examples illustrate the freedom of movement associated with collation, which finds in the text of Scripture a source of fertile, endlessly proliferating connections.

Herbert avails himself of this freedom, bringing together both "like" and "unlike places" and linking them in a variety of ways. "Lesse then the least / Of all thy mercies" in "The Posie," as we have seen, conflates two texts marked by the word "least" (Gen. 32:10, Eph. 3:8). In "the Prince of peace; peace that doth passe / All understanding" ("The Sacrifice," 118–19), the repetition of "peace" on both sides of the caesura rivets the two verses together (Isa. 9:6, Phil. 4:7). "Take not his name, who made thy mouth, in vain" ("The Church-porch," 55) has a tongue-and-groove construction, the dovetailed relative clause providing the rationale for the third commandment (Ex. 4:11, 20:7). The refrain of "The Church Militant" is pieced together from different psalms and bound by rhyme: "*How deare to me, O God, thy counsels are! / Who may*

---

15. Whitaker, *Disputation,* 472. (The biblical quotations in this paragraph are from the AV rather than from Whitaker.)

with thee compare?" (47–48, Pss. 139.17, 89.6).[16] Herbert
also likes ironic juxtapositions, where the verses jostle
and clash, most notably in "The Sacrifice":

> But, *O my God, my God!* why leav'st thou me,
> The sonne, in whom thou dost delight to be?
>
> (213–14)

The anguished cry from the Cross (Matt. 27:46; cf. Ps.
22:1) seems doubly poignant when it is made to rhyme
with the heavenly assurance at Christ's baptism and
transfiguration: "This is my beloved Sonne, in whom I am
well pleased" (Matt. 3:17, 17:5; cf. Isa. 42:1).

The marriage of two texts almost invariably generates
new meanings. To paraphrase Eliot's well-known analogy, the elements with which Herbert starts do not remain inert but rather, in the presence of the catalyst of his
mind, fuse to form something different.[17] Consider the
central metaphor of "The Altar":

> A broken ALTAR, Lord, thy servant reares,
> Made of a heart, and cemented with teares:
>   Whose parts are as thy hand did frame;
>   No workmans tool hath touch'd the same.
>
> (1–4)

The *altar* comes from a passage in Deuteronomy where
Moses commands certain sacrifices to be offered "on the
day when you shall passe over Jordan":

> And there shalt thou build an Altar unto the LORD thy
> God, an altar of stones: thou shalt not lift up any yron toole
> upon them.

---

16. On this refrain see Stanley Stewart, "Time and *The Temple*,"
Studies in English Literature 6 (1966), rpt. *Essential Articles for the Study of
George Herbert's Poetry*, ed. John R. Roberts (Hamden, Conn., 1979), 370–
73; Raymond A. Anselment, "'The Church Militant': George Herbert
and the Metamorphoses of Christian History," *Huntington Library Quarterly* 41 (1978): 308–9.

17. T. S. Eliot, "Tradition and the Individual Talent," *Selected Essays*, 3d ed. (London, 1951), 17–19.

Thou shalt build the Altar of the LORD thy God of whole stones: and thou shalt offer burnt offerings theron unto the LORD thy God.

(Deut. 27:2, 5–6; cf. Josh. 8:31)

The prohibition against "any yron toole" is glossed in Ex. 20:25: "for if thou lift up thy toole upon it, thou hast polluted it." Herbert specifies the nature of the desecration in *workmans tool*, for "workeman" (Heb. *ḥarash*) in the diatribe of the prophets is always a maker of idols.[18] But if the *altar* comes from a passage that prescribes sacrifices, the *broken heart* comes from one of the Penitential Psalms that explicitly denies the value of material offerings:

For thou desirest no sacrifice, els would I give it thee: but thou delightest not in burnt offerings.
The sacrifice of God is a troubled spirit: a broken and contrite heart, O God, shalt thou not despise.

(Ps. 51:16–17)

From these two texts with their differing emphases Herbert brings together *altar* and *broken heart* to form a new compound: "A broken ALTAR . . . Made of a heart." However familiar its components, the image has the power to startle: is it not irreverent, one asks, to raise a *broken* altar to God? The Book of Deuteronomy distinctly specifies "*whole* stones." But Herbert's altar is the *heart*, and the more broken the better. In this imaginative "combination," Herbert reconciles contradictions and activates a whole complex of associations relating to sacrifice and penitence.

Sometimes, at its extreme, Herbert's use of collation is so rapid, so dense, that the modern reader may well find it difficult to follow. Look, for example, at lines 19–22 of "The Church Militant":

Where th' Ark did rest, there *Abraham* began
To bring the other Ark from *Canaan*.
Moses pursu'd this: but King *Solomon*
Finish'd and fixt the old religion.

18. Isa. 40:19–20, 44:11; Jer. 10:3, 9; Hos. 8:6.

Hutchinson points out that in these couplets, "obscure through their compression and allusiveness," Herbert is bringing together passages about two different kinds of *ark*, Noah's vessel of gopher wood (Heb. *tevah*, Gen. 8:4) and Moses' ark of the covenant (Heb. *aron*, Ex. 25), as well as a number of other texts linked by the words *Philistines* (Gen. 21:34, 1 Sam. 5:1) and *Moriah* (Gen. 22:2, 2 Chron. 3:1)—words that are not even mentioned!—connecting the history of Abraham with that of his descendants in the days of David and Solomon.[19] That Herbert allows himself these multiple associations is a clear indication that he sees all of Scripture as potentially related; that he moves so swiftly from text to text, without pausing to amplify or explain, shows how much he could expect of his readers. We may miss some of these connections without a commentary like Hutchinson's, but as Tuve reminds us, and as we must keep reminding ourselves, Herbert did not need commentary in his own day.[20]

Now that we have seen collation at work in a variety of poems, we may turn to "The Sacrifice," where it provides a major structural device. Some of the most brilliant ironic effects in the poem come from the studied juxtaposition of two texts that are linked by a single word: *thorns, pence, garment, spit, blinde, binding, bloud, come down, live, stonie, rock, strike, reed, weep, breath, vailed, shine, warre*. In each case, a verse from the Passion story "marks" another verse elsewhere in the Bible with the same (or a similar) word, which offers a striking contrast. Sometimes Herbert states both terms explicitly, as in "I suffer *binding*, who have loos'd their *bands*" (47) or "*Weep* not, deare friends, since I for both have *wept*" (149); sometimes he names one and implies the other: "For thirtie *pence* he did my death devise, / Who at three hundred did the ointment prize"

19. "Commentary," *Works*, 544; cf. Frye, *Great Code*, 177, on the movement of biblical history "from ark to ark."
20. Tuve, *A Reading*, 110.

(17–18), or "*now come down.* / Alas! I did so . . ." (221–22).
Either way, he strikes sparks from the play of text against
biblical text. What I am suggesting is that the writing of
the poem involved the "diligent Collation of Scripture
with Scripture," the "industrious, and judicious comparing of place with place."

In saying this I am proposing to qualify Rosemond
Tuve's account of the poem's genesis. In her learned and
passionate essay on "The Sacrifice," Tuve brings to life
the traditional materials that lie behind Herbert's poem:
the Sarum Missal and Breviary, Latin hymns by Pruden-
tius and Venantius Fortunatus, Middle English lyrics and
the drama of the guilds, the *Biblia Pauperum* and the
Speculum humanae salvationis, illustrated Books of Hours,
sermon manuals, the *Golden Legend* and the *Cursor Mundi,*
to name only the most frequently cited. Although she
believes that "deliberate borrowing is involved," she is
careful to point out that these are not Herbert's "sources"
but rather examples of "a very widely diffused tradition."
Tuve argues persuasively that "read by the illumination
of the tradition in which it was conceived [the poem]
takes on a richness, a depth, complexity and moving
power" that we should not willingly forego.[21] Her notion
of Herbert's tradition, however, extensive as it is, leaves
out one essential constituent: the Bible.

Tuve is interested in the Bible primarily as it is medi-
ated by liturgy and iconography, and one comes away
from this essay with the impression that Herbert knew
the Bible at two removes. Even where she grants that
Herbert's "actual phrasings . . . are scriptural," she looks
elsewhere for his "actual sources": "It would perhaps be
easy," she suggests in a typical passage, "to make a case
for the *Speculum humanae salvationis.*"[22] As William Halewood has written, the Reformation tends "to become in-

21. Ibid., 42, 32.
22. Ibid., 75.

visible in her long view of antecendent Christianity."[23]
And that exemplar of the Reformation, the Protestant believer with his Bible "laid open," avidly reading the sacred text for himself, plays no part in her detailed historical reconstruction. There is no doubt that the tradition
Tuve describes lies behind many features of the poem.
But I find it inconceivable that a seventeenth-century Protestant clergyman would compose a long poem about a
biblical subject without drawing directly on his own reading and knowledge of Scripture, and the evidence of "The
Sacrifice" bears this out. Before Tuve wrote this essay,
one would not have needed to argue such a point, it
seems so self-evident; but her exclusively "liturgical and
'Catholic' preoccupations"[24] prompt us to take a closer
look at how Herbert uses the Bible in his poem.

Let us begin with the stanzas about *thorns*, which we
have already had occasion to notice:

Then on my head a crown of thorns I wear:
For these are all the grapes *Sion* doth bear,
Though I my vine planted and watred there:
                Was ever grief like mine?

So sits the earths great curse in *Adams* fall
Upon my head: so I remove it all
From th' earth unto my brows, and bear the thrall:
                Was ever grief like mine?
                        (161–68)

Tuve writes that Isaiah's parable of the vineyard is already linked with Christ in the liturgy of Holy Week, and
that Herbert takes the process one step further when
"from the vineyard of Sion choked with thorns in Isa. v. 6
[he] makes our minds leap simultaneously to the curse of

23. William H. Halewood, *The Poetry of Grace: Reformation Themes
and Structures in English Seventeenth-Century Poetry* (New Haven, 1970),
88–89.
24. Tuve, *A Reading*, 47.

thorns in Genesis and to the thorns of Christ's bloody crown."²⁵

It is not the liturgy, however, that invites such a "leap." Christ's crown of thorns is recalled during Holy Week, of course, because of its part in the Passion story. But there is no mention in the Sarum Missal Easter service of Adam's thorns, and oddly enough, though Isaiah's parable figures on three separate occasions, the thorns of the vineyard are not heard of once. The abbreviated version of Isaiah's parable sung on Easter Even is made up of verses 1, 2 and 7 of chapter 5, omitting all reference to the thorns of verse 6. The English reads:

> My well-beloved hath a vineyard in a very fruitful hill.
> And he fenced it, and gathered out the stones thereof, and planted it with the choicest vine, and built a tower in the midst of it.
> And also made a winepress therein; for the vineyard of the Lord of Hosts is the house of Israel.²⁶

Tuve notes this without seeing that it disallows her point about the "thorns in Isa. v. 6." Moreover, neither the *Improperia* nor the Responsories of Good Friday, which cite Isaiah, mention thorns; the first contrasts Christ as "planter" of his people with their bitter gift of vinegar and gall, and the second with their choice of Barabbas.²⁷ It is clear that what makes Herbert's mind leap from the *thorns* of Isaiah to those of Genesis and the Gospels is not the liturgy but rather his way of reading Scripture. That he was collating biblical texts is apparent too when we notice how much else in these two stanzas, aside from the

25. Ibid., 62; cf. 60.
26. See *The Sarum Missal*, ed. J. Wickham Legg (Oxford, 1916), 120, or *The Sarum Missal in English*, trans. Frederick E. Warren, 2 vols. (London, 1913), I, 275, from which this passage is quoted.
27. Tuve quotes both texts on p. 61. For the *Improperia*, see the Latin *Sarum Missal*, 113, or the *Sarum Missal in English*, I, 258. For the Responsories, see the *Breviarum ad usum . . . Sarum*, ed. F. Procter and C. Wordsworth (Cambridge, 1882), I, dcclxxxix.

image of *thorn*, is taken from the passages in question: *on my head* and *crown* from the Gospels; *grapes*, *vine* and *planted* from Isaiah; and Adam's *curse* from Genesis. I would add that Herbert does more than supply the "last, minute, logical link between thorns and thorns," which Tuve calls "the measure of Herbert's 'originality' in this image."[28] In the Gospels it is the soldiers who crown Jesus with a wreath of thorns, but Herbert's Christ performs that action himself—"so I remove it all / From th' earth unto my brows, and bear the thrall" (166–67)—literally taking Adam's curse upon his head. Thus, in a few words, and without calling attention to his boldness, Herbert invents a startling new image for one of the oldest of Christian commonplaces. This imaginative recreation of traditional materials is the very hallmark of his art; herein lies his originality, his poetic energy, the breath of life that animates his lines. Notice too the pun on *bear*, which reinforces the opposition of thorn and thorn. In line 162 *bear* has the sense of "bring forth," "produce," alluding to Gen. 3:18 and Isa. 5:6; Herbert uses the verb again in line 167 in the sense (it has come to seem peculiarly Christian) of "carry," "endure" (cf. Matt. 27:32, Heb. 9:28). Herbert's elaborations of Scripture characteristically involve surprises of this order, so quietly presented that they often go unnoticed.

When he writes about Judas's treachery, Herbert again modifies the Gospel account:

> For thirtie pence he did my death devise,
> Who at three hundred did the ointment prize.
>
> (17–18)

Matt. 26:15 tells us that Judas "covenanted" with the chief priests for "thirtie pieces of silver" (Gk. *argurion*, cf. Zech. 11:12–13); John reports an earlier incident in which Judas protested the anointing of Jesus' feet: "Why was not this

---

28. Tuve, *A Reading*, 62–63.

ointment sold for three hundred pence, and given to the poore?" (Gk. *denarion*, John 12:5). Herbert connects these passages about Judas because they both mention specific sums of money, but he makes Judas bargain for pennies in order to heighten the irony.[29]

In a number of stanzas Herbert juxtaposes a text from the Passion story with another that reveals Christ's divine powers. The coat the soldiers cast lots for is seen to be the very *garment* that once brought healing (John 19:23–24, cf. Ps. 22:18; Matt. 14:36):

> They part my garments, and by lot dispose
> My coat, the type of love, which once cur'd those
> Who sought for help, never malicious foes.
>
> (241–43)

The mocking of Jesus (Matt. 26:67; cf. Isa. 50:6) evokes another miracle of healing (John 9:6–7; cf. Isa. 42:7):

> Behold, they spit on me in scornfull wise,
> Who by my spittle gave the blinde man eies,
> Leaving his blindnesse to my enemies.
>
> (133–35)

Tuve cites a "parallel but not identical antithesis" from the *Speculum*, where "they covered the eyes of Him who gave light to them as a pillar of fire"; Herbert's "originality," she says, "consists in sharpening the contrast to a more biting point."[30] It seems to me, however, that Herbert is not touching up a contrast from the *Speculum* that is more-or-less similar, but rather clashing together two biblical passages that are linked by a common word. He

---

29. The *argurion* (in Greek the word means both "silver" and "money," like the French *argent*) was worth considerably more than the *denarion* (translated "penny" in the AV), an ordinary day's wages for a laborer (cf. Matt. 20:9–10). According to *The Interpreter's Dictionary of the Bible*, 4 vols. (New York, 1962), III, 428, thirty pieces of silver = thirty shekels, and one shekel = four pence. Hence Judas's thirty pieces of silver would be equivalent to 120 pence.

30. Tuve, *A Reading*, 64.

does so again in line 135, contrasting the *blind* man whose sight was restored with the Pharisees, "blinde leaders of the blinde" (Matt. 15:14; cf. John 9:39). The same process also generates "I suffer binding, who have loos'd their bands" (47). Tuve remarks that Herbert "quite probably never saw the anticipation of his antithesis in an earlier *Popule meus* poem . . . or in a Gregorian hymn," because he is drawing upon "an established and diffused tradition."[31] But here too the process of collation seems more direct; Herbert could have found these antitheses simply by bringing together passages from the Bible. The binding of Christ (Matt. 27:2) "marks" many verses about redemption from bonds or from the house of bondage, for example, "I am the LORD your God, which brought you forth out of the land of Egypt, that yee should not be their bondmen, and I have broken the bandes of your yoke" (Lev. 26:13). "Thou hast loosed my bonds" (Ps. 116:16 AV), from one of the Hallelujah Psalms, is part of the "hymne" (Matt. 26:30) that Jesus and his disciples sang together at the end of the Passover feast before going out to Gethsemane[32]—a connection that makes the irony all the more harrowing.

Herbert finds in the taunts of the multitude a deeper level of meaning; indeed, they know not what they say. When they "wish *my bloud on them and theirs*" (107; cf. Matt. 27:25), they are calling for Jesus' death, but, irony of ironies, "These words aright / Used, and wished"—referring to the purging of sin through sacrificial blood[33]—"are

31. Ibid. and n. 19.
32. John Donne, *The Sermons of John Donne,* ed. George R. Potter and Evelyn M. Simpson, 10 vols. (Berkeley and Los Angeles, 1953–1962), VI, 293, writes that "it hath beene traditionally received, and recommended by good Authors, that that *Hymne,* which Christ and his Apostles are said to have sung after the Institution and celebration of the Sacrament, was a *Hymne* composed of those six Psalmes, which we call the *Allelujah Psalmes,* immediatly preceding the hundred and nineteenth."
33. Cf., e.g., Rom. 5:9, Eph. 1:7, Col. 1:14, Heb. 9:12.

the whole worlds light" (109–10). The cry *come down* elic-
its a bitter pun:

> *Now heal thy self, Physician; now come down.*
> Alas! I did so, when I left my crown
> And fathers smile for you, to feel his frown.
>
> (221–23)

Tuve says that Herbert is introducing the Incarnation here
"in his own new way,"[34] but Herbert's startling play on
words depends on a way of reading Scripture that is
neither new nor his own. In the synoptic Gospels the
crowd mocks Jesus: "Save thy selfe, and come downe
from the Crosse" (Mark 15:30); in John, however, *come
down* is used in quite another sense: "For I came downe
from heaven, not to doe mine owne will, but the will of
him that sent me" (6:38; cf. 3:13, 6:51).

One other antithesis is of this type:

> *It is not fit he live a day*, they crie,
> Who cannot live lesse then eternally.
>
> (98–99)

The image of Christ as the embodiment of eternal life
appears in the Fourth Gospel: "I give unto them eternall
life"; "I am the resurrection, and the life"; "I am the Way,
the Trueth, and the Life" (John 10:28, 11:25, 14:6, etc.).
Tuve seems puzzled that in retelling the Passion of Christ
Herbert should borrow a line from the story of Paul:
"Away with such a fellow from the earth: for it is not fit
that he should live" (Acts 22:22); she remarks that "this
specific juxtaposition based on 'I *am* the Life'" is one of
the few passages for which she has "noticed no suggestion in the traditional materials."[35] But Herbert's use of
Acts here is not surprising when we understand how, in
collating passages, he takes all Scripture for his province.

34. Tuve, *A Reading*, 64.
35. Ibid., 53.

He is drawn to the verse about Paul apparently because it contains the word *live*.

Herbert twice refers to the complex of imagery that we found in "Sepulchre":

> He clave the stonie rock, when they were drie;
> But surely not their hearts, as I well trie.
>
> (122–23)
>
> Then with the reed they gave to me before,
> They strike my head, the rock from whence all store
> Of heav'nly blessings issue evermore.
>
> (169–71)

In lines 122–23 it is the word *stonie* that provides the link between two Old Testament texts: "Hee brought waters out of the stonie rocke" (Ps. 78:17); "I will take away the stonie heart out of your flesh" (Ezek. 36:26). The second passage is particularly rich in affiliations. The *rock* that brought forth water in the wilderness is given a new meaning by Paul: "that Rocke was Christ" (1 Cor. 10:4). Another set of allusions is connected in the original by *smote:* "He smote the stonie rocke indeed, that the water gushed out" (Ps. 78:21); "And they . . . tooke the reed, and smote him on the head" (Matt. 27:30); here, as in line 142, Herbert substitutes "strike" for the bibilical "smite."[36] Finally, the *reed* that the soldiers mockingly thrust into Jesus' hands appears again two stanzas later—"since mans scepters are as frail as reeds" (177)—recalling Old Testament images of the king of Egypt as a "bruised reed," a "broken reede" (2 Kings 18:21, Isa. 36:6).

Let me mention briefly a few more instances. "*Weep not, deare friends, since I for both have wept*" moves

---

36. It may be that Herbert wanted a colloquial form here; *strike* is part of his normal vocabulary, occurring in various forms six times in *The Temple,* while *smite* does not occur once. Or perhaps he found *strike* a shade more forceful in its sound because of the initial triconsonantal cluster. In any event, the sequence of *strike-rock-store* in line 170 produces a tighter sound pattern than smite-rock-store.

from Jesus' words to the daughters of Jerusalem to his own weeping over the city and thence to the Agony in the Garden, "when all my tears were bloud" (149–50; Luke 23:28, 19:41, 22:44); Herbert forges the second link by turning the bloody sweat of the Agony into bloody tears. Paul's words on Mars Hill, "hee giveth to all, life and *breath*" (Acts 17:25), are connected to Gen. 2:7:

> Then they condemne me all with that same breath,
> Which I do give them daily, unto death.
> Thus *Adam* my first breathing rendereth.
>
> (69–71)

Perhaps too Herbert has in mind a verse from the Psalms: "false witnesses are risen up against me, and such as breath out crueltie" (Ps. 27:12 AV). Moses' *vail* is mentioned as a parallel to the blindfolding of Christ:

> My face they cover, though it be divine.
> As *Moses* face was vailed, so is mine.
> Lest on their double-dark souls either shine.
>
> (137–39)

Here the Old Testament source, "And the children of Israel saw . . . that the skinne of Moses face *shone:* and Moses put the *vaile* upon his face againe" (Ex. 34:35), calls up both Matthew's account of the transfiguration ("his face did shine," Matt. 17:2) and Paul's commentary on *vaile* (2 Cor. 3:13–16). Finally, in line 77 Herbert paraphrases Luke 23:11, which reads: "And Herod with his men of warre set him at naught"; the word *warre*, which Herbert does not repeat, explains the transition (otherwise puzzling) to Psalm 144:1 in the next line: "Blessed be the Lord my strength: which teacheth my hands to warre, and my fingers to fight."

While it is true that the *Improperia* of Good Friday furnish the basic pattern of Herbert's "Reproaches," that pattern has been considerably refined in "The Sacrifice." The *Improperia* of the Sarum Missal contrast God's beneficence and man's cruelty in a series of broad strokes:

Because I brought thee up out of the land of Egypt, thou hast prepared a cross for thy Saviour. . . . Because I led thee through the wilderness forty years, and I fed thee with manna, and brought thee into a land sufficiently good, thou hast prepared a cross for thy Saviour. . . . I planted thee indeed, O my vineyard, with fair fruit, and thou art become very bitter unto me; for thou gavest me to drink in my thirst vinegar mingled with gall, and piercedst thy Saviour's side with a spear.[37]

Suggestive as they are, the *Improperia* do not rely on the clashing of word against scriptural word that we find in Herbert's most telling ironies. Nor is pointed rhetorical antithesis typical of the vernacular lyrics influenced by the *Improperia*. The contrasts in these anonymous medieval lyrics are as a rule looser than Herbert's, as in "thou hast a garland, I have a crown of thorns; thou white gloves, I bloody hands."[38] Tuve concedes that despite a "similarity of tone in the liturgical, the medieval, and the Herbert 'reproaches,'" there is "plenty of verbal independence."[39] But where Herbert is verbally independent of tradition, he is often directly dependent on Scrip-

---

37. *Sarum Missal in English,* I, 258. Tuve, *A Reading,* quotes the second and third of these Reproaches on p. 37, and the first and second on p. 41. She cites one more contrast on p. 41, which proves to be from the Roman Missal: "Before thee I *opened* the sea, and thou hast *opened* my side with a spear" (my italics). This looks like Herbert's antitheses, though its source is not scriptural: cf. "The LORD caused the Sea to goe backe" (Ex. 14:21); "one of the souldiers with a speare pierced his side" (John 19:34). Of the twelve Reproaches in the Roman Missal, four others involve some wordplay, but only one of these has a basis in Scripture: "Ego propter te Chananaeorum reges *percussi:* et tu *percussisti* arundine caput meum" (cf. Josh. 12, Matt. 27:30).

38. Tuve, *A Reading,* 44, citing Carleton Brown, ed., *Religious Lyrics of the XIVth Century* (Oxford, 1924), 225 (no. 126). The one *Popule meus* poem quoted by Tuve that approaches Herbert's practice—"In bem of cloude ich ladde the; / And to pylate thou ledest me" (38–39)—is by a known author, Friar William Herebert. Of course we have no idea which medieval lyrics Herbert actually knew, as Tuve recognizes; we can only conjecture about manuscripts he may or may not have seen at Cambridge (cf. Tuve, *A Reading,* 64 n., 45).

39. Tuve, *A Reading,* 40.

ture. With the basic pattern of the *Improperia* and the medieval lyrics in mind, I am suggesting, Herbert went back to the Bible and found some of his sharpest ironies by collating passages of Scripture.

On this point Tuve raises an objection that must be met. "Phrasings being largely scriptural," she writes, "Herbert's independence of tradition here would be conceivable; in that case the marked absence of scriptural materials *not* liturgically marked out for emphasis would call for explanation."[40] Now, "phrasings" cannot be dismissed quite so lightly; they must be regarded as a crucial issue when we are studying the work of a poet. If Herbert follows one source in his tone or choice of emphasis but employs the exact words of another, that surely is of some consequence. Where the Sarum Missal or the Prayer Book quotes the Bible verbatim, as in the case of the Passion narrative, there is no way of knowing whether the Bible or the liturgy was Herbert's source; the two can hardly be separated.[41] When we turn, however, to what Tuve calls "the other prong of the two-pointed irony,"[42] which comes from outside the Passion story, it is worth noting that the great majority of the examples I have quoted are not even mentioned, much less stressed, in the Sarum liturgy for Holy Week.[43] On the other hand, given Tuve's argument, one may justifiably wonder why Herbert does not refer to

40. Ibid., 48 n. 12.

41. Tuve suggests, for example, that in the first section of the poem, which deals with the Agony in the Garden and Jesus' betrayal and arrest, Herbert "follows roughly" the Responsories of Maundy Thursday in his "choices from the four Gospel Passions" (p. 48). But the Responsories are for the most part "adapted from" or "based on" verses of Matt. 26–27, according to the notes in *Sarum Missal in English*, I, 245–47, whereas Herbert borrows many important details from Luke and John as well, e.g., Luke 22:44 (line 22), 22:48 (41), 23:12 (74–75); John 12:5–6 (13, 18), 18:3 (35), 18:24 (53–54).

42. Tuve, *A Reading*, 62.

43. The exceptions are "pence," John 12:5; "loosed . . . bonds," Ps. 116:16 AV; and "I am the . . . Life," John 14:6 (*Sarum Missal in English*, I, 230, 243 n. 3, 251).

certain relevant materials that were in fact "liturgically marked out for emphasis": for example, Jesus washing his disciples' feet, in the Sarum Maundy Thursday service, or the binding of Isaac, a Proper Lesson for Good Friday in the Book of Common Prayer. It is clear, in short, that while Herbert's familiarity with the liturgy has helped to shape "The Sacrifice," it in no way takes the place of his own reading of the Bible.

By speaking as if there were hardly any difference between them, Tuve blurs the distinction between the medieval Latin liturgy, in which Herbert would have had a historical interest, and that of the Church of England, which he himself celebrated. Certainly the Book of Common Prayer was available to him in a much more immediate way than the Sarum service books; when Herbert wrote "The Sacrifice," the Sarum Use had been out of use for three generations. Although the Prayer Book borrowed a great deal from the Sarum Missal, the distinction between them, as I see it, has some bearing on the matter at hand. In the Latin liturgy, selected verses from the Bible, often freely adapted, are one of a number of elements—vestments, candles, incense, holy water, bells—that combine to form a dramatic ritual of considerable power. The Prayer Book, on the other hand, makes the Bible central, and in its more austere way lets the word of God speak for itself. It is not surprising that in the Latin poem *Passio Discerpta*, where Herbert meditates on many of the same themes as in "The Sacrifice" (the bloody sweat, pierced side, spitting and mocking, crown of thorns, reed and scarlet robe, buffeting, portioned garments, nails of the cross, bowed head, and veil of the Temple rent), he shows no special interest in the wording of the Vulgate.[44] The Latin poem, like the Latin liturgy, is

44. Even when he brings together texts that are related by a single word, he does not draw this to our attention. For example, no. XV ("Inclinato capite," *Works*, 407) avoids the play on *caput* that its sources

a free meditation on Scripture. "The Sacrifice," on the other hand, closely follows the language of the English Bible, in keeping with the spirit of the Prayer Book.

Although Tuve's discussion of the liturgical tradition is invaluable for the student of Herbert, her flat map of the Bible is misleading. Herbert's Christ, she insists, "is not the Christ we know in Luke's or Matthew's straightforward narrative—but He *is* the Christ of the liturgy of Holy Week."[45] By now it should be clear that there is no such thing as "straightforward narrative" in the Bible, least of all in the New Testament. The web of symbolic cross-reference that Tuve locates in the "liturgical and homiletic habit of attaching Old Testament phrasings to New Testament events"[46] is found first of all in the Scriptures. Giving witness to a sense of prophecy come true, the Gospels are dense with allusions to the Old Testament—allusions that figure importantly in Herbert's poem. The Christ of the Gospels is Isaiah's Suffering Servant, "a man of sorrows, and acquainted with griefe," "brought as a lambe to the slaughter," "numbred with the transgressours" (Isa. 53:3, 7, 12), and he speaks in the voice of the psalmist: "My God, my God, . . . why hast thou forsaken mee?" "They pearsed my hands and my feet," "They part my garments among them," "They gave me gall to eate: and when I was thirstie, they gave me vineger to drinke" (Pss. 22:1, 17, 18; 69:22). In pursuing the connections between various biblical passages, the liturgy is carrying

---

make possible: "Et inclinato *capite* tradidit spiritum" (John 19:30); "Filius autem hominis non habet ubi *caput* reclinet" (Matt. 8:20). The opposition of Zacchaeus and Jesus in no. XII comes closest to the wordplay of "The Sacrifice": "Zacchaeus, ut Te cernat, arborem *scandit:* / Nunc ipse *scandis*" (*Works,* 406). The first part of this contrast echoes the Vulgate's "ascendit in arborem" (Luke 19:4). The second is traditional—it is, as Tuve notes, "the veriest commonplace" (*A Reading,* 31)—but it is not scriptural.

45. Tuve, *A Reading,* 41.
46. Ibid., 58.

on a process initiated in Scripture itself. And as we have seen, Herbert believes that the reader of the Bible may—indeed, should—participate in this process, diligently comparing text with text in order that he may learn "how all [its] lights combine."

TRANSFORMATIONS: "MAKING A SCEPTER OF THE ROD"

Herbert brings to the "book of starres" his own light, such as it is. He often adapts Scripture to suit his poetic purposes, and as we have seen, his modifications, far from being presumptuous, demonstrate his active involvement with the text—precisely what the Bible requires of its readers. In the preceding pages I noted some examples of Herbert's boldness in handling biblical texts, for example in "Sepulchre," where he rewrites the story of Christ's burial to intensify its pathos, or in "The Sacrifice," where he has Christ set the crown of thorns on his own head. It is now time to consider Herbert's method and purpose in transforming his biblical materials.

Helen Vendler deals with this subject at length in *The Poetry of George Herbert*. The great strength of her book is that it subjects to scrutiny Herbert's "inventive transformations," which have never received adequate attention. "A question crying out for answer," Vendler writes, "is what [Herbert] makes of the traditional base":

> Certainly "tradition" is used differently by different poets, and each poet decides what décor he will choose from the Christian storehouse in order to create his stanzas. Though every single image in a poem may be "traditional," the choice of emphasis and exclusion is individual and revealing.[47]

This seems to me just and true—with the exception of one word: Herbert's borrowings from the Bible are not mere "décor" ("embellishment," he would say) but the very substance of his art.

47. Vendler, *Poetry of Herbert*, 4, 29.

I cannot agree, however, with her assumptions about why Herbert "reinvents" his biblical materials. Vendler argues that Herbert's true originality lies in his opposition to the Bible. In her view Herbert "often finds the original conception inadequate, whether the original conception be the Church's, the Bible's, or his own. Nothing is exempt from his critical eye." The Bible is one of the sources of "the safe, the bland, the familiar, and the taken-for-granted" that Herbert turns inside out in his campaign to "criticize the received idea."[48] Now, while it is true that Herbert rigorously examines and corrects his own too-easy formulations of thought or feeling, his reverence for the Bible (his own and that of his church, his readers, his age) makes it unlikely that he would have approached that text in quite the same way. Herbert would hardly have classified his scriptural materials as "cliché[s] of religious expression"[49] in need of refurbishing, and he would have been shocked by the notion that he was "criticizing" or "correcting" an "inadequate" account. To argue in this way, he surely would have objected, is to have "too slight a regard of the Scripture."[50]

Vendler sees as the primary subject of Herbert's poems "the workings of his own mind and heart rather than the expression of certain religious beliefs," and construes every "departure from scriptural authenticity" as an assertion of self.[51] That Herbert felt no such conflict is apparent in "The H. Scriptures, II":

> Such are thy secrets, which my life makes good,
>   And comments on thee: for in ev'ry thing
>   Thy words do finde me out, & parallels bring,
> And in another make me understood.

(9–12)

48. Ibid., 29, 56.
49. Ibid., 29.
50. Quoted from Herbert's "Notes on Valdesso," *Works*, 317. Herbert finds Valdesso's disparagement of the Scriptures "unsufferable" (318; see 306–7, 309–10, 317–18).
51. Vendler, *Poetry of Herbert*, 4, 206.

In the balanced interplay of "thy/thee" and "my/me," he says "thou art mine, and I am thine" to the Bible in the accents of a lover. To Herbert, Bible and self are not mutually exclusive but rather mutually illuminating. He works *through* Scripture, not *against* it, departing from the text, as we have observed, to enter it more fully. And what he seeks to express are not simply personal discoveries but universal Christian truths. In another context Vendler reminds us that it is wrong to "think of 'strict form' as offering only 'obstacles,'" or to "suggest that such 'obstacles' preclude 'individual thought and feeling.'"[52] But the same principle applies to Herbert's attitude toward his sources. These can be liberating, not confining, in the same way that formal demands can be liberating.

Because she assumes that Herbert's biblical sources are constricting, Vendler tends to interpret them in a negative light. In her account of "The Invitation," for example, she writes that Herbert is "probably remembering, in the beginning, Paul's statement (Rom. 14:21) that it is good neither to eat flesh nor to drink wine, and he begins his invitation with the Pauline view of sinners as prodigal gluttons and winebibbers":

> Come ye hither All, whose taste
>   Is your waste;
> Save your cost, and mend your fare.
> . . . .
> Come ye hither All, whom wine
>   Doth define,
> Naming you not to your good.
>
>   (1–3, 7–9)

But "St. Paul's revulsion is not congenial" to him, she goes on, and "the poem amounts, though implicitly, to a

52. Ibid., 203.

total critique of the usual scorn toward sinners."[53] Vendler is remembering only the first half of Romans 14:21; the verse in its entirety reads: "It is good neither to eate flesh, nor to drinke wine, nor any thing whereby thy brother stumbleth, or is offended, or is made weake." Paul is urging the Christian to abstain not from food or drink but rather from any action that may be an occasion of sin to another. He is not expressing "revulsion" toward sinners but, quite the contrary, admonishing those who hold their weaker brethren in contempt; as he says earlier: "Let us not therefore judge one another any more: . . . there is nothing uncleane of it selfe" (14:13–14). Far from being a "critique" of Paul's attitude, "The Invitation" in fact reflects his generosity of spirit.

Again, in her discussion of "Aaron," Vendler finds a "divergence from the Pauline position," or as she calls it, "Paul's harsher mode"[54]—as if the speaker's sweetness and light were to be gained only at the price of putting off Paul. I doubt that Herbert would have thought of Paul as harsh; he characteristically dwells on Paul's most "ravishing" texts.[55] As for "Aaron," the image of dying unto sin that Herbert takes from Paul speaks about "newnesse of life" (Rom. 6:4), death as a prelude to resurrection. In the serenity and joy that suffuse the final lines, we find Herbert embracing not his own nature but Paul's theology of redemption. Vendler wants to read the poem as "a movement of the heart rather than a proposition in theology,"

53. Ibid., 30–31.
54. Ibid., 121. See my discussion of "Aaron" in chap. 3.
55. We have already noticed the texts he chooses from the Epistles as subjects for poems: the Holy Spirit grieves for us, our life is hid in Christ, we may be a sweet savor to God (see my discussion in chap. 1). In "The Parson preaching" Paul is held up as an example: "For there is no greater sign of holinesse, then the procuring, and rejoycing in anothers good. And herein St *Paul* excelled in all his Epistles" (*A Priest to the Temple, Works,* 234). Again, when Herbert writes to his ailing mother, it is Paul's words of solace that he quotes: "*Rejoyce in the Lord alwaies, and again I say rejoyce*" (*Works,* 374; cf. Phil. 4:4).

but "Aaron" shows precisely how a proposition in theology may induce a movement of the heart.[56]

The "free play of ideas" that Vendler associates with "Herbert's true originality"[57] is more often than not the free play of *biblical* ideas. Consider "The Call." In Vendler's reading the poem departs from Jesus' self-definition in John 14:6, "I am the Way, the Trueth, and the Life," and progresses to something "far less 'Biblical' and far more 'Herbertian' "—though she concedes that nothing in the ending "lacks Biblical authorization."[58] "The Call," however, is a tissue of scriptural verses; the beginning is hardly "joyless" and the end is as biblical as the beginning:

> Come, my Way, my Truth, my Life:
> Such a Way, as gives us breath:
> Such a Truth, as ends all strife:
> Such a Life, as killeth death.
>
> Come, my Light, my Feast, my Strength:
> Such a Light, as shows a feast:
> Such a Feast, as mends in length:
> Such a Strength, as makes his guest.
>
> Come, my Joy, my Love, my Heart:
> Such a Joy, as none can move:
> Such a Love, as none can part:
> Such a Heart, as joyes in love.

Vendler's view of the first stanza is like a negative of a photograph, with dark and light values reversed. The speaker's joyous faith that "Jesus will give him breath, end strife, and kill death" yields the somber realization that he is "the strayed sheep, the mind in darkness, and the soul imprisoned by the body of this death," and it is shadowed too by "Jesus' stern implication in the original Gospel source that unbelievers will perish if they do not

56. Vendler, *Poetry of Herbert*, 121. This is the central point of Strier's *Love Known:* "We can grasp the human content of Herbert's poetry only through, not apart from, the theology" (xxi).

57. Vendler, *Poetry of Herbert*, 56.

58. Ibid., 209.

find the way, the truth, and the life."[59] But Jesus' teaching is more hopeful than foreboding ("Let not your heart be troubled," John 14 begins), and it is amplified by Herbert in the second and fourth lines of the poem by allusions to Paul's words of comfort: "Hee giveth to all, life and breath"; "Our Saviour Jesus Christ . . . hath abolished death" (Acts 17:25, 2 Tim. 1:10).

Vendler names some texts that figure in the second stanza: lines 5 and 6 are "quite close to things Jesus did in fact say—'I am the light of the world,' and 'I am the living bread'" (John 8:12, 6:51). But the third stanza, which she finds the most intimate and self-assured, seems to her by definition the least biblical. "For the first time," she writes, "the titles by which Jesus is addressed come from the speaker himself rather than from his Scripture reading." But if " 'Come, my Joy, my Love, my Heart' seems close in feeling to 'My true love hath my heart and I have his,' " its obvious source is the repeated invitation of the Song of Songs, "Come, my beloved" (7:11; cf. 2:10, 2:13, 4:8, 4:16). And surely it is stretching a point to call the implied " 'I am Love' " "almost Blakean" if Herbert is "using" John's words "God is love" (1 John 4:16). Vendler traces the stanza's "bold exclusive claims" to the "identity of self and Jesus [that] has finally been achieved"; as a result, "Herbert knows that 'none can move' this joy, 'none can part' this love."[60] But this knowledge comes to him directly from the Bible: "Your heart shall rejoyce, and your joy no man taketh from you"; "Who shall separate us from the love of Christ?" (John 16:22, Rom. 8:35). Indeed the intimacy and certainty of the final stanza are firmly rooted in Scripture.

The opposition of "biblical" and "Herbertian," in short, rests on an inadequate accounting of just how much Herbert owes to the Bible. "To think that such a

59. Ibid., 205–6.
60. Ibid., 206–8.

poem could be constructed on a 'source' of only nine words," Vendler exclaims of "Love, III," "is to stand astonished at Herbert's powers."[61] That Herbert needed one source only, and a brief one at that, seems proof of his originality. But Herbert's "source" for a poem is rarely a single text of Scripture; his usual practice, as we have just seen, is to work with a variety of texts, generating new meanings from their interaction. When we discover that what is most Herbertian has a direct source in the Bible, I think we remain no less astonished at his powers.

Vendler's Herbert leaves his biblical sources far behind in the heat of creation; I see him rather as clinging tenaciously to the old symbols and making them serve his need to say something new. To modify a biblical image is not to abandon it but rather to preserve it, to secure it for the present. Let us look for a moment at stanza 5 of "Praise, III":

> I have not lost one single tear:
>   But when mine eyes
> Did weep to heav'n, they found a bottle there
>   (As we have boxes for the poore)
> Readie to take them in; yet of a size
>   That would contain much more.
>
> (25–30)

Herbert starts with an odd image from Psalm 56:8, "put my teares into thy bottel," enlarging on it in ways that make it both more accessible to the reader and more explicitly Christian.[62] The tenor of the metaphor is clear (our very tears are all numbered by God), but the vehicle, as

---

61. Ibid., 276. Earlier, however, Vendler refers to the centurion's words (Luke 7:6) and Paul's definition of Charity (1 Cor. 13) as "sources" (55, 275).

62. Herbert presents his prayer as already answered, in keeping with the conclusion of the verse ("Are not these things noted in thy booke?") and of the psalm ("Thou hast delivered my soule from death, and my feete from falling," 56:8, 13). See my discussion of the psalmist's "certainty of a hearing" in chap. 5.

Herbert recognized, requires a gloss. The psalmist's "bottel" (Heb. *nod*) was an animal skin used to store water, wine, milk or oil (cf. Judg. 4:19, 1 Sam. 16:20). Herbert compares the ancient waterskin to an object familiar to his contemporaries, the church's poor box, his reflections on the state of the poor box leading him back to the "bottel" with a wry qualification: it is "of a size / That would contain much more." If the psalmist implies that he has wept a good deal, Herbert has the image say precisely the opposite: we are as chary with penitential tears as we are with alms for the poor.

In the next stanza Herbert works one more change in the metaphor. A single tear of Christ's makes the heavenly cup run over: "But after thou hadst slipt a drop / From thy right eye, / . . . The glasse was full and more" (31–32, 36). (I deliberately pass over the three lines in parentheses, which refer to Christ's tear, not the bottle.) Herbert first stretches the bottle, then fills it to overflowing, making it into a vessel of Christian teachings about human inadequacy and divine grace. The psalmist's old leather "bottel," it appears, can be filled with new wine— if I may be allowed to invert a biblical figure as Herbert so often does. When Jesus said that men do not "put new wine into old bottles" (Matt. 9:17), he was referring specifically to the Pharisees' religious practices, not the Hebrew Scriptures; of those he said, "I am not come to destroy, but to fulfill" (Matt. 5:17). The New Testament, which sets out to document how the Scriptures have been fulfilled, may be seen precisely as an attempt to put new wine into old bottles. This is an apt figure for Herbert's process of transformation: he does not leave the old symbols behind but lovingly restores them, making them fit for use under the new dispensation. When Herbert reworks Old Testament images in the light of his experience as a Christian, he is participating in a process initiated in the pages of the New Testament, as we noted earlier in our discussion of "constellations" like *lamb* and *thorn*.

Herbert's poetics are formed on the Gospels and Epistles, from which he learns how to take liberties that do not destroy but fulfill.

"Prayer, I" reveals with particular clarity how Herbert typically goes about transforming his sources, making new symbols of old ones. Half of the fourteen lines are based on biblical images (my italics):

> Prayer *the Churches banquet,* Angels age,
> *Gods breath in man returning to his birth,*
> The soul in paraphrase, *heart in pilgrimage,*
> *The Christian plummet sounding heav'n and earth;*
> *Engine against th' Almightie, sinners towre,*
> *Reversed thunder, Christ-side-piercing-spear,*
> *The six-daies world transposing in an houre,*
> A kind of tune, which all things heare and fear;
> Softnesse, and peace, and joy, and love, and blisse,
> *Exalted Manna,* gladnesse of the best,
> Heaven in ordinarie, man well drest,
> The milkie way, the bird of Paradise,
> Church-bels beyond the starres heard, *the souls bloud,*
> *The land of spices;* something understood.

The sonnet celebrates, among other things, the transforming power of prayer, a power that Herbert imitates in his poetic re-creation of biblical images. In "Prayer, I" he "stretches" his materials with minimal means, usually just an adjective or a participial phrase; in a few cases the equation the title calls for ("Prayer is X") is enough to alter the meaning of the image or event. The reader is expected to draw upon his knowledge of Scripture in order to expand the highly compressed phrases and render them intelligible. If he pursues the biblical allusions to their sources, as I intend to do in the next few paragraphs, he will discover some striking examples of Herbert's image-making process.

In *reversed thunder* we have a paradigm of poetic transformation: Herbert takes a biblical image, charged with ancient terror, works a small but significant change in it, and sends it off in a new direction. In the Old Testament, *thunder,* often accompanied by smoke, fire, darkness and lightning (e.g., Ps. 18:7–15) is a sign of God's might. At the Creation, "the voice of [God's] thunder" subdues the primeval waters (Ps. 104:7); at Mount Sinai it reduces the Israelites to fear and trembling (Ex. 19:16, 20:18); later it defeats the Philistines (1 Sam. 7:10) and leaves Job speechless: "Hast thou an arme like God? or canst thou thunder with a voyce like him?" (40:9). Praying, man steals God's thunder: *reversed* thunder is man's weapon, his "engine against th' Almightie." Similarly, the plummet or "plumb-line," originally a metaphor of judgment (2 Kings 21:13, Isa. 28:17, Amos 7:7–9), is "reversed" in Herbert's *Christian* plummet, "sounding heav'n and earth," which speaks consolingly about the boundless reaches of prayer. These images convert divine threat into human privilege, "making a scepter of the rod," as Herbert writes in "Affliction, III."

Other images suggest that prayer can remake the world, redress the ravages of history. Two have their source in the biblical story of Creation. The power of prayer rivals God's own, enabling man to "transpose" the *six daies world* in a mere "houre" on his knees. *Gods breath in man returning to his birth* envisions a new Adam who will not abuse the gift of life. *Towre* and *spear* both recall incidents of human aggression against God; in prayer the impulse to aggression is rendered harmless—or indeed productive. *Sinners towre* is Babel revisited. We are told in Genesis how men in their pride attempted to build "a tower, whose top may reach unto heaven" (11:4); here that sinful tower of "bricke . . . and slime" is replaced by a tower of penitent words, just as the "brasse and . . . stone" of the Hebrew Temple give way to the "grones" of the heart in "Sion." *Christ-side-piercing spear* is the only image from the New Testament to be reinterpreted in this fashion, the soldier's affront to Christ (John 19:34) being converted into an expression of human urgency.

Where the Old Testament images were already "baptized" in the tradition—*banquet, Manna, pilgrimage, bloud*—Herbert chooses "modifiers" that call attention to that modification: "*Churches* banquet," "*exalted* Manna," "*heart* in pilgrimage," "*souls* bloud." Herbert is following the allegorical interpretation of the Song of Songs when he reserves the "banketting house" of 2:4 for *the Churches banquet*. *Manna*, the food of the wandering Israelites (Ex. 16, Ps. 78:25–26) was understood as a type of Christ ("Your fathers did eate Manna in the wildernesse, and are dead. . . . I am the living bread, which came downe from heaven. If any man eate of this bread, he shall live for ever," John 6:49–51). The epithet *exalted*, pointing as it does to Christ (Acts 5:31, Phil. 2:9), reminds us of the new range of meaning.[63] In the Old Testament, *pilgrimage* refers simply to a temporary sojourn—in Canaan (Ex. 6:4) or more generally, on earth (Gen. 47:9). In the New Testament the image implies the faith in an afterlife: "These all . . . were strangers and pilgrims on the earth. . . . But now they desire a better countrey, that is, an heavenly" (Heb. 11:13–16); "I beseech you as strangers and pilgrimes, abstaine from fleshly lusts" (1 Peter 2:11). The adjective *heart*, which, as Lewalski points out, is frequently used "as synecdoche for the Christian himself," claims the *pilgrimage* as a metaphor for the Christian life.[64] Finally, *bloud* reflects Old Testament notions of sacrifice, redefined in Christ: "Neither by the blood of Goats and

63. On the further implications of *exalted*, see Mario A. Di Cesare, "Herbert's 'Prayer (I)' and the Gospel of John," in *"Too Rich to Clothe the Sunne": Essays on George Herbert*, ed. Claude J. Summers and Ted-Larry Pebworth (Pittsburgh, 1980), 107–8. For other readings of the poem, see E. B. Greenwood, "George Herbert's Sonnet 'Prayer': A Stylistic Study," *Essays in Criticism* 15 (1965): 27–45, and Sidney Gottlieb, "How Shall We Read Herbert? A Look at 'Prayer' (I)," *George Herbert Journal* 1 (1977): 26–38.

64. Lewalski, *Protestant Poetics*, 101; cf. also her discussion of the pilgrimage trope, p. 93.

Calves: but by his owne blood" (Heb. 9:12). *Soul* completes the transformation of the image, locating the Christian's sacrifice of praise in the temple of the spirit.

The images I have singled out—*thunder, plummet; sixdaies world, Gods breath; towre, spear; banquet, Manna; pilgrimage, bloud*—dramatize how the old is made new for the Christian in prayer. All of these were generated in the same way, by pressing the symbols of the past into the service of the present. I have not attempted to account for everything in the poem; indeed some of Herbert's most striking conceits—"The milkie way, the bird of Paradise, / Church-bels beyond the starres heard" (12–13)—make no reference to the Bible. My purpose, rather, has been to focus on a particular strain of images that casts light on Herbert's process of composition. Just as "The Sacrifice" illustrates how Herbert typically combines biblical texts, so "Prayer, I" reveals how he modifies what he borrows. In the first he draws a line between points in the text, letting them comment on one another; in the second, he draws a line between various Old Testament images and the Christian's life—also a form of commentary, according to "The H. Scriptures, II" (9–10). I am suggesting that we think of Herbert's "inventive transformations" of biblical materials not as "critique"—far too narrow and negative an approach—but rather as commentary. Herbert's poems are written as it were in the margins of the Bible.

Here an analogy will be helpful. The biblical tales invite retelling much in the same way that they (in Erich Auerbach's phrase) "demand" interpretation.[65] Retelling, indeed, is a form of interpretation, elaborating what the Bible only hints at or leaves in darkness and adapting the ancient stories to the needs and perceptions of a later day. We see the impulse at work in the Towneley Master as well as in Thomas Mann, but I am thinking in particular of the rabbinic legends of the Bible, sprightly and fanciful tales that occur alongside grammatical parsings and knotty legal

65. Auerbach, *Mimesis*, 12.

disquisitions in the Talmud and Midrash. The rabbinic materials were well known to biblical scholars in the Renaissance, and it is entirely possible that Herbert was aware of them.[66] But that is not my point; here I am not tracking down an influence but rather proposing an analogy. Although these legends are often startling in their departures from Scripture, the rabbis saw them as reverent commentary, permitting them to be transmitted only in oral form for centuries in order to set them apart from the revealed truth of Holy Writ. To elaborate is not necessarily to reject. A variation on a theme is a form of homage, not of criticism.

I have been arguing that Herbert's transformations are not critiques but commentaries, and that we should not think of the Bible as "inadequate" to his expressive needs. But let me go further: in my view the Bible is not constricting but enabling for Herbert, opening the "closets" of the heart,[67] freeing him to speak more fully, more truthfully, than he might otherwise have done. When Herbert writes "Thy words do finde me out," he means "find out" not only in the sense of "to come upon by searching" but also "to penetrate the disguise of" (*OED*); the word of God is "a discerner of the thoughts and intents of the heart" (Heb. 4:12). From this point of view, I would like to consider "Affliction, I" and "The Forerunners" and then, in some detail, "Love, III."

"Affliction, I" is a recital of grievances, reviewing a long period of fruitless service. For most of the poem's sixty-six lines, the speaker complains bitterly of his "master," charging him with fraud: thou didst "entice," "entwine,"

---

66. Arnold Williams, *The Common Expositor: An Account of the Commentaries on Genesis, 1527–1633* (Chapel Hill, 1948), 12, reports that "certain commentators made this Jewish material their chief concern. Thus Steuchus Eugubinus in the early sixteenth century and Mercerus toward the end of the century are especially notable for the amount of material they derived from Talmud, midrash, and rabbinical commentary. Succeeding commentators used their work extensively."

67. "Confession," 3.

"betray"; I was "argu'd into hopes," "entangled"—strong
language for *The Temple*. His anger mounts until the uncharacteristically bitter irony of the ninth stanza:

> Yet lest perchance I should too happie be
> In my unhappinesse,
> Turning my purge to food, thou throwest me
> Into more sicknesses.
> Thus doth thy power crosse-bias me, not making
> Thine own gift good, yet me from my wayes taking.
>
> (49–54)

In this indictment, summed up in the startling phrase
"thou troublest me" (61), the master is made to seem a
petty tyrant, at best scheming and at worst malicious.
Herbert rarely allows himself to accuse God so openly.
Usually he will express his anger against God only as it is
transmuted into sorrow ("O that thou shouldst give dust
a tongue / To crie to thee, / And then not heare it crying!") or diverted against himself ("I know it is my sinne,
which locks thine eares").[68] Vendler finds "a remarkable
lack of censorship" in "Affliction, I," naming the Psalms
and the Book of Job as precedents.[69]

There is another precedent worth mentioning, one directly related to the language of the poem. Consider the
second stanza:

> I looked on thy furniture so fine,
> And made it fine to me:
> Thy glorious houshold-stuffe did me entwine,
> And 'tice me unto thee.
> Such starres I counted mine: both heav'n and earth
> Payd me my wages in a world of mirth.
>
> (7–12)

The words *furniture, houshold-stuffe* and *wages* seem, at
first glance, to be examples of Herbert's characteristic

---

68. "Deniall," 16–18; "Church-lock and key," 1.
69. Vendler, *Poetry of Herbert,* 43–44.

kind of wit, which looks to everyday reality rather than
to abstruse learning—the province of the metaphysi-
cals—for its comparisons. *Furniture* is used in the Book
of Exodus (e.g., 31: 7–9) to designate the appurtenances
of the tabernacle; hence "thy furniture" is not as
quaintly domestic as one might think. What is particularly arresting, however, is the fact that *furniture, houshold-stuffe* and *wages* occur together, along with the title
"Affliction," within the space of a few verses, in the account of Jacob's angry confrontation with his exploitative
master, Laban: Rachel hides Laban's household gods in
the camel's *"furniture"*; Jacob reproaches Laban, who has
pursued him and searched his goods, "What hast thou
found of all thy *household stuffe*?" "I *served* thee [twenty
years]," he complains, "and thou hast changed my *wages*
ten times . . . God hath seene my *affliction* (Gen. 31:34–
42, my italics). Surely it is no coincidence that this
cluster of words appears in "Affliction, I," a poem about
a disaffected servant brooding on his ill-treatment and
accusing his master of duplicity.

One can see why this story would be suggestive for
Herbert. Laban, the reader will remember, first welcomes
his nephew Jacob with demonstrative warmth, offering
what seem to be attractive terms of employment. It is not
until Jacob has labored for seven years that he discovers
he has been cheated. "Wherefore then hast thou beguiled
me?" he protests, when Leah is substituted for Rachel
(29:25). "Let me goe," he pleads after working for another
seven years, "for thou knowest my service which I have
done thee" (30:26). But Laban smoothly urges him to
"tary" (30:27). "With all my power I have served your
father," Jacob complains to his wives on the eve of their
flight, "and your father hath deceived mee" (31:6–7). In
the final confrontation with Laban quoted above, Jacob
gives voice to his pent-up bitterness in a defiant speech:
he has given years of good service and has in turn gotten

nothing but abuse. The key words in the narrative are
service and *wages*.[70]

It seems to me very likely that the plight of Jacob was
in Herbert's mind when he wrote "Affliction, I." Earlier
versions of the poem may have contained more overt references to Jacob's history; the readings in the Williams
manuscript make that a plausible conjecture:

> I looked on thy furniture so *rich*,
> And made it *rich* to mee:
> Thy glorious houshold stuff did mee bewitch
> Into thy *familie*.[71]

> (7–10, my italics)

Herbert identifies himself with Jacob in other poems. His
personal motto, *"Lesse then the least / Of all thy mercies"*
("The Posie," 3–4), comes from the following chapter in
Genesis, when Jacob offers thanks to God for "all the
mercies . . . which thou hast shewed unto thy servant"
(32:10). And the episode of Jacob's wrestling with God
(32:24–32), remembered in "Decay," is the type of Herbert's own spiritual "wrastling."[72] But if in those poems
Herbert is Jacob and God is God, here God is—at least so
long as the spate of temper lasts—an exploitative master
like Laban. The analogy is never overt (Herbert *knows*
God is not Laban) and is summoned up only to be dismissed. As soon as the speaker threatens to seek "some
other master," he recalls with a gasp ("Ah my deare
God!" 64–65) who his Master is and, all passion spent,
renews his vows of love. Herbert includes "Affliction, I"
in *The Temple* as a record of his own petulant willfulness:

70. See the illuminating stylistic and structural analysis of the Hebrew text in J. P. Fokkelman, *Narrative Art in Genesis* (Assen/Amsterdam,
1975), 123–96.

71. *The Williams Manuscript of George Herbert's Poems*, facs., intro.
Amy M. Charles (Delmar, N.Y., 1977), fol. 48$_v$.

72. Garret Keizer discusses Herbert's use of the biblical motif of
combat with God in "Artillerie," "Sion" and other poems in "George
Herbert and the Tradition of Jacob," *Cithara* 18 (1978): 18–26.

it is, finally, an indictment of himself, not God. Still, the expression of anger is allowed to stand. I think the story of Jacob and Laban made possible the undiluted vehemence of the poem, the directness with which Herbert expressed the full force of his frustration.

In "The Forerunners" it is the uncharacteristically rude language of the middle stanzas that requires explanation—or what is more puzzling, the peculiar combination of tenderness and abuse:

> Farewell sweet phrases, lovely metaphors.
> But will you leave me thus? when ye before
> Of stews and brothels onely knew the doores,
> Then did I wash you with my tears, and more,
>> Brought you to Church well drest and clad:
> My God must have my best, ev'n all I had.
>
> Lovely enchanting language, sugar-cane,
> Hony of roses, whither wilt thou flie?
> Hath some fond lover tic'd thee to thy bane?
> And wilt thou leave the Church, and love a stie?
>> Fie, thou wilt soil thy broider'd coat,
> And hurt thy self, and him that sings the note.
>
> Let foolish lovers, if they will love dung,
> With canvas, not with arras, clothe their shame:
> Let follie speak in her own native tongue.
>
> (13–27)

Hutchinson politely evades the issue in his note: "Herbert sought at first to dedicate to sacred use the language which before had been used by others in the service of Venus."[73] But "stews and brothels," "stie," "dung" and "shame" are hardly associated with the worship of Venus and Cupid that Herbert fusses about in his youthful sonnets.[74] The very words are foreign to Herbert (with the obvious exception of "shame"): "stews," "brothels" and

73. Hutchinson, "Commentary," Works, 539.
74. See especially "My God, where is that ancient heat . . . ," Works, 206.

"stie" occur only here in *The Temple,* and "dung" only in passages about animals.[75]

I do not think that Herbert would have written in this vein without the example of the prophets, who often represent Israel's idolatry with images of sexual betrayal (e.g., Jer. 3, Ezek. 23). Of particular interest is a passage from Ezekiel, where God reproves Israel:

> Then *washed* I thee with water: yea, I throughly washed away thy blood from thee, and I anointed thee with oyle. I *clothed* thee also with *broidred* worke. . . .
>
> And thy renowme went foorth among the heathen for thy *beautie:* for it was perfect through my comelinesse which I had put upon thee, sayth the Lord GOD.
>
> But thou diddest trust in thine owne beauty, and playedst the harlot. . . .
>
> And in all thine abominations and thy whooredomes, thou hast not remembered the dayes of thy youth, when thou was naked and bare, and wast polluted in thy blood.
>
> (Ezek. 16:9–22, my italics)

When he tells us that he has washed and clothed the language of brothels, Herbert is drawing directly on Ezekiel.

Equally important here is the story of Hosea, who is commanded to marry "a wife of whoredomes" (1:2) in order to make plain the meaning of Israel's apostasy. Hosea tries to teach his wife, with a tenderness and devotion that mirror God's redemptive love, to "put away her whoredomes," but she plays the harlot and leaves him, shamelessly decking herself out in her jewels and proclaiming, "I will goe after my lovers" (2:2, 5). That Hosea was present to Herbert's mind is suggested by the phrase *Thou art still my God.*[76] In Hosea's tale of sexual betrayal,

75. "The fly / That feeds on dung, is coloured thereby," ("The Church-porch," 233–34); "Sheep eat the grasse, and dung the ground for more" ("Providence," 69).

76. This phrase summons up a constellation of texts about covenant loyalty: Jer. 24:7, 30:22, 31:33, 32:38; Ezek. 11:20, 36:28, 37:27; Zech. 13:9; cf. 2 Cor. 6:16; Heb. 8:10. "Thou art . . . my God" is also a formula of trust found in the Psalms; see chap. 1, pp. 25–26.

the prophet is commanded to name one of his bastard children *Lo-ammi* (Heb. "not my people") to symbolize that "yee are not my people, and I will not be your God" (1:2, 9), but he dreams of a day when God's love for Israel will be reciprocated: "I will say to them which were not my people: Thou art my people, and they shall say, Thou art my God" (2:23).

The opening chapters of Hosea are a welter of mixed emotions, love and tender longing vying with righteous anger and revulsion. The story of Hosea is echoed in "The Forerunners" with some of the intensity of its conflicting and unresolved passions. Herbert complains that he has taken the language of "stews and brothels," washed it with his tears, redeemed it—and that it has betrayed him. In his complaint we hear the baffled rage and resignation of the cuckold. Seen in the light of its biblical allusions, then, "The Forerunners" is about a man in pain turning to God for help, and at the same time about the casting away of "whoredoms," the purification of the heart. Ezekiel and Hosea give Herbert access to a world of sexual passion, jealousy and betrayal where he would scarcely have ventured alone, a world that he would seem to have excluded from his poems when as a young man he loftily turned away from "*filth*" to write chaste songs of praise.[77]

In "Affliction, I" and "The Forerunners," which Vendler numbers among Herbert's "three greatest autobiographical poems,"[78] the Bible provides Herbert with the means to self-understanding, sets him up a glass that shows him who he is. In the process it "mends" his eyes: when Herbert sees himself the aggrieved servant of an exploitative master, it is the scriptural word *master* that makes him look again and see more truly; when he is

77. "Sure, Lord, there is enough in thee . . ." (13), *Works*, 206.
78. Vendler, *Poetry of Herbert*, 41. The third is "The Flower," which I discuss in chaps. 4 and 5.

distressed by the betrayal of language, the phrase *Thou art my God* lets him perceive his loss in a new light. Autobiography in *The Temple* is the story of the self reflected and improved in the mirror of Scripture. This is in part what Herbert means when he writes in "The Dedication" that his poems are *"not mine neither: for from thee they came"* (2). The self, moreover, makes no claims to uniqueness. By using the Bible as a vehicle of discovery, Herbert is saying in effect that the truths he finds there are not his alone.

In Vendler's view Herbert had to choose between two alternatives. "Decking the given" at best could produce poems of "relative shallowness . . . , no matter how intricate and polished"; this, she thinks, may have been his initial goal, and proved a slough he fell into later "in moments of less-than-adequate insight or inspiration." On the other hand, his greatest poems seem to her "a faithful tracing of the interior disposition of the unique individual soul," a "searching interior enquiry" that inevitably left "the given" far behind.[79] But there is another possibility, which I believe best describes Herbert's method: searching the given, laying *stone* to *stone*, and in the process, making the old new. Herbert's poems of "interior enquiry" usually begin—and end— with his looking into "the thankfull glasse, / That mends the lookers eyes"; and even in his transformations he carries forward a process of elaboration and reinterpretation sanctioned in Scripture itself.

A READING OF "LOVE, III":
"HOW ALL THY LIGHTS COMBINE"

In this chapter I have spoken about how certain luminous words of Scripture light up Herbert's lines; about how the exegetical method of collating texts informs his poetic practice; and how his transformations involve a kind of

79. Vendler, *Poetry of Herbert,* 197.

"stretching" of these texts to make them fit the circumstances of his own life. By way of summary I would like to examine in detail a poem in which we can see all these processes at work. "Love, III" is one of Herbert's most subtle and complex achievements—and indeed one of the most beautiful lyrics in the English language. Typically Herbertian in its dramatization of theological issues, its deceptive simplicity, its colloquial ease, its candor and tact, its knowledge of the human heart, it has often been thought to be the quintessential Herbert poem:

> Love bade me welcome: yet my soul drew back,
>> Guiltie of dust and sinne.
> But quick-ey'd Love, observing me grow slack
>> From my first entrance in,
> Drew nearer to me, sweetly questioning,
>> If I lack'd any thing.
>
> A guest, I answer'd, worthy to be here:
>> Love said, You shall be he.
> I the unkinde, ungratefull? Ah my deare,
>> I cannot look on thee.
> Love took my hand, and smiling did reply,
>> Who made the eyes but I?
>
> Truth Lord, but I have marr'd them: let my shame
>> Go where it doth deserve.
> And know you not, sayes Love, who bore the blame?
>> My deare, then I will serve.
> You must sit down, sayes Love, and taste my meat:
>> So I did sit and eat.

"Love, III" presents an analytic task very different from that of explicitly biblical poems like "Coloss. 3.3" or "The Bunch of Grapes." Here the presence of Scripture is as unobtrusive as it is pervasive; indeed one must overcome a certain reluctance to unravel what appears to be a seamless unity. Neither Herbert's editors nor his critics have noticed how much "Love, III" owes to the Bible. In his notes to the poem, Hutchinson does not mention the Bible, while Patrides, who is especially attentive to scriptural allusions, refers only to Luke 12:37.

Even if one were to read the poem with no awareness of the Bible, as many readers undoubtedly do, it would still speak movingly on a considerable theme: how impotence is overcome by love. But it would not be the poem Herbert wrote. For, as in much of *The Temple,* the Bible provides the means by which an experience is translated into words and given poetic form. The subject is conceived biblically, as it were, and expressed biblically: the dramatic situation, the images, the tension of ideas, the very shape of the plot, all have their source in Scripture. "Love, III" is a consummate example of the way in which Herbert uses biblical materials—and makes them speak with his own voice.

Herbert's poem is about the love of man and God—on earth, as it is in heaven—not simply "the entrance of the redeemed soul into Paradise," as has been suggested.[80] The feast of love to which God has invited man is at once the earthly communion (with the implied pun on Host) and the heavenly marriage supper it anticipates. The Prayer Book makes that association inevitable by invoking the parables of the marriage feast and the wedding garment, which were told of the kingdom of heaven, in the communion service. Vendler finds the awkward hesitation of the guest surprising ("the originality of conception takes us aback") and the "ordinariness of the conversation" seems to her "daring . . . in view of the awe natural to the subject,"[81] but these give no occasion for surprise once we recognize the poem's larger concerns.

Some other readers have assumed that the poem "takes place in Heaven"[82] because it follows four poems

80. Ibid., 55; cf. Patrides, ed., *English Poems,* 192n.
81. Vendler, *Poetry of Herbert,* 55, 275.
82. Mary Ellen Rickey, *Utmost Art: Complexity in the Verse of George Herbert* (Lexington, Ky., 1966), 128. Rickey (p. 37) cites Joseph Summers, who in turn cites Herbert's seventeenth-century commentator George Ryley on this point. Summers, however, does not limit the poem's subject as Rickey and Vendler do; he is aware of "the relationships it establishes between this world and the next" (*George Herbert,* 89). So too Martz, *Poetry of Meditation,* 319.

about the traditional "last things": "Death," "Dooms-day," "Judgement" and "Heaven." But "Love, III," in which a fully visualized narrator recounts an intensely human experience, does not entirely belong to this sequence of impersonal eschatalogical poems (though it gains in complexity if we read it with the sequence in mind). Herbert imagines celestial scenes in these and a few other poems ("The Starre," "The Glance"), but he is not really comfortable with such imaginings—"Onely the present is thy part and fee," he rebukes his "busie enquiring heart" in the "The Discharge"; "Raise not the mudde / Of future depths" (21, 27–28)—and it is unlikely that he would wish to end a book whose "frame and fabrick is within" ("Sion," 12) by reinventing Paradise. Because "Love, III" is the final poem in "The Church,"[83] we must consider it in relation to the entire volume, not just the concluding sequence. Herbert's real subject, as his title tells us, is not an idea about heaven but an experience of love.[84]

The image of a feast to which God invites man has many sources in the Bible which, with their overlapping

83. Annabel M. Endicott [Patterson], "The Structure of George Herbert's *Temple:* A Reconsideration," *University of Toronto Quarterly* 34 (1965), rpt. *Essential Articles*, 360–62, and Lee Ann Johnson, "The Relationship of 'The Church Militant' to *The Temple*," *Studies in Philology* 68 (1971); 200–206, have argued that Herbert never intended "The Church Militant" to be considered a part of *The Temple*. There is a particularly firm sense of closure at the end of "The Church," not only in "Love, III," but in the entire final sequence. "Love, III" is followed, too, by an explicit "FINIS" (which appears in both manuscripts) as well as the doxology, *"Glory be to God on high / And on earth peace / Good will towards men,"* which recalls the conclusion of the Communion service. Herbert was surely aware that one of the changes in the 1552 Prayer Book of Edward VI was the "moving of the *Gloria in excelsis,* which became now the triumphant ending of the whole service" (George Hedley, *Christian Worship* [New York, 1953], 192). Finally, there is no poem of transition from "The Church" to "The Church Militant" as there is between "The Church-porch" and "The Church." It seems likely that Herbert intended "Love, III," with its ringing coda, as the conclusion of *The Temple*.

84. See chap. 4 on learning through experience.

and somewhat conflicting motifs, provide the framework for Herbert's poem. A bare listing of the most prominent sources, to start with, will show us where we stand. From the Old Testament: "Hee brought me to the banketting house, and his banner over mee, was love" from the Song of Songs (2:4), which was understood as an allegory of Christ's love, and the figure of God as gracious host in the Twenty-third Psalm.[85] From the New Testament: the messianic banquet promised in the Gospels (Matt. 26:29, Luke 12:37) and in the Book of Revelation (3:20); the invitations to drink of the water of life (John 7:37, Rev. 22:17; cf. Isa. 55:1); the parables of the great supper (Matt. 22:1–10, Luke 14:15–24, cf. 14:7–14) and the wedding garment (Matt. 22:11–14); and, finally, Jesus' provocative practice of dining with publicans and sinners (Luke 5:29–32, 19:2–10). Some of this was shaped for Herbert by its use in the Anglican liturgy, but we shall see plenty of evidence of Herbert's own shaping hand in the choice of resonant language, the juxtaposition of a variety of texts, and the inventive application of these materials to his own life.

The guest in Herbert's poem is reluctant to partake of God's feast, as in the parable of the great supper, where the chosen guests ungraciously spurn an invitation. His reason ("guiltie of dust and sinne") is deeply felt, unlike the alibis of the parable—it is a state of soul rather than a matter of business—but all the same, his balking clearly puts him in the wrong. The Prayer Book exhortation to those who are "negligent to come to the holy Communion" had already used the parable of the great supper as Herbert was to use it:

85. Some of Herbert's elaborations on the biblical text in his verse translation of this psalm clearly recall "Love, III": "The God *of love* my shepherd is, / *And he that doth me feed*: . . . Nay, thou dost *make me sit and dine*" (1–2, 17; my italics). "The 23d Psalme" was probably written after "Love, III" since, unlike that poem, it does not appear in the Williams manuscript.

Ye know how grievous and unkind a thing it is, when a man hath prepared a rich feast, decked his table with all kinde of provision, so that there lacketh nothing but the guests to sit downe, and yet they which be called (without any cause) most unthankefully refuse to come. . . . If any man say, I am a grievous sinner, and therefore am afraide to come: wherefore then doe you not repent and amend? When God calleth you, be you not ashamed to say yee will not come?[86]

In the parable the guests are unceremoniously condemned, for "they which were bidden, were not worthy" (Matt. 22:8). But Herbert's guest is patiently coaxed until he finally accedes, nor is his initial reluctance held against him. For Herbert is retelling the parable with Love as host, and when the beloved "draws back," as in the Song of Songs—"I opened to my beloved, but my beloved had with drawen himselfe, and was gone" (5:6)—Love is not angered but determined to win him back.

Knowing himself "guiltie of sinne," the guest is immobilized by the very thought of his unworthiness: he does not deserve to sit at Love's table. Here again the Prayer Book's use of the Bible provides a valuable insight. In the Anglican communion service, where not the sacramental elements but the communicants are to be transformed, it becomes vital for these to make themselves "woorthy partakers." The liturgy invokes the parable of the wedding garment, as well as Paul's warning to the communicants

to consider the dignitie of the holy mysterie, and the great perill of the unworthy receiving thereof, and so to search and examine your owne consciences, as you should come holy and cleane to a most godly and heavenly feast, so that in no wise yee come but in the mariage garment required of God in holy Scripture, and so come and be received, as woorthy partakers of such a heavenly table [cf. 1 Cor. 11:27].[87]

86. *The Booke of Common Prayer* (London, 1604), sig. [P8ᵥ].
87. Ibid., sig Qᵥ.

At the same time, the Prayer Book assumes the intrinsic unworthiness of the communicants in the penitential preparation for the sacrament, in the Prayer of Humble Access ("Wee be not worthy so much as to gather up the crummes under thy Table"), and in the concluding thanksgiving ("And although wee bee unworthy, through our manifolde sinnes, . . . yet we beseech thee to accept this our bounden duetie and service, not weighing our merits, but pardoning our offenses. . . .").[88] Thus too Herbert, in "The Parson in Sacraments," justifies the kneeling posture at communion, the subject of some debate in his day:

> The Feast indeed requires sitting, because it is a Feast; but man's unpreparednesse asks kneeling. Hee that comes to the Sacrament, hath the confidence of a Guest, and hee that kneels, confesseth himself an unworthy one, and therefore differs from other Feasters.[89]

How does a human being who is unworthy, and convinced of his unworthiness, respond when he is called by God? As in many of Herbert's poems, the guest must work through the historical stages of religious consciousness, from the Old Dispensation to the New, before he can resolve his difficulties. When Herbert starts with an Old Testament voice, letting the poem unfold by stages, he dramatizes the human dilemma, and offers a poetic analogue for the experience of conversion, when resistance is overcome by grace and the soul responds to the saving truth.[90]

The guest's initial response "copies out" those Old Testament scenes in which the prophets are summoned by God to his service. Moses, Isaiah and Jeremiah, it will be

88. Ibid., sigs. [Q5–Q5ᵥ]. John Booty, in his essay "History of the 1559 Book of Common Prayer" in *The Book of Common Prayer, 1559* (Charlottesville, 1976), 327–82, discusses the penitential emphasis of the Ante Communion service; cf. especially 357–59, 369, 374, 378–81.
89. *A Priest to the Temple, Works*, 259.
90. See my discussion of putting off the "old man" in chap. 3.

remembered, all resist God's call out of a sense of personal inadequacy, but God reasons with them, or reaches out to touch them, sweeping aside their objections. When Moses pleads, "O my lord, I am not eloquent, . . . but I am slow of speach, and of a slow tongue," God retorts, "Who hath made mans mouth?" (Ex. 4:10–11). Jeremiah cries, "Ah Lord GOD, behold, I cannot speake, for I am a childe," but God comforts him by word and gesture: "the LORD put foorth his hand, and touched my mouth" (Jer. 1:6–9). In Isaiah the note of self-abasement is at its most intense: "Woe is me; for I am undone, because I am a man of uncleane lippes, . . . for mine eyes have seene the king, the LORD of hostes." Only after a seraph touches his lips with a live coal from the altar, symbolically purging his sin ("thine iniquitie is taken away"), does Isaiah feel enabled to serve (Isa. 6:5–8).

These archetypal scenes have dictated the shape of Herbert's second stanza. In line 9, "I the unkinde, ungratefull?" the guest speaks with the self-reproach of the prophets—at this point the only conceivable human response—while "I cannot look on thee" echoes ancient taboos about man's confronting God directly (Ex. 33:20, Judg. 13:22, Isa. 6:5). Love's rejoinder—"Who made the eyes but I?"—is as pointed as God's reply to Moses. This is the God of the Old Testament speaking, though with a distinctly Herbertian smile. The guest, however, resists Love's assertion of omnipotence, as he did Love's fiat ("You shall be he"), and parries the argument from Creation with a reference to the Fall: "let my shame / Go where it doth deserve."[91] The word *shame*, like *dust* earlier, has the effect of focusing the consequences of man's first sin (cf. Gen. 2:25, 3:7)—including the most important, which the guest has for the moment forgotten: the redemptive sacrifice of Christ.

91. This phrase may reflect Hebrew idiomatic usage: cf. "And I, whither shall I cause my shame to goe?" (2 Sam. 13:13).

It is only in the middle of the third stanza, when Love, with the greatest delicacy, reminds him—"And know you not . . . who bore the blame?"—that the guest is convinced. The word *bore* points to a constellation of texts: "For hee shall beare their iniquities" (Isa. 53:11); "So Christ was once offered to beare the sinnes of many" (Heb. 9:28); "Who his owne selfe bare our sinnes in his owne body on the tree" (1 Peter 2:24). The conflict again is resolved by means of single words of Scripture, weighty with implication: *shame* is refuted by *bore* as man's whole history of sin is canceled by Christ's death. "For as by one mans disobedience many were made sinners: so by the obedience of one, shall many bee made righteous"; "but where sinne abounded, grace did much more abound" (Rom. 5:19–20)—these Pauline formulations lie behind the dialectic of Herbert's final stanza.

Love's logic is incontestable as his manner is disarming, and at this point one would assume that the debate is over. But Herbert's personae have a way of clinging, with a stubborn, almost comic dignity, to their old selves, even as they are being renewed. Thus in the last three lines the poem takes one final turn. In "My deare, then I will serve," the guest, it appears, accedes gracefully to Love's overpowering argument, but he is careful to insist upon terms of submission: "I will suffice," "I will serve you," "I will be the servant of the Lord," as Moses and Isaiah, among others, are called. The word *serve*, however, also calls to mind those New Testament passages in which Jesus, who "tooke upon him the forme of a servant" (Phil. 2:7), washes his disciples' feet (John 13:5–17) or instructs them in watchfulness and humility:

> Blessed are those servants, whom the Lord when he commeth, shall find watching: Verily, I say unto you, That he shall girde himselfe, and make them to sit downe to meate, and will come foorth and serve them.
>
> (Luke 12:37)

For whether is greater, hee that sitteth at meat, or hee that serveth? Is not he that sitteth at meat? But I am among you as he that serveth.

(Luke 22:27)

Such passages alert us to the density of Herbert's line: "then I will serve the Lord who serves his servants." But we realize its full complexity only when we see that the line belongs, in effect, to both speakers: the guest pronounces it, but Love appropriates it by performing the action.

Love's final invitation, "You must sit down and taste my meat," echoes the Old Testament again: "Shake thy selfe from the dust: arise, and sit downe, O Jerusalem" (Isa. 52:2); "O taste and see how gracious the Lord is" (Ps. 34:8); "Let my beloved come into his garden, and eate his pleasant fruits" (Song 4:16). In *The Temple* the note of passionate or ecstatic fulfillment is rare, and usually carries with it echoes of the Song of Songs, as in "Clasping of hands," "The Glance," "The Odour" and "The Banquet."[92] Here too the expression of achieved joy, "So I did sit and eat," recalls the Song of Songs: "I sate downe under his shadow with great delight, and his fruit was sweete to my taste" (2:3). When the problems posed by the Old Testament voice are finally resolved by Christ, Herbert's poem tells us, those ancient words find their true fulfillment.

In the end, the guest is rewarded when he expects to be punished, like the prodigal son whose loving father sweeps away his protestations of unworthiness ("I have sinned against heaven, and in thy sight, and am no more worthy to be called thy sonne," Luke 15:21)—and orders a joyful feast. In the movement of its plot from sorrow to rejoicing, "Love, III" echoes the hopeful turn of so many of the psalms and parables, as well as the Gospel narratives of Jesus' death and resurrection: "They that sow in

92. Cf. Song 2:16, 4:9, 1:3, 5:1.

teares: shall reape in joy" (Ps. 126:6); "the last shall be first" (Matt. 20:16); "hee that humbleth himselfe, shalbe exalted" (Luke 14:11). This biblical promise has impressed itself on most of Herbert's poems, and on the ordering, too, of the volume, where "Love, III" takes its place as the final poem. Herbert believes, of course, that man's nature is sinful. But he also believes (and the belief is equally orthodox) that God is ready to embrace man as he is—inadequate, dusty, troubled, with all his imperfections on his head; that, surely, is how we understand the meaning of love, whether human or divine.

In "Love, III" man's sin and God's love are weighed in the balance. These two are set forth as the proper study of mankind in "The Agonie," and throughout *The Temple* are opposed to one another in a variety of formal structures that embody the tension of contrary forces. There is no doubt about the outcome: "We are darknesse, and weaknesse, and filthinesse, and shame," as Herbert writes in "The Authour's Prayer before Sermon," "but thou Lord, art patience, and pity, and sweetnesse, and love."[93] "Dialogue," a forerunner of "Love, III," offers a pointed rebuke to the nearsighted creature who cannot comprehend this: *"What, Child, is the ballance thine, / Thine the poise and measure?"* (9–10). And "Love, III," which contains *The Temple* in brief, proceeds by a series of careful balancings, tipping first to the one side and then to the other, until it comes to rest in the last line emphatically on the side of God's love.

The tension of ideas in "Love, III," which Herbert carries over from his sources, is in part what makes it so convincing a representation of human experience. The

---

93. "Prayer before Sermon," *Works,* 288. Herbert goes on to say "Thou hast exalted thy mercy above all things; and hast made our salvation, not our punishment, thy glory: so that then where sin abounded, not death, but grace superabounded" (cf. Rom. 5:20). Herbert's emphasis throughout *The Temple* on mercy and grace, on the incomprehensible wonder of God's love for man, is strictly Pauline.

biblical and liturgical texts that were present to Herbert's mind when he wrote the poem teach, to a certain extent, conflicting lessons: when Love calls, we must respond—but woe to us if we come without a wedding garment; we must be humble—we shall be served; we must be worthy—how can we be worthy?—our worthiness, finally, is irrelevant in the eyes of God. In "Love, III" the need to be humble and the need to be worthy (not always in accord) are among the guest's nobler impulses, yet they prevent him from responding to what he needs most: God's love. His behavior seems, from one point of view, unimpeachable—surely we would not want him presumptuous?—yet he is exalted, in the end, not because of his humility but, paradoxically, in spite of it. In some of his overtly didactic verse, Herbert oversimplifies the issues in order to point a moral, but here, as in all his greatest lyrics, he explores, with sympathy and without censorship, the painful contradictions of the human condition.

The biblical precedents have guided Herbert, too, in imagining the dialogue of God and man. Herbert manages the colloquial tone of this dialogue so persuasively because he has perfectly mastered the way man and God converse in the pages of the Bible. Not only this poem but the whole of *The Temple* is remarkable for the unaffected ease of the speaker's discourse with God. The note of directness and openness that the patriarchs, the prophets or the psalmists use in speaking to God, the tender intimacy of the lovers in the Song of Songs, the familiarity with which Jesus addresses his Father in Heaven as "Abba"—these have helped to form Herbert's style, though of course they do not account for all of its virtues.

As we have seen, Herbert's vocabulary—*guiltie, dust, sinne, shame; guest, worthy; made, bore; serve; sit, taste, eat;* and of course, *love*—finds its primary definition in biblical contexts: parables about host and guest, master and servant, father and son; the lives of the prophets; the symbolism of the Song of Songs; and Paul's theology of sin and redemption. The words are the words of Scripture, but the voice is Herbert's own. Out of these many sources, Herbert has fashioned a new parable, about an abashed but loving man and a tactful, fine-grained, sweetly insistent God who wins him through love. In Herbert's parable Love issues the invitation; the guest, feeling unworthy, hangs back at the threshold; Love doesn't punish but gently persuades him; the guest offers to serve but instead is served by Love. Knowing the biblical sources, we can watch Herbert's mind in the process of creation: elaborating or excluding, choosing among possibilities, making something that is neither old nor new. Herbert presents a private rather than a public occasion, and a quieter mood than any of his sources. Characteristically, he softens the harsh elements of the materials he is working with: the severity of the host, the rudeness of the guest, and the threat of punishment in the parables; the overtones of sublimity and dread in the experience of the prophets; the extremity of passion in the Song of Songs.

This process of creative transmutation has its most remarkable effect in the figure of God, who does not resemble the vengeful or august presences of most of Herbert's sources. Herbert's God is intimately addressed as "my deare" and presented through a series of tender, one might say feminine, images of solicitude: "quick-ey'd," "sweetly questioning," "took my hand," "smiling did reply"—images that are fully absorbed into the traditional figure of Christ in the final stanza. In trying to imagine the New Testament definition "God is love" (1 John 4:8) as part of a concrete dramatic situation, Herbert may be recalling certain descriptive details in the Song of Songs: the "doves eyes" and "sweet . . . voice" of the beloved, the embracing hands of the lover (1:15, 2:14, 2:6).

In any event, the allegorical interpretation of the Song of Songs, where sexual images of the "feast" are understood spiritually, gives Herbert a warrant, an associative predisposition, to visualize the love of man and God in terms of an erotic relationship between a man and a woman. Perhaps this is the best way of accounting for the suggestion in the first lines of the poem, and again in the final couplet, of a sexual encounter between an inhibited or impotent man and a gently loving, patient woman. It is possible that in his presentation of this situation Herbert has been unconsciously guided by the memory or imagination of a human sexual encounter;[94] it is unlikely that he would have intended an explicitly sexual scene. At all events, I hardly think Herbert would have used the sexual metaphor here without the precedent of the Song of Songs. I would suggest that in this respect the Bible has freed his imagination to more direct expression than he would otherwise have attempted.

We cannot take the true measure of Herbert's originality without a careful accounting of his sources. As Tuve so eloquently argues, this kind of work (and work it often is, for what we know is so different from what Herbert knew) is a necessary step in any reading that is to be more than impressionistic. Tuve is right in describing " 'Herbert's method' " as an " 'originality' . . . where nothing is new," which "reanimates connexions among elements already carrying weighty meanings":[95]

94. This reading gains support from critics' observations about implicitly sexual imagery elsewhere in *The Temple.* Vendler notes the "tentative sexuality" of " 'budding' and 'shooting up' and later 'swelling' " in "The Flower" (*Poetry of Herbert,* 51; cf. Strier, *Love Known,* 252 n. 63). Strier speaks of the "phallic sexuality of 'burnish, sprout, and swell' " in "Jordan, II" (*Love Known,* 39 n. 30); of the "uncannily literal phallic dimension of 'staffe of flesh' " in "Divinitie," Herbert's conception of the intellect "in terms of aggressive sexuality" and his "desire to escape from masculine sexuality" (48 n. 45); and of the implicitly sexual vocabulary of stanza 3 of "The Pearl" (89 and n. 16). It is not surprising to find such imagery in "Love, III"; as Northrop Frye remarks, "Wherever we have love we have the possibility of sexual symbolism" (*Great Code,* 231).
95. Tuve, *A Reading,* 61, 63 n. 18.

112 · *Spelling the Word*

> The basic metaphor, the first great Invention, was found for Herbert; but of such tiny new little movements of the mind as that which his mind has made in using the tradition is genius and poetic greatness made.[96]

But Tuve speaks as an archaeologist, unearthing a temple hidden by the dust of centuries, when she calls the movements of Herbert's mind "tiny." A fully satisfying reading of *The Temple* must not neglect to ask by what means traditions are made into poems. "Tradition" is hardly some monolith that the poet, and the reader after him, is forever pushing uphill, and Herbert's poetry is more than the sum of its sources. We have seen the imaginative freedom with which Herbert uses the tradition, bringing together disparate and even contradictory passages, elaborating on their suggestions, and ranging them dramatically, so that what they say strikes us with the force of discovery. Only by paying attention to these movements of Herbert's mind can we understand how a poet so deeply indebted to traditional materials writes poems of such astonishing freshness.

96. Ibid., 63.

· 3 ·

From Old to New

THE CHRISTIAN TEMPLE: "A BRAVER PALACE"

In the language of *The Temple*, as we have seen, Herbert is concerned with making the old new. His efforts are motivated not only by a desire for freshness of expression that he shares with other poets, but also by a view of history that he shares with other Christians. Herbert's mind typically works by contraries. We have already observed that God's Word is opposed to the language of men in "The Quip," "The Forerunners" and other poems; the hidden life to the "diurnall" in "Coloss. 3.3"; and the love of God to the attractions of the world in "The Pearl." One further opposition, that between Old and New—the organizing principle of the Christian Scriptures—lies at the very heart of his thinking. The relations between Old and New, both in the history of salvation and the life of the individual, is a subject returned to so often that it comes to seem the central preoccupation of *The Temple*. "Poem after poem," Tuve rightly says, "is clarified by this realization of an underlying theme."[1]

To the Christian, history reveals "a providential design according to which the created order advances onward."[2] The Old Testament envisions a day when man will be renewed; the New Testament proclaims that day is at hand. But the New is of two minds about the Old. "No

1. Tuve, *A Reading*, 123.
2. Patrides, ed., *English Poems*, 26. See also C. A. Patrides, *The Grand Design of God: The Literary Form of the Christian View of History* (London, 1972), 1–12.

man putteth a piece of new cloth unto an olde garment" (Matt. 9:16), Christ teaches; yet at the same time he insists, "I am not come to destroy, but to fulfill" (Matt. 5:17). "Old things are past away, behold, al things are become new" (2 Cor. 5:17), Paul writes sweepingly; still, he reminds the Gentiles that they are a wild olive tree grafted onto good Jewish stock: "Boast not against the branches: but if thou boast, thou bearest not the root, but the root thee" (Rom. 11:18). The New leaves the rags of the Old behind; the New crowns the Old—these seemingly opposed notions are resolved in the paradox of new-yet-old, in its way as profound a mystery as maid-yet-mother, man-yet-God, three-yet-one.

That paradox is central to all Christian self-definition. Because the Incarnation is a unique event, all other events must be understood in relation to it. Thus the Church divides all time into B.C. and A.D., making "old" virtually equivalent to "obsolete": "In that he saith, A new Covenant, he hath made the first olde" (Heb. 8:13). The very name "Old Testament" reflects a Christian scale of values; in Hebrew, the Scriptures are called simply *Tanakh,* an acronym formed from *Torah* (the Pentateuch or Law), *Nevi'im* (the Prophets) and *Ketuvim* (the Hagiographa or Sacred Writings). On the other hand, because the Incarnation is seen as the fulfillment of the promises to Israel, the Church looks to the Old Testament for proof-texts and prophecies and resolves to bind up the Old with the New in one book. The Old Testament is retained as part of the Christian Scriptures—despite pressures in the early Church to abandon it—but in the process, it is radically reinterpreted as prologue to the New.

In the Reformation the paradox of new-yet-old is reasserted in its full intensity. As Lewalski explains, Protestants "insisted, none more vigorously, that Old Testament ceremonies and practices have been abrogated"; at the same time they were convinced of the "essential spiritual identity of the two Testaments," rejecting the "medieval dichotomy of shadow and substance." In their own view they were both like and unlike the ancient Israelites. When they contemplated their spiritual state—still waiting in hope for the final fulfillment at the end of days—they saw themselves as "correlative types" of the ancient Israelites; when, however, they considered the greater perfection of the New Dispensation, they were "antitypes," in whose lives the promises of Scripture had been made good.[3]

When Herbert writes about what it means to be a Christian, he typically measures his good fortune with comparatives that recall the past: "Faith sets me *higher* in his glorie"; "I have their fruit *and more*"; "a *braver* Palace *then before*."[4] "Justice, II" and "Death" define the opposition of *then* and *now* in its simplest terms: "O dreadfull Justice, what a fright and terrour / Wast thou *of old*, / . . . *But now* that Christs pure vail presents the sight, / I see no fears" (1 2, 13–14); "Death thou wast *once* an uncouth hideous thing, / . . . [But] we do *now* behold thee gay and glad" (1, 17). *Now* in these poems, as often in *The Temple*, refers not to Herbert's own day but to the new age ushered in by Christ: "*now* by Faith all arms are of a length"; "Christ keepeth *now*"; "*now* both sinne is dead, / And all thy promises live and bide"; "Wonders of anger *once*, but *now* of love."[5] It is Paul's *now*, and it carries the same unmistakable emphasis that it has in the Apostle's preaching: "But nowe the righteousnesse of God without the Lawe is manifested"; "beholde, now is the accepted

3. Lewalski, *Protestant Poetics*, 125, 127, 130.
4. "Faith," 20; "The Bunch of Grapes," 23; "The World," 20 (my italics throughout).
5. "Faith," 27; "The Holdfast," 14; "Longing," 67–68; "The Church Militant," 38 (my italics throughout). Cf. also "now thy Architecture meets with sinne" ("Sion," 11); "thy sithe a hatchet was, / Which now is but a pruning-knife," "Thou art a gard'ner now, and more" ("Time," 9–10, 16); "now each Christian hath his journeys spann'd" ("The Bunch of Grapes," 10); "Thy promise now hath ev'n set thee thy laws" ("Artillerie," 24).

time, behold, now is the day of salvation" (Rom. 3:21,
2 Cor. 6:2, etc.).

We soon discover in reading *The Temple* that in this
now the past looms large. Vendler speaks of the "retrospective immediacy, perfected by Herbert": "All of Herbert's recapitulatory poems . . . purport to retell yesterday's events, but in fact seem rather to transport us back
into yesterday as a present experience, tenses notwithstanding."[6] This is true even in "Justice, II" and "Death,"
with their sharp demarcation of Old and New, their triumphant dismissal of the past. One would have expected to read, "Once *men* saw justice as frightening;
now *I* see it as lifting us to heaven." Instead, as Vendler
points out, Herbert writes, "For then I saw through a
glass, darkly; but now through a pure veil fearlessly,"
presenting the past as something that he himself has
experienced, not merely heard about. Similarly, Stein observes that in the first stanza of "Death," where the "formal time [is] . . . the finished past," "a sense of the feel-
ing-present dominates."[7] These perceptions are accurate
and suggestive. I would add that Herbert's "retrospective
immediacy"—in which the past that has been super-
seded seems painfully present again for a moment—is
one of the peculiarities of his style and requires some
encompassing explanation.

It seems to me that Herbert is imaginatively drawn to
the nodal point of history as it is recorded in Scripture,
the juncture between Old and New, precisely because he
encounters it time and again in his own experience. He
finds in biblical history the paradigm of his spiritual
struggles, his movement toward God and his miserable
backsliding. The new man in him has learned to "aim and
shoot at that which *Is* on high," but the old man is still
"wrapt *In* flesh, and tends to earth." Torn between new

6. Vendler, *Poetry of Herbert*, 132, 95–96.
7. Ibid., 77; Stein, *Herbert's Lyrics*, 41.

hopes and old habits, he straddles two worlds: "restor'd" yet "full of rebellion"; "new drest" yet "guiltie of dust."[8] Hence he is keenly aware "not only of the pastness of the past," in Eliot's phrase, "but of its presence" as well.[9]

At times the past seems a good deal more attractive than it does in "Justice, II" and "Death." Herbert looks back with some nostalgia to tribal memories of the "sweet . . . dayes" of Adam, Abraham, Moses and Solomon: "we *at first* did board with thee"; "there was a Prince *of old*"; "thou *once* didst write in stone"; "with what glorie wast thou serv'd *of old*."[10] Moreover, the triumph of the New is rarely as swift, or as final, as in "Justice, II." "The Church Militant" chronicles the difficult course of the Church, dogged in its progress westward by sin; and as the poems of "The Church" attest, the reversals of history find their parallel in the experience of the believer. The "finished past," it appears, is never really finished, but continues to impose its burdens, and its ideals too, on the life of the present.

The title and unifying metaphor of the collection embodies, as perhaps no other word could, the charged dialectic of Old and New. The range of associations for *temple* extends through both Testaments, and the Christian senses of the word—Christ's body, the Church, the body of the individual Christian—can be fully understood only in relation to its primary Hebrew meaning. As Rickey has said, Herbert's title "indisputably suggests the place of worship of the Old Testament, at the same time that it does the living temple of the Pauline epistles," since many of the poems "are 'about' the relationship of the two temples."[11] Herbert's title is a particularly telling in-

8. "Coloss. 3.3," 8, 5; "The H. Communion," 37, "Nature," 1; "Aaron," 20, "Love, III," 2.
9. Eliot, "Tradition and the Individual Talent," 14.
10. "Decay," 1; "Affliction, V," 11; "Peace," 22; "The Sinner," 14; "Sion," 1 (my italics throughout).
11. Rickey, *Utmost Art*, 4–5.

stance of the density, the specifically biblical density, of his language.

The Old Testament Temple in Jerusalem, like the desert tabernacle, is thought of as a dwelling place for God: "an house of habitation for thee, and a place for thy dwelling for ever" (2 Chron. 6:2; cf. Ex. 25:8). It is "the centre of all holiness,"[12] for God's presence, it is believed, actually rests there: when the "two Tables of stone" of the Law are placed within the holy of holies, the Temple is filled with "the glory of the LORD" (1 Kings 8:9–11; cf. Ex. 40:34). Because of this special claim to holiness, we find an extensive description of the Temple and its furnishings; of the priesthood, its vestments and duties; and all the minute details of the sacrificial cult. At the same time, however, the Old Testament presents a radical critique of the Temple cult. It is given to Solomon himself to raise the essential question in his prayer of dedication: "I have surely built thee an house to dwel in, a setled place for thee to abide in for ever. . . . But will God indeede dwell on the earth? Behold, the heaven, and heaven of heavens cannot conteine thee: how much lesse this house that I have builded?" (1 Kings 8:13, 27; cf. Isa. 66:1). The prophets are relentless in their criticism of the empty and outward forms of religion: "To what purpose is the multitude of your sacrifices unto me, sayth the LORD?" (Isa. 1:11); "For I desired mercie, and not sacrifice; and the knowledge of God more then burnt offerings" (Hos. 6:6).[13]

In the New Testament *temple* acquires a symbolic meaning of considerable evangelical force: "The most high dwelleth not in temples made with hands" (Acts 7:48, 17:24). Opposition to the Hebrew Temple, first of all, is a sign of Jesus' messianic consciousness. Purging the Temple, Jesus

12. Johannes Pedersen, *Israel: Its Life and Culture*, 4 vols. in 2 (London, 1940), III–IV, 276.
13. Cf. also Jer. 6:20, 7:4, 21–23; Amos 5:21–24; Micah 6:6–8; Ps. 51:16–17.

summons up the prophets: "And he taught, saying unto them, Is it not written, My house shalbe called of all nations the house of prayer? but ye have made it a den of theeves" (Mark 11:17, conflating Isa. 56:7 and Jer. 7:11). In the Gospels, Christ refers to himself as the new temple: "Destroy this temple, and in three dayes I will raise it up. . . . But he spake of the temple of his body" (John 2:19–21). In the Epistles, the new temple is the community of believers, with Christ as its "foundation" or "corner stone."[14] The image is most fully developed by Paul in a number of passages that are of primary importance for Herbert:

> Knowe yee not that yee are the Temple of God, and that the Spirit of God dwelleth in you?
> If any man defile the Temple of God, him shall God destroy; for the Temple of God is holy, which Temple ye are.
> (1 Cor. 3:16–17)

> For ye are the Temple of the living God, as God hath saide, I will dwell in them, and walke in them, and I will be their God, and they shall be my people.
> (2 Cor. 6:16; cf. Lev. 26:11–12, Ezek. 37:27)

> Now therefore yee are no more strangers and forreiners; but fellow citizens with the Saints, and of the houshold of God,
> And are built upon the foundation of the Apostles and Prophets, Jesus Christ himselfe being the chiefe corner stone,
> In whom all the building fitly framed together, groweth unto an holy Temple in the Lord:
> In whom you also are builded together for an habitation of God thorow the Spirit.
> (Eph. 2:19–22)

The topos occurs too in the first epistle of Peter, where "spirituall house" stands for "temple": "Ye also as lively stones, are built up a spirituall house, an holy Priesthood

14. Bertil Gärtner, *The Temple and the Community in Qumran and the New Testament* (Cambridge, 1965), 47–142.

to offer up spirituall sacrifice, acceptable to God by Jesus Christ" (2:5). Finally, and most important for Herbert, *temple* refers not only to the community but also to the individual Christian, who is seen as the antitype of the Old Testament Temple: "What, know ye not that your body is the Temple of the holy Ghost which is in you, which yee have of God, and ye are not your owne?" (1 Cor. 6:19).[15]

Our familiarity with these texts and our distance from them in time have blunted their polemical thrust. Paul, we must remember, is addressing new Christians at Corinth and Ephesus who have heard about the Temple in Jerusalem with its claims to holiness. With Christ's coming, he insists, they have no need of that material Temple: they have a temple within, happier far. Once they were only "strangers and forreiners"; now the Spirit of God "dwells" in them, the community of the faithful, its new "habitation." There is challenge as well as comfort in this notion; hence Paul's image of the living temple is accompanied by exhortations to purity (1 Cor. 6:9–20, 2 Cor. 6:11–7:1). When Paul wrote his Epistles, the Temple— that is, the "third Temple," Herod's magnificent edifice— was still standing; with the conquest of Jerusalem a few years later, in 70 A.D., Paul's words were felt to be confirmed by an act of God, for Christians saw in the destruction of the Temple a proof that the promises of God had passed to the New Israel.

Paul defines the present reality as the fulfillment of the prophets' vision of a new covenant, when God would write his Law in man's heart and put his spirit within man (Jer. 31:31–33, Ezek. 36:26–28). But at the same time, in declaring the Hebrew Temple obsolete, Paul marks a

15. Cf. also Hebrews 9:11–12, where Christ is both the "high Priest . . . by a greater and more perfect Tabernacle" and the perfect sacrifice. The vision of the New Jerusalem in the Book of Revelation has "no Temple therein: for the Lord God Almightie, and the Lambe, are the Temple of it" (21:22).

sharp break with the past. This affirmation of both continuity and change, sameness and difference, is reflected, as we shall see, in the formulas of Christian typology. It is significant that Paul, who stands at the crucial juncture of Judaism and Christianity, did not invent a vocabulary to describe what he perceived, after all, as a new reality, but instead laid claim to ancient images and invested them with new meaning. Thus words like *temple, altar, sacrifice* and *priesthood*, in Christian usage, not only define the relations of God and man but also preserve a memory of their historical development. When Herbert uses these words to describe the present Christian reality, he is, like Paul, saying something about how that reality came to be.

Herbert's imagery of the temple is characteristically Pauline in its emphases. Though the word *temple* also implies a "classical structure for pagan worship," and some poems do present a "contrast between the life of grace offered by the Church and the natural values of the ancients,"[16] this concern is firmly subordinated to the Pauline dialectic of Law and Grace, Works and Faith, the Letter and the Spirit, the Old Covenant and the New. For Paul, addressing himself to an audience of Gentile converts, it was a matter of political necessity to define his faith in opposition to the Jews and Jewish Christians rather than to the Gentiles. Paul's antitheses, taken up later by Augustine in his campaign against Pelagius and by the Reformers in their attack on the medieval church,[17] furnish Herbert with a set of terms that helps him to fathom his own divided mind. In the "wrastling," the "combate," the "warres"[18] of *The Temple*, which take place on the ground of the self, we can hear the echoes of historic battle.

16. Rickey, *Utmost Art*, 5, 38; Rickey notes the references to the Greek *perirrhanterium* or ceremonial sprinkling brush and the *procul esti profani* of Roman ritual (6–8).

17. Cf. Meeks, ed., *Writings of Paul*, 216, 220–50.

18. "The Crosse," 8; "Artillerie," 26; "Employment, II," 17.

It should be clear by now why Herbert named the volume *The Temple* and not, as the central portion of it is called, "The Church." Though *church* has a certain range of significance—it is at once the actual church building and the community of believers, both visible and invisible—it has nothing like the associative richness of *temple*. Amy Charles considers the title "pretentious" and suggests that it is not "appropriate to Herbert's thought."[19] In taking this position she is reviving the objection of Edmund Dowden, who found the title "somewhat too stately" for Herbert's poems: "as far as they are concerned with the public ordinances of religion," he wrote in 1901, " 'The Parish Church' would have been sufficient."[20] Charles protests that "for Herbert, the natural place for the worship of God is a church, not a temple"; but to urge this objection is to make Herbert more literal-minded than he is. The problem arises again with some

19. Charles, *Life of Herbert*, 185–86. Charles claims that "during the seventeenth century, the little volume was generally referred to as 'The Church.' " But the titles of Harvey's *The Synagogue, or, The Shadow of the Temple . . . In Imitation of Mr. George Herbert* (1640)—often bound up with *The Temple*—and Crashaw's *Steps to the Temple* (1646) suggest otherwise. Moreover, if Barnabas Oley gave the name *A Priest to the Temple* to Herbert's tract on the country parson (see Summers, *George Herbert*, 13), he too probably thought of the volume of poems as *The Temple*. Charles cites Walton's comment that "this excellent Book . . . now bears the name of *The TEMPLE*" as evidence that it may once have had a different title, but as she herself recognizes, we must be careful about taking Walton's words literally. The same caveat applies to Aubrey's remark that Herbert wrote a book of "Sacred Poems, called 'The Church' " (*Brief Lives*, 137), in view of Aubrey's notorious carelessness.

Even if it could be shown conclusively that the title is in Ferrar's handwriting, as Charles claims, we would still have no real evidence that it is his and not Herbert's. *The Temple* is a distinctly idiosyncratic title. If someone other than Herbert had been pressed to name the collection, one imagines he would have settled on a neutral descriptive phrase like *Divine Poems* or *Sacred Poems and Private Ejaculations* (the latter being the subtitle added in 1633). We may never know whether the title is really Herbert's; all we can say with certainty is that it is in keeping with the central patterns of imagery in the volume (cf. Lewalski, *Protestant Poetics*, 485 n. 16).

20. Edmund Dowden, *Puritan and Anglican* (New York, 1901), 107.

other titles that would have had a suspect ring in Herbert's day. Why did Herbert call his poem "The Priesthood" and not "The Ministry"? Why "The Altar" and not "The Communion Table"? (And why, one should add, is that altar made of stone and not of wood?)[21] To Helen White, the "altar" is "the essential thing for a man in Herbert's ecclesiastical party."[22] But to draw inferences about Herbert's "party" sympathies from such titles is to misunderstand his use of symbolic language. Herbert is concerned here not with church government or architecture but with biblical metaphor.

The metaphor of the temple, moreover, was a familiar one to the seventeenth-century reader, as many critics have shown;[23] hence it is not likely to have been thought pretentious. One source of visual information about the Hebrew Temple and its furnishings, which would have made the metaphor accessible to a wide audience, was the popular Geneva Bible. This was provided not only

21. Summers, *George Herbert*, 141: "The canons of Herbert's time directed that the Table should be made of wood rather than stone." Or, to choose an example from the other end of the spectrum, why does the guest "sit and eat" at the end of "Love, III" when sitting at Communion was a practice Herbert explicitly rebuked? Strier, *Love Known*, 78 n. 41, citing *A Priest to the Temple*, *Works*, 259 ("man's unpreparednesse asks kneeling"), explains that the poem is not "primarily Eucharistic in reference"; I would argue, rather, that Herbert's choice of verb is determined by biblical metaphor, not actual church practice. For the biblical context of "sitting" as a metaphor of fulfilled joy see my discussion of "Love, III" in chap. 2.

22. Helen C. White, *The Metaphysical Poets: A Study in Religious Experience* (New York, 1936; rpt. 1962), 158. On the omission of the word "altar" from the Order for Holy Communion in the 1552 Prayer Book, see *The Annotated Book of Common Prayer*, ed. John Henry Blunt (London, 1892), 370. On the altar controversy see G. W. O. Addleshaw and Frederick Etchells, *The Architectural Setting of Anglican Worship* (London, 1948), 108–47.

23. See, for example, Summers, *George Herbert*, 85; Endicott [Patterson], "Structure of Herbert's *Temple*," 351–57; Stanley E. Fish, *The Living Temple: George Herbert and Catechizing* (Berkeley and Los Angeles, 1978), 68–77; Patrides, ed., *English Poems*, 16–17; Lewalski, *Protestant Poetics*, 100–101.

with marginal annotations but also with a series of illustrative woodcuts as an aid to the reader. Twenty of the
twenty-six woodcuts are concerned with the Tabernacle
or the Temple. Of particular interest to readers of Herbert
are those entitled "The Garments of the High Priest,"
which helps us to visualize "Aaron"; "The Temple Un-
covered," which shows the incense altar, almost exactly
in the shape of Herbert's "Altar," and the two cherubim
with wings outstretched, perhaps suggested in "Easter-
wings"; "The Temple Covered"; and "The Sea or Great
Caldron" mentioned in "Sion."[24]

Herbert's temple imagery constitutes a central system
of allusions in the volume. Fish counts "no less than
sixty-two poems in the sequence [that] can be directly
related to the temple topos (and these sixty-two are
spaced so that there are never more than three poems in
succession without such a direct relationship)." Lewalski
goes even further, calling it "the governing trope" of the
collection, which "affects to some degree all the poems in
the volume": "all the biblical texts relating to the stony
heart, the Old Testament altars of unhewn stone, and the
designations of the Christian as God's building and
temple are laid under contribution in the complex development of this trope."[25]

Images of this type are concerned either with the
temple as a place or with the notion of sacrifice. Let me
cite a few examples of each to give some notion of the
variety of treatment to which this topos lends itself. The
biblical epigraph on the title page, "*In his Temple doth every
man speak of his honour*" (Ps. 29:8), is an example of the

24. *The Bible* [Geneva] (1560), pt. 1, fols. 38, 151ᵥ, 152, 153ᵥ. On the
cherubim and "Easter-wings" see C. C. Brown and W. P. Ingoldsby,
"George Herbert's 'Easter-wings,'" *Huntington Library Quarterly* 35
(1972), rpt. *Essential Articles*, 466–67.
25. Fish, *Living Temple*, 88; Lewalski, *Protestant Poetics*, 105–6. Cf.
also Florence Sandler, "'Solomon ubique regnat': Herbert's Use of the
Images of the New Covenant," *Papers on Language and Literature* 8 (1972),
rpt. *Essential Articles*, 258–67.

first type. One would expect as epigraph one of the familiar Pauline texts about the Christian temple of the heart; instead Herbert chooses a verse from the Psalms that summons up as a physical presence the ancient Hebrew Temple, reminding us at the outset of the historical substructure of his present reality. Since some of the biblical synonyms for *temple* are *house, habitation* and *palace,*[26] we are in the presence of this complex of ideas when we read that "Love built a stately house" and after its destruction by sin "built a braver Palace then before" ("The World," 1, 20), or when we find man represented as "a stately habitation" or "so brave a Palace" ("Man," 2, 50). "O dwell in it," Herbert exclaims at the end of "Man" (50), pointing up the allusion. In this group too belong all those poems in which God is said to "dwell" in man, to seek or to take up "lodging" in the heart, or in which the heart must be purged to make it a worthy receptacle: "For where thou dwellest all is neat" ("The Familie," 8; cf. "Good Friday," "The Starre," "Christmas"). Finally, there is the sequence of poems, early in the volume, that finds in an actual church building a series of emblems for the life of the spirit: "Church-monuments," "Church-musick," "Church-lock and key," "The Church-floore" and "The Windows." In this last poem, Herbert explicitly refers to Paul's metaphor: through God's grace, the preacher is given to be a window "in thy temple"(3), transmitting God's Word by his very life.

The imagery of sacrifice begins with "The Dedication," which is prefaced to the poems:

> *Lord, my first fruits present themselves to thee;*
> *Yet not mine neither: for from thee they came,*
> *And must return.*

Here Herbert is echoing Deut. 26:1–10, a liturgy for the offering of the first fruits of the harvest, which concludes

---

26. *house:* 1 Kings 8:13, Ps. 23:6; *habitation:* 2 Chron. 6:2, Ps. 26:8; *palace:* 1 Chron. 29:1.

with the words "And now behold, I have brought the first fruits of the land, which thou, O LORD, hast given mee." Although the "fruits of the land" is replaced by the "fruit of our lippes, giving thankes to his Name" (Heb. 13:15), the ancient rite is summed up in a variety of poems. "The Sacrifice" might well have been called "The Passion"; instead Herbert chose a typological title that alludes to the Temple cult. "The Altar," "Aaron" and "The Priesthood" evoke the cult as a type of the spiritual sacrifices of the Christian. So does "The Odour," which refers to the "sweet savour" of the Old Testament burnt offerings, perfected in Christ. It is "the offerers heart" rather than a sacrifice of "fruit" or "fold" that is required by God in "Love unknown," "An Offering" and "Ungratefulnesse." Finally, Man is called "the worlds high Priest" in "Providence," where he presents "the sacrifice for all"—a sacrifice of praise.

The metaphor of the temple, in short, is a remarkable instance of the economy of biblical language, compressing the history of salvation into one word. "How neatly doe we give one onely name,"[27] Herbert might well have written, to the new covenant inscribed in the heart, the indwelling Spirit, the sacrifice of praise, the body as a sanctified vessel, and the Church as inheritor of God's promises to Israel. There is no better example of the way the historical consciousness of biblical faith, the progression from Old to New, informs Herbert's dense multivalent language.

That consciousness is embodied also in the very shapes of Herbert's poems, which present the Christian faith as a living process of development from the forms of Old Testament religion. The plot of many of the poems, like the "plot" of the Bible itself, is about the "long . . . and weary way"[28] traveled from the Old to the New. The les-

27. "The Sonne," 5.
28. "The Pilgrimage," 3.

son that Herbert teaches is never abstract but is always embodied in the matrix of a specific emotional experience.

In what follows I will be studying Herbert's typological poems, in which the New crowns the Old, and poems of discovery, in which, at the eleventh hour, the New leaves the rags of the Old behind. In "Sion," "Aaron" and "The Bunch of Grapes," Herbert confronts the misery of the human condition and the inescapability of sin—the point at which the correspondence of Old and New is most apparent—but he ends by affirming that the New fulfills and surpasses the ideals of the Old. The second group of poems—"Redemption," "The Holdfast," "The Collar" and others—is given over to the voice of the "old man." Written in a present still dominated by "dust and sinne," these poems dramatize the difficulty of putting off the old man and putting on the new.

APPLIED TYPOLOGY: "THEIR FRUIT AND MORE"

It is always a help to regard one's sufferings in perspective, and the historical long view that begins with the Old Testament is particularly consoling to the Christian believer. Herbert occasionally contemplates "this wretched world"[29] under the aspect of eternity, which has the effect of mitigating pain by distancing pain and joy alike, as in "The Foil," "Vanitie, II" or "The Rose." But he clearly prefers the biblical perspective of history, which sets in relief his present good fortune and allows him to end by affirming gratitude without denying the reality of pain. Herbert's typological poems—"Sion," "Aaron," "The Bunch of Grapes" and (with a difference) "Decay"—are about learning from history. They show us how the Christian mind makes use of the past to understand the present, applying a "doctrine" of history to the "life" of the individual. Because he believes that the Bible is a true

29. "The Foil," 7.

record of man's spiritual development, Herbert is continually measuring himself against its scheme of events and promises. And because he assumes that Aaron or the Exodus is as much a part of the reader's past as of his own, his references to biblical history are intended to convey a sense of shared experience.

Typology is a mode of interpretation that discerns in history a meaningful pattern—the "grand design of God."[30] In typological exegesis, persons, institutions and events in the Old Testament are seen as prefigurations of Christ, of the Church as the Body of Christ, or of events in New Testament history. Adam is a type of Christ, the Exodus a type of the Redemption and the Temple a type of the Church (1 Cor. 15:22, 10:1–4, 3:16–17). This view of history implies not only purpose but also progress: the Old means the New, but the New surpasses the Old. To put it another way, the assumptions of typology may be expressed in two paradoxically related formulas: *A is equal to B*, but *B is greater than A*. "New" used in a typological sense (in "New England" and "New World" as surely as in "New Covenant" and "New Jerusalem") invariably means "better"—a word that sounds a recurrent note in Hebrews. Finally, it cannot be said strongly enough that for the believer typology is not of merely academic interest. As A. C. Charity puts it, "typology is, in the Bible, 'applied.'" Its purpose is "to confront man with the action of God," and its essential reference is "to the life of its hearer or reader": history is "laid before the present as a challenge."[31] When we speak of "applied typology," we are referring to its power to challenge, to work change in the life of the hearer.

The twofold plan of the Christian Scriptures required that the Old Testament be extensively reinterpreted,

30. Patrides borrows the title of *The Grand Design of God* from a phrase of Jonathan Edwards (as he notes on pp. xiii, 119).

31. A. C. Charity, *Events and Their Afterlife: The Dialectics of Christian Typology in the Bible and Dante* (Cambridge, 1966), 8, 58, 8, 74.

"changed," in Erich Auerbach's words, "from a book of laws and a history of the people of Israel into a series of figures of Christ and the Redemption." Paul played a significant role in this development:

> The Church Fathers often justify the figural interpretation on the basis of certain passages in early Christian writings, mostly from the Pauline Epistles. The most important of these is I Cor. 10:6 and 11, where the Jews in the desert are termed *typoi hēmōn* ("figures of ourselves"), and where it is written that *tauta de typikōs synebainen ekeinois* ("these things befell them as figures").

Auerbach reminds us that typological interpretation grew out of "a definite historical situation, the Christian break with Judaism and the Christian mission among the Gentiles; it had a historical function." Paul's thinking, he writes, "eminently combined practical politics with creative poetic faith."[32] Paul and the evangelists addressed themselves to new converts, still shaky in their faith, who kept slipping back into retrograde habits of thought and practice. Since the break between Christianity and Judaism was then in its initial stages, they were much concerned with the superiority of the New Dispensation to the Old. This issue dominates the most "Pauline" of Paul's Epistles, Galatians and Romans, with their contrast between the Law and justification by faith, and it is prominent in the Gospels, too, where Christ is shown to be superior to the Temple, the Sabbath, and so forth.

According to Paul, the Jews were unable to divine the true meaning of the Scriptures. When Moses descended from Mt. Sinai with the two tablets of the Law, the Jews could not bear to behold the radiance of his face, and he had to cover it with a veil (Ex. 34:29–35); so now too, Paul

---

32. Erich Auerbach, "Figura," trans. Ralph Manheim, in *Scenes from the Drama of European Literature* (New York, 1959), 52, 49, 56, 51. See also K. J. Woollcombe, "The Biblical Origins and Patristic Development of Typology," *Essays on Typology*, Studies in Biblical Theology, no. 22 (London, 1957), 39–75.

argued, their minds are blinded, "for untill this day remaineth the same vaile untaken away, in the reading of the old testament: which vaile is done away in Christ" (2 Cor. 3:14; cf. 3:7). Paul's use of typology, then, was intended to encourage new converts, to strengthen them in their faith by revealing their good fortune. It is remarkable that, centuries later, when Judaism was no longer a political threat and the success of the Christian mission had long been assured, Paul's reading of history should still speak with such immediacy. On the face of it, the superiority of the New Dispensation would seem to need no urging to a Christian audience in the seventeenth century. But Herbert makes it a live issue in *The Temple* because he regards it as a truth that man must keep discovering, must struggle to repossess. He writes with the excitement of the New Testament authors, who were conscious of bearing a message of hope, of "good news." In Herbert's poems the Christian believer recapitulates within himself the experience of the race, having to fight Paul's battles as if Paul had never fought them, and celebrating Paul's victory in Christ, each time as if for the first time. Detached from their original circumstances, the antagonists of the Epistles are discovered at war on the battleground of the self, the battle still raging and the comfort still real.

Every student of Herbert's typology is indebted to Tuve's subtle and learned exegesis. The sheer quantity of information she has retrieved for us illuminates a great many puzzling references and helps us to overcome the handicap of three and a half centuries' distance from the text. But in her enthusiasm for patristic and medieval literature, she does not make it clear that Herbert's typology is essentially Pauline in its emphases, focusing on Paul's major themes: Adam and the Exodus, Creation and Covenant.[33] Nor is she concerned with how these are "ap-

33. See Woollcombe, "Typology," p. 68; E. E. Ellis, *Paul's Use of the Old Testament* (London, 1957), 134.

plied" (to use Charity's term) by the poet to his own experience, and how in consequence they inform the structure and movement of his poems.

Lewalski has redressed the balance by elucidating the specifically Protestant approach to typology. Of particular importance is the "Reformation emphasis upon the application of all scripture to the self, the discovery of scriptural paradigms and of the workings of Divine Providence in one's own life." Whereas the traditional formula finds in Christ's life the primary antitype of the Old Testament types, the Protestant exegetes focus on the individual believer, whose life becomes the stage where the historical drama of promise and fulfillment is played out. Protestants also stressed the "essential spiritual identity of the two Testaments," which were now seen to differ in degree rather than in kind. They believed that Old Testament persons and events are not mere shadows of the truth but that they embodied, however imperfectly, "true spiritual realities."[34] These beliefs make themselves felt in the poems I will now consider, poems in which a seventeenth-century Christian uses his knowledge of typology as a way of coming to terms with his own life. That Herbert regards himself as both correlative type and antitype accounts for their complexity.

A good point of departure is "Sion," where Herbert elaborates on Paul's temple typology from a Protestant perspective. "This great poem," as Sara Hanley writes, "which is placed at the exact center of *The Temple* . . . makes the most explicit statement in the volume of the parallel between the Old Dispensation temple, the New Dispensation Church, and the temple of the heart."[35] Herbert starts by describing Solomon's Temple, whose sumptuous decor offers such a contrast to the invisible temple

34. Lewalski, *Protestant Poetics*, 131, 125–26.
35. Sara William Hanley, "Temples in *The Temple*: George Herbert's Study of the Church," *Studies in English Literature* 8 (1968): 130.

of the heart. Herbert's view of the Temple seems at first almost nostalgic. He lingers appreciatively over the details of its material splendor, giving us an image of "Solomon in all his glory" (Matt. 6:29):

> Lord, with what glorie wast thou serv'd of old,
> When Solomons temple stood and flourished!
>   Where most things were of purest gold;
>   The wood was all embellished
> With flowers and carvings, mysticall and rare:
> All show'd the builders, crav'd the seeers care.

(1–6)

Herbert is drawing upon the account in 1 Kings that tells us the Temple's walls were embellished "with carved figures of Cherubims, and palme trees, and open flowers" (6:29) and enumerates its costly vessels—the golden altar, table, candlesticks and tongs, the "boules, and the snuffers, and the basons, and the spoones, and the censers of pure gold" (7:48–50). We learn from other poems what we may suspect here: that for Herbert, "embellished" or "gold" or even "glorie" are not necessarily terms of approbation.[36] But if there are ironies here, they are not insisted upon. The Old apparently had its value: God was "serv'd" and the Temple "flourished," tangible evidence of the Israelites' "care."

The negative implications of the first stanza become overt, however, in the second:

> Yet all this glorie, all this pomp and state
> Did not affect thee much, was not thy aim;
>   Something there was, that sow'd debate:
>   Wherefore thou quitt'st thy ancient claim.

(7–10)

The Lord seeth not as man seeth. God is unimpressed with the massive tomblike splendor of the Temple, how-

36. *Embellishment:* "The Forerunners," 33. *Gold:* "The H. Communion," 2; "Vanitie, II," 12; "Businesse," 31; "Self-condemnation," 14; "The Church Militant," 251. *Glorie:* "Frailtie," 13, "The Quip," 13; "The Church Militant," 143.

ever much it may impress man, and he renounces his claim to it. "And now . . .," Herbert goes on, but where we expect a statement of the greater perfections of the New, Herbert takes us instead into the dark center of the poem:

> And now thy Architecture meets with sinne;
> For all thy frame and fabrick is within.
>
> There thou art struggling with a peevish heart,
> Which sometimes crosseth thee, thou sometimes it:
>   The fight is hard on either part.
>   Great God doth fight, he doth submit.
>
> (11–16)

"Sion" is not a simple statement of the superiority of New over Old. God in the first stanza was sumptuously "serv'd"; in the second, he quit his claim by active choice. Now, as a result, he is locked in battle with man's peevish heart; indeed, one is startled to hear, "he doth submit."

But if life is more strenuous now, for God as well as for man, Herbert insists that it is better:

> All Solomons sea of brasse and world of stone
> Is not so deare to thee as one good grone.
>
> And truly brasse and stones are heavie things,
> Tombes for the dead, not temples fit for thee:
>   But grones are quick, and full of wings,
>   And all their motions upward be;
> And ever as they mount, like larks they sing;
> The note is sad, yet musick for a King.
>
> (17–24)

In God's paradoxical balance, "all" Solomon's brass and stone is less precious than "one" good groan. There is no place in the Christian universe, Herbert says, for a temple of brass and stones. But far from rejecting the obsolete Old Testament image, he deliberately invokes it in the manner of Paul as a way of defining the new Christian reality: the Temple is dead, long live the temple!

In the final stanza, God's in his heaven again, a

"King," served by man with his chosen music. We tend to think of groans as "heavie things," but Herbert represents them with images of motion and music, suggesting a spiritual quickening; in restrospect, we can see that what looked like "glorie" was really a form of material torpor. At the end of "Sion," his *"griefs . . . sing,"* as in "Josephs coat," a poem whose typological title extends the range of its concerns.

In "Sion," Herbert presents not only the opposition between the Old Dispensation and the New, but also what historians have called the "interiorization of the religious life" that characterized the Protestant Reformation, the "movement away from the institutional and toward a more spiritual concept of the church."[37] One of the Ninety-Five Theses of Luther reads: "First of all we should rear living temples, next local churches, and only last of all St. Peter's, which is not necessary for us."[38] This is part of Herbert's subject in "The H. Communion" ("Not in rich furniture, or fine aray, / Nor in a wedge of gold," 1–2), where, as Hutchinson notes, "a contrast is intended between the simple accessories of Anglican worship and those of the Roman Catholic rite."[39] As we have noted, the word *furniture* is used in the Book of Exodus (e.g., 31:7–9) to designate the furnishings and utensils of the tabernacle; here it suggests the panoply of the Mass. By implication, then, "Sion" and "Aaron" contain an implicit criticism of the Roman Catholic church with its sacrificial liturgy of the Mass, its splendid churches and elaborate vestments.

"Aaron" like "Sion" begins with the Old Testament type seen in its most positive aspect. The first stanza alludes to Aaron's ceremonial attire:

Holinesse on the head,
Light and perfections on the breast,

37. George and George, *Protestant Mind*, 375, 317.
38. Quoted in Bainton, *Here I Stand*, 80.
39. Hutchinson, "Commentary," *Works*, 493.

Harmonious bells below, raising the dead
To leade them unto life and rest:
Thus are true Aarons drest.

(1–5)

If these images seem recherché today, they were certainly not so in Herbert's day. In the Geneva Bible the woodcut accompanying Exoduṣ 28 shows in detail "The Garments of the High Priest," and every reader of the AV would have been able to identify on the title page, opposite a simply draped Moses, the figure of Aaron with his exotic turban and elaborate vestments, a row of small bells encircling the hem, and on his chest the heavy breastplate with its twelve inset stones. Aaron is singled out among Old Testament priests because it was his family, a branch of the tribe of Levi, that received a promise of perpetual priesthood (Ex. 29:9, 40:15). Like Moses he is a traditional type of Christ; Hebrews tells us that Christ is superior because he is a "high Priest of good things to come, by a greater and more perfect Tabernacle, not made with hands" (9:11; cf. 7:11). Moreover, all Christians are constituted a "kingdome of Priestes," as the ancient Israelites were once called (Ex. 19:6, 1 Pet. 2:5). Thus Aaron's ceremonial vestments are figures of the spiritual qualities of the true Christian priest, and by extension, of any believer.

Exodus 28 prescribes the making of Aaron's "holy garments . . . for glory and for beauty" (28:2). Herbert is not interested in the purely functional attire, like the sash (girdle) or the linen breeches. Of the garments described here in detail, he singles out three that correspond to "head," "breast" and "musick": the gold plate, engraved with the words "HOLINES TO THE LORD," to be worn on the "forefront of the miter . . . upon Aarons forehead" (28:36–38); the breastplate of judgment, containing the "Urim and the Thummim," literally "lights and perfections,"[40] to be worn "upon Aarons heart" (28:30); and the

40. *The Bible* [Geneva] (1560), pt. 1, fol. 38ᵥ, marginal gloss on Ex. 28:30: "Urím signifieth light, and Thummím perfection: declaring that

golden bells sewn at the hem of his robe so that "his sound shall be heard when he goeth in unto the holy place before the LORD, and when he commeth out, that he die not" (28:33–35). These seem particularly mysterious, lending themselves to symbolic interpretation. They are already invested, moreover, with a spiritual significance, which Herbert proceeds to elaborate in Christian terms, just as Paul adapts Isaiah's "brestplate" of "righteousnesse" and "helmet of salvation" for the Christian soldier (Isa. 59:17, Eph. 6:13–17).

The second stanza moves directly from the Old Testament type to its antithesis. Man relying on his own resources is a perversion, a dark parody of the ideal:

> Profanenesse in my head,
> Defects and darknesse in my breast,
> A noise of passions ringing me for dead
> Unto a place where is no rest:
> Poore priest thus am I drest.
>
> (6–10)

Is such a man fit to be priest? The Old Testament regulates the lives of the priests with a multiplicity of laws in order to assure their ceremonial purity:

> They shalbe holy unto their God, and not profane the name of their God: for the offrings of the LORD made by fire, and the bread of their God they doe offer: therefore they shall be holy. . . .
> Speake unto Aaron, saying, Whosoever he be of thy seed in their generations, that hath any blemish, let him not approche to offer the bread of his God.
>
> (Lev. 21:6, 17)

This is precisely Herbert's burden in "The Priesthood":

---

the stones of the brest plate were moste cleare, and of perfect beautie: by Urím also is ment knolage, and Thummím holynes, shewing what vertues are required in the Priests." The Urim and Thummim appear to have been employed in divining the will of God; cf. Num. 27:21, 1 Sam. 28:6. Yehezkel Kaufmann, *The Religion of Israel*, trans. Moshe Greenberg (Chicago, 1960), suggests that the "Urim oracle" was " a kind of lot" (92).

But th' holy men of God such vessels are,
As serve him up, who all the world commands:
. . . .
O what pure things, most pure must those things be,
   Who bring my God to me!

(25–26, 29–30)

The blemishes singled out in Leviticus are all physical ("a blind man, or a lame, or he that hath a flat nose . . .," 21:18), whereas Herbert is concerned with defects of the spirit. In the final stanza we shall see the superiority of the antitype expressed again, as in "Sion," in the contrast of external and internal, matter and spirit: Aaron's garments are worn "on" the head and breast, whereas the true Christian priest's adornments are within.

The new Aaron must be "most pure" both as a priest and as a Christian who belongs to a kingdom of priests. But how can the Old Testament ideal be bettered, let alone fulfilled, given man's defects? As in "Sion," Herbert moves from original glory to sin and thence to redemption, setting out the drama of salvation in its historical progression so that we may fully appreciate what has been gained. This time at the final stage we see not just the temple of the heart but Christ, who dwells within:

Christ is my onely head,
My alone onely heart and breast,
My onely musick, striking me ev'n dead;
That to the old man I may rest,
And be in him new drest.

So holy in my head,
Perfect and light in my deare breast,
My doctrine tun'd by Christ, (who is not dead,
But lives in me while I do rest)
Come people; Aaron's drest.

(16–25)

The paradox "I live, yet not I, but Christ liveth in me" (Gal. 2:20) lies behind these lines, as Vendler has noticed,[41]

41. Vendler, *Poetry of Herbert*, 119.

resolving the dilemma posed by the first two stanzas in distinctly Pauline terms. Like Paul, Herbert feels keenly the misery that attends on the old way of being, and the joy that he is enabled to leave it behind. In the firmness and conviction of the last line—"Come people; Aaron's drest"—we can measure how far the speaker has traveled. It is a new man indeed who pronounces those words.

The nostalgia of "Sion" and "Aaron" reaches its climax in "Decay." The poem begins with memories of a lost paradise:

> Sweet were the dayes, when thou didst lodge with Lot,
> Struggle with Jacob, sit with Gideon,
> Advise with Abraham, when thy power could not
> Encounter Moses strong complaints and mone:
> Thy words were then, *Let me alone.*
>
> One might have sought and found thee presently
> At some fair oak, or bush, or cave, or well:
> Is my God this way? No, they would reply:
> He is to Sinai gone, as we heard tell:
> List, ye may heare great Aarons bell.
>
> (1–10)

This passage breathes with a sense of the easy familiarity between man and God in the good Old Testament days. And not only that: it suggests the extent of man's former mastery, his favor with God. In each of these incidents, man succeeds in prevailing upon God: Lot persuades the reluctant angels to lodge with him; Jacob wrestles the angel to a draw; Gideon wheedles three signs of his election; Abraham convinces God to spare Sodom if ten righteous souls are found; and Moses, braving God's wrath, pleads for the backsliding Israelites until God relents.[42] The "oak, or bush, or cave, or well" of the second stanza speak not only of the omnipresence of God, but also of his present help in danger. Each of these places is readily associated

---

42. *Lot,* Gen. 19:1–3; *Jacob,* Gen. 32:24–32; *Gideon,* Judg. 6:17–24, 36–40; *Abraham,* Gen. 18:23–32; *Moses,* Ex. 32:7–14.

with an Old Testament figure. The Lord appears at an *oak* to Gideon with a plan of rescue from the Midianite oppression; charges Moses at the burning *bush* to lead the Israelites out of Egypt; manifests himself to Elijah near a *cave* on Mt. Horeb; reveals a *well* in the desert to the banished Hagar.[43] When God appears, offering relief and promise for the future, each of these figures is in desperate need of help. The first two stanzas, then, do not merely contemplate God's bonhommie or omnipresence; they cite numerous specific instances in which God once responded to man's persuasions or his deeply felt needs.

Up to this point "Decay" follows the pattern of Hebrews 11, which recalls, among others, the names "of Gideon, and of Barak, and of Sampson, and of Jephthah, . . . who through faith subdued kingdomes, wrought righteousnesse, obteined promises, stopped the mouthes of Lions." That passage concludes, "And these all . . . received not the promise: God having provided some better thing for us" (11:32–33, 39–40). But "Decay" ends very differently. Instead of rejoicing in "some better thing" that is provided for us, Herbert complains that God is hounded by Sinne and Satan in "one corner of a feeble heart" (12). We are not surprised that God "meets with sinne" in his new quarters, though we still expect to hear, as in "Sion," that the present state of affairs, whatever its difficulties, is nonetheless preferable to the old. What is disturbing in "Decay" is that there appears to be no hope of recovery. Herbert summons up an idealized past as a reproach to the present, leaving us with a despairing vision of a world in which we can look forward only to the final conflagration.

In no other poem does Herbert invoke the Last Judgment with such fury. "Vertue," like "Decay," starts with sweet days and ends with the whole world in flames, but "then" the "vertuous soul . . . chiefly lives" (13, 16). In "Love, II" Herbert prays that "those fires, / Which shall

43. *Oak,* Judg. 6:11; *bush,* Ex. 3:2; *cave,* 1 Kings 19:9; *well,* Gen. 21:19.

consume the world" may first "consume our lusts, and make thee way" (2–3, 5); the final couplet offers a vision of men on their knees praising God. Nor does Herbert represent the process of historical deterioration in such grim colors elsewhere. Although "Whitsunday" traces a decline from the time when God kept "open house" during the glorious apostolic age to a gloomy present when "thou shutt'st the doore, and keep'st within," the sense of falling off is poignant, not embittered; the poem concludes with a hopeful prayer to the "sweet God of love and light" (7, 21, 26). Finally, "The Church Militant" regards the Church's loss of its primitive purity with a "prophetic irony," as Anselment calls it, that discerns in the course of history the workings of divine providence.[44] In this light one can accept the fact that the Church will keep moving westward, pursued by sin, till it reaches its point of origin "where judgement shall appeare" (277).

In "Decay," however, the case is different: the period that is presented elsewhere as a prelude to the Christian era seems, poignantly enough, like a lost Golden Age. The Old Testament figures have about them a primal innocence, an ease and familiarity with God, like Adam's before the Fall: "He might to heav'n from Paradise go, / As from one room t'another," Herbert writes in "The H. Communion" (35–36). In "Decay" the orthodox formulas of typology clash with a felt sense of deterioration. Because Herbert elsewhere assumes the progressive unfolding of the typological scheme, "Decay" seems so anomalous. It required a steadfast truthfulness on Herbert's part to include a poem that contradicts his own most firmly held beliefs. He would not have done so, however, if "Decay" represented only a momentary faltering: it gives us an unretouched picture of Christian despair, and thus earns a place in the story. Moreover, by bringing into focus the shadows in the other typological poems, it helps

44. Anselment, " 'The Church Militant,' " 303.

us to see more clearly the triumphs of faith that Herbert celebrates there.

Those shadows are particularly disturbing in "The Bunch of Grapes." Although this belongs as well to the poems of discovery I will discuss next, I wish to consider it here because it provides Herbert's most explicit statement of the meaning of typology for the life of the believer. The title of Herbert's poem refers to the episode in Numbers 13–14 where the scouts sent to spy out the land of Canaan bring back a branch with one cluster of grapes, so heavy that "they bare it betweene two upon a staffe" (13:23). The Israelites ignore the obvious meaning of this sign—that the promised land is rich and fruitful—and begin to "murmur." Misled by the scouts, fearful that Canaan is populated by giants, they foolishly reject their own good and are punished by a lifetime of wandering in the desert:

> Surely they shall not see the land which I sware unto their fathers, neither shall any of them that provoked me, see it. . . . to morrow turne you, and get you into the wildernesse, by the way of the Red sea. . . .
> And your children shall wander in the wildernes forty yeres.
>
> (14:23, 25, 33)

Because of their murmurings, they are "brought back to the Red sea," once the scene of God's triumphs, now their "sea of shame." Herbert telescopes the complex series of events that we call the Exodus into this single telling incident. Invoked in psalm and prophecy, history and law, the story of the Exodus symbolizes par excellence God's redemptive activity in the Old Testament, and it is the type of the Redemption in the New.

In "The Bunch of Grapes," unlike the other typological poems, Herbert begins at once with the problem of man's peevish, murmuring, forgetful heart. Depressed by the sterile repetitiveness of his life ("I am where I began," 3), the speaker identifies himself in the first three stanzas with the errant Israelites who never reached the goal of their wanderings.[45] What is happening now has already happened, in some form, long ago; the life of the individual recapitulates the history of the race:

> I did towards Canaan draw; but now I am
> Brought back to the Red sea, the sea of shame.
>
> For as the Jews of old by Gods command
>   Travell'd, and saw no town;
> So now each Christian hath his journeys spann'd:
>   Their storie pennes and sets us down.
>   A single deed is small renown.
> Gods works are wide, and let in future times;
> His ancient justice overflows our crimes.

$(6-14)$

The analogy had already been suggested by Paul, who interpreted the events in the wilderness—the pillar of cloud and miraculous Red Sea crossing, the manna and

45. For a very different account of the poem see Barbara Leah Harman, *Costly Monuments: Representations of the Self in George Herbert's Poetry* (Cambridge, Mass., 1982), 171–81. I do not see that it is at all "difficult" (176, 177) for the speaker to acknowledge the parallels between his experience and that of the Israelites; his use of the vocabulary of the Exodus story in stanza 1 ("Canaan," "Red sea") shows him doing so from the start without hesitation. Nor do I find evidence in the poem that the speaker initially attempts to "exempt" himself from the "realm of encounter" with God, to "escape and conduct *his own journey*" (174; cf. 176), or that he uses biblical vocabulary "without realizing in any way the collective nature of his involvement in sacramental history" (177). Lines 1–2 offer no grounds for this assumption, and the first person pronoun in "*I* did towards Canaan draw" (6) is no more suspect than that in "*I* have their fruit" or "pressed for *my* sake" (23, 28); cf. line 10: "*each* Christian hath his journeys spann'd." The speaker does not consider the Exodus "first as narrative and then as historical account": the Exodus is a significant chapter in the history of salvation and to the believer is always "biblical history," not just "biblical story" (181). Finally, Herbert would not have said that "the story that takes the place of his own was *never* his own" (176), that it is "the story of others rather than the story of the self" (196). Harman reads the Bible from the point of view of a secular twentieth-century reader who values autonomy and individuality. But where she sees loss, Herbert sees gain. For Herbert the story of the self is made intelligible and resonant precisely by the fact that it has been enacted time and again by others like himself.

water from the rock—as types of the Christian sacraments of baptism and communion:

> Moreover brethren, I would not that yee should be igno-rant, how that all our fathers were under the cloud, and all passed thorow the Sea:
> And were all baptized unto Moyses in the cloud, and in the sea;
> And did all eat the same spirituall meat:
> And did all drinke the same spirituall drinke: (for they dranke of that spirituall Rocke that followed them: and that Rocke was Christ).
>
> (1 Cor. 10:1–4)

In the third stanza, the speaker outdoes Paul in dis-covering signs of God's providence:

> Then have we too our guardian fires and clouds;
>   Our Scripture-dew drops fast:
> We have our sands and serpents, tents and shrowds;
>   Alas! our murmurings come not last.
>
> (15–18)

The "Scripture-dew" or manna (Num. 11:9) is a type of Christ as the "living bread" (John 6:49–51); the "serpent of brasse" that Moses lifted up to cure the people bitten by "fierie serpents" (Num. 21:6–9), a type of "the Sonne of man . . . lifted up" (John 3:14). That despite all these signs he remains despondent shows how closely he re-sembles his ancient counterparts. "Alas! our murmurings come not last," he confesses, with acerbic understate-ment. Complaint and rebellion are the very substance of the parallel that Herbert is so meticulously setting forth. And as if to demonstrate that he is fully the equal of the Israelites, he at once produces his own petulant demand: "But where's the cluster? where's the taste / Of mine in-heritance?" (19–20).

Paul's enumeration of types, we must remember, is couched as an urgent warning. The Israelites too had their signs of God's grace, Paul cautions, yet "with many of them God was not well pleased," and they perished in the wilderness. "Now these things were our examples, to the intent wee should not lust after evil things"; "Now all these things happened unto them for ensamples: and they are written for our admonition" (1 Cor. 10:5–6, 11; cf. 9:10). Paul exhorts the Christian to stand fast against the sins of the Israelites, to avoid idolatry and fornication, to avoid tempting Christ—and concludes, significantly: "Neither murmure ye, as some of them also murmured, and were destroyed of the destroyer" (10:10). Calvin comments: "For what could a historie profit deade men? And how could it profyt those that are alyve, except they being admonished by the examples of other men should repente?" This is an ominous moment: the poem briefly raises the specter of deserved judgment ("His ancient justice overflows our crimes"). "If God punished them," Calvin warns, echoing Rom. 11:21, "he will not spare us."[46]

But the speaker's complaint marks the moment at which his identity with the Israelites becomes most explicit (*A is equal to B*); thus it leads naturally to the assertion that his state surpasses theirs (*B is greater than A*). The very words of his complaint—"Where's the *taste* / Of mine *inheritance?*"—point the way to recovery, for the question carries within itself an implicit answer: "O taste and see how gracious the Lord is"; "The Lord himselfe is the portion of mine inheritance, and of my cup" (Pss. 34:8, 16:6). Single words of Scripture, as so often, are bearers of a hidden truth, and the central action of the poem is the discovery of that truth: the veil done away in Christ.

What the speaker remembers is that the grape cluster, the "taste of his inheritance," is a type of Christ. In the context of the poem, "cluster" subordinates all the earlier figures and becomes the ultimate proof of the superiority of the New Dispensation. The signs of God's providence

46. John Calvin, *A Commentarie upon S. Paules Epistles to the Corinthians*, trans. Thomas Tymme (London, 1577), fols. 117, 117ᵥ.

mentioned in lines 15–17 are temporary measures in the wilderness—the manna, for example, ceases when the Israelites enter the Promised Land (Josh. 5:12). But the "cluster" signifies the fruitfulness of the Promised Land itself, which makes it an ideal symbol of the new order of things. Herbert's *bunch of grapes* is a veritable "cluster" of significances, gathering all the implications of the other types—sacrifice and communion and heavenly promise—into one triumphant emblem.

"All of this," as Fish says, "is potentially contained in the title of the poem, but, paradoxically, it is brought out only because it is suppressed."[47] The strategy of the poem is to keep the speaker so engrossed in his complaint that he ignores the consoling truth—until it bursts upon him in the final stanza with the force of a discovery:

> But can he want the grape, who hath the wine?
> I have their fruit and more.
>
> (22–23)

At last he stops the petulant whining that was the outward sign of his lack of faith. In the very process of complaining, he has realized that he is not like the rebellious Israelites, after all. They were condemned to die in the wilderness, never to taste the fruit of the Promised Land, while he may rejoice in "sweet wine . . . pressed for my sake" (27–28). At last we hear the words that till now have been missing: "more," "much more" (23, 26). The final stanza is composed of a series of comparisons—*grape/wine; their fruit/more; sowre juice/sweet wine; Noahs vine/God himself*—that hammer home the point. And in the final "for my sake" (as touching in its way as "Grieved for me?" in "Ephes. 4.30"), the speaker recognizes just how much has been done for him. He speaks as a representa-

47. Stanley E. Fish, "Catechizing the Reader: Herbert's Socratean Rhetoric," in *The Rhetoric of Renaissance Poetry*, ed. Thomas O. Sloan and Raymond B. Waddington (Berkeley and Los Angeles, 1974); rpt. *Essential Articles*, 204.

tive Christian, at the same time acknowledging a personal sense of gratitude, like Paul's "The sonne of God . . . loved mee, and gave himselfe for me" (Gal. 2:20).

In "The Bunch of Grapes" Herbert wishes to show how the example of history can "profyt those that are alyve." The Israelites were punished for refusing a fulfillment offered them. So long as the Christian goes on murmuring, refusing his joy, he is condemned to a lifetime of murmuring: the punishment fits the crime. The final movement of the poem enacts his release from this abortive history. When his eyes are "mended," gratitude overcomes frustration and complaint gives way to praise. The Christian reader learns that just as he transcends the fate of the ancient Israelites, so he can free himself from the old groove of faults, the nagging dissatisfactions of his own life. He is not doomed to go on repeating himself forever, but can move out of bondage to the past into an eternally present fulfillment. That much is clear. Still, the last stanza of the poem lacks the perfectly achieved assurance of "Aaron." The speaker is working hard at being joyful, the mind instructing the feelings: "But much more him I must adore" (26). From the show of effort just perceptible beneath the profession of joy, we may guess at the difficulty of putting off the old man, the subject to which I now turn.

PUTTING OFF THE OLD:
"THY WORDS DO FINDE ME OUT"

Although most of Herbert's poems have notoriously "happy endings," it is remarkable how little he has to say about the state of grace. What does it feel like to "sit and eat"? Herbert presents grace by indirection, as theologians define God by negatives. We are shown not the "feast" but the "way to it"; we are given only an occasional "glimpse of blisse," a "glance," a fleeting intuition. Herbert is less concerned with the experience of illumination than with the confused or troubled mind of the person who goes astray for lack of it, blundering "betwixt this world and that of grace."[48] In his psalmlike complaints and thanksgivings, as we shall see, Herbert presents the state of "betwixt" as one of gradual movement toward God: by "tuning" man's breast, pruning his branches, helping him to wings, God teaches man to "climbe" to him.[49] But in the poems we are about to consider, nothing less than spiritual rebirth can save the poor wretch: "Except a man be borne againe, he cannot see the kingdome of God" (John 3:3); "If any man be in Christ, hee is a new creature" (2 Cor. 5:17).

In these poems about putting off the old man and putting on the new[50]—what we might call "the making of the Christian"—Herbert dramatizes not just theological propositions but the way in which these enter a human life. He presents the saving truth, with the full stress on the active meaning of the participle: that is, the truth in the very act of saving. Perhaps "conversion" is too grand a word for that moment of recognition, of discovery, that we find so often in *The Temple*. Still, the shape of the experience is similar. Resistance or rebellion or despair is followed by miraculous, instantaneous illumination, as in the archetypal Christian conversions: Paul hears Christ's voice addressing him; Augustine perceives that a sentence of Paul's, chanced upon, is meant for him; Luther wrestles with a text in Romans and will not let go until it blesses him. In *The Temple* the moment of discovery is often marked by two of the classic insignia: the heavenly voice

48. "Love, III," 18; *A Priest to the Temple, Works,* 258; "Miserie," 75; "The Glimpse"; "The Glance"; "Affliction, IV," 6.

49. "The Temper, I," 23; "Paradise," 11; "Praise, I," 5; "Mattens," 20.

50. It is no accident that two of the three key passages about putting off the old man and putting on the new (Eph. 4:22–24 and Col. 3:9–10; the third is Rom. 6:4–6) are connected with texts that Herbert chooses as subjects for poems. See my discussion of "Ephes. 4.30" and "Coloss. 3.3" in chap. 1.

with its shattering message, and the suddenness of its appearance on the scene.

Herbert's poems of discovery focus on either the narrator's misguided zeal or his stubborn resistance. In "Redemption," "The Thanksgiving," "Jordan, II" and "The Holdfast," he is like an earnest child, trying almost too hard to please; in "Affliction, I," "The Crosse" and "The Collar," tired of trying, he bangs on the table in a rage. He is patiently nudged toward salvation in "The Holdfast," dragging his feet every step of the way; more often he pursues his wayward course unimpeded until the penultimate moment when suddenly, unexpectedly, he sees the light. There is no shared ground here between Old and New, as in the typological poems, but rather the sharpest possible contrast, a contrast pointed up by a pronounced structural imbalance. These are horizontal poems with abrupt vertical endings. All the chapters of folly or wretchedness are spelled out in detail—and then brushed aside in the final lines of the poem by a powerful word or phrase. "Thy words do finde me out": in each case, as in "The Bunch of Grapes," it is a word (or words) from the New Testament—*died, passion, friend, love, master, cross, child*—that signals the change of direction, teaching the speaker his proper relation to God.

The narrator of these poems is a familiar presence in *The Temple*. "I resolved to be bold," he swaggers; "I threatned," he declares loftily, "to observe the strict decree / Of my deare God." "Were it not better," he grows politic, "to bestow / Some place and power on me?" "But where's the cluster?" he sulks; "I disclaim the whole designe." "Things sort not to my will," he grouses; "I will . . . seek / Some other master out." "No more," he raps the table, "I will abroad."[51] These protagonists have

51. "Redemption," 2; "The Holdfast," 1–2; "Submission," 5–6; "The Bunch of Grapes," 19; "Dialogue," 23; "The Crosse," 19; "Affliction, I," 63–64; "The Collar," 1–2.

a distinctly biblical complexion. Men of little faith, stiff-necked, self-righteous, they resemble the stock figures of murmuring and rebellion in the Old Testament, and those in the New Testament who resist the fullness of grace by clinging to the Law—the contentious Pharisees of the synoptic Gospels, the literal-minded wranglers of the Gospel of John, the erring Jews for whom Paul prays:

> For I beare them record, that they have a zeale of God, but not according to knowledge.
> For they being ignorant of Gods righteousnesse, and going about to establish their owne righteousnesse, have not submitted themselves unto the righteousnesse of God.
> For Christ is the end of the Law for righteousnes to every one that beleeveth.
>
> (Rom. 10:2–4)

When he presents the old man in bondage to the flesh, Herbert dramatizes the contrast between the Old and the New, making palpable the very need for grace, and the mysterious way in which grace invades the human sphere.

We observe these creatures from just enough of a distance (or so we persuade ourselves) to find most of them comic. As Northrop Frye remarks, "For a Christian audience an Old Testament or pagan setting is ironic" because its characters are "in a state of lower freedom than the audience," moving "according to the conditions of a law, whether Jewish or natural, from which the audience has been, at least theoretically, redeemed."[52] The final words offer an important qualification. If these personae were too remote from the reader, the poems would lose some of their sting. We cannot help noticing that the boundary between Herbert and his personae is a fluid one (compare, for example, "Jordan, II" with "Redemption," "The Thanksgiving" and "The Holdfast"; or "Affliction, I" and "The Crosse" with "The Collar"). The personae Herbert

52. Northrop Frye, *Anatomy of Criticism* (Princeton, 1957), 221.

presents with such knowing irony are versions of his retrograde self, like the wordly antagonists of "The Quip,"
and like the misguided or rebellious speakers of the autobiographical poems. Nor are they so different, truth to
tell, from ourselves: I think we are meant to note our own
resemblance to them, to feel the tug of their resistances
and the shock of their discoveries. Even as we laugh at
them, we cannot help wincing a little, too.

The narrator of "Redemption" stands literally at the
juncture of Old and New. Though he wears an air of
bravado ("I resolved to be bold," "I straight return'd"),
he is a poor lost soul, searching for his Lord in all the
wrong places:

> Having been tenant long to a rich Lord,
>   Not thriving, I resolved to be bold,
>   And make a suit unto him, to afford
> A new small-rented lease, and cancell th' old.
> In heaven at his manour I him sought:
>   They told me there, that he was lately gone
>   About some land, which he had dearly bought
> Long since on earth, to take possession.
> I straight return'd, and knowing his great birth,
>   Sought him accordingly in great resorts;
>   In cities, theatres, gardens, parks, and courts:
>
> (1–11)

In the end, almost despite himself, he stumbles upon
Christ, who has the last word, leaving him not even one
iamb for a reply:

> At length I heard a ragged noise and mirth
>   Of theeves and murderers: there I him espied,
>   Who straight, *Your suit is granted*, said, & died.
>
> (12–14)

God's prevenient grace has rendered all his efforts absurd. Significantly, Christ has the last action too: Herbert
did not write (the banal rhyme aside), "there I him did
see, / Who straight, *Your suit is granted*, said to me." Some
of the power of the ending lies in the abrupt "& died."

The point is not simply that Christ died before the suitor could say "Please" or "Thank you," but that he *died*, with that act effecting man's redemption.

With this blundering persona, Herbert dramatizes the theological doctrine that "while we were yet sinners, Christ died for us" (Rom. 5:8), drawing out in fourteen packed lines Paul's amazed, grateful "while." And he gives Paul's *pro nobis* its full imaginative sweep by deliberately confounding the dramatic time of the poem. While the stage set (manor, resorts, cities, theaters, gardens, parks, courts) points to Herbert's England, the speaker seems, remarkably, to be unaware that there has been a New Dispensation, till he finds himself at Calvary at the very moment of the crucifixion. By linking *once* and *now* in a kind of poetic time warp, Herbert is saying that each man must discover the cross for himself if it is to have any meaning for him. The surprise of the final couplet enacts that experience of awakening in which one comes face to face with what he already knows. The discovery seems so abrupt because the narrator is looking elsewhere, but it can be so briefly put because he has already grasped it in the innermost recesses of his mind.

One of Herbert's great virtues as a religious poet—a rare one, indeed—is that he has a sense of the comic. In "Redemption" he pokes fun at the spiritual obtuseness of the narrator; in "The Thanksgiving," Jordan, II" and "The Holdfast," the object of his irony is the inefficacy of works, the absurdity of the old man's efforts to "get ahead" in the world of the spirit. Simone Weil, the twentieth-century religious philosopher whose affinity for Herbert is well known, puts the matter much as Herbert does:

> There are people who try to raise their souls like a man continually taking standing jumps in the hopes that, if he jumps higher every day, a time may come when he will no longer fall back but will go right up to the sky. Thus occupied he cannot look at the sky. We cannot take a single step to-

ward heaven. It is not in our power to travel in a vertical direction.[53]

The narrator of "The Thanksgiving" is just such a figure: he has, in Paul's words, "a zeale of God, but not according to knowledge." The question he poses so insistently is the essential question of the Christian life: "But how then shall I imitate thee?" (15). At first he throws up his hands in dismay at the plain impossibility of such an attempt, but quickly rallies, producing what seems at first glance an exemplary plan of action: charity to the poor, honor to God, chastity, public works, psalms of praise. He is ambitious to reform both the outer and the inner world: "I'le build a spittle, or mend common wayes, / But mend mine own without delayes" (33–34). What could be more commendable than to write hymns of praise ("My musick shall finde thee," 39)? (That Herbert is referring to his own book of poems is obvious from the deictic "'tis here," 44.) Surely nothing could be better than to study the Bible ("Nay, I will reade thy book," 45). But one cannot miss the fact that all these noble New Year's resolutions are bracketed by two couplets of pure swagger:

> Surely I will revenge me on thy love,
>   And trie who shall victorious prove.

> Thy art of love, which I'le turn back on thee:
>   O my deare Saviour, Victorie!
>
> (17–18, 47–48)

"O my deare" notwithstanding, the speaker is too much the braggart warrior.

We may be aware of his self-preoccupied air and his skewed sense of priorities:

> As for thy passion—But of that anon,
>   When with the other I have done.
>
> (29–30)

---

53. Simone Weil, *Waiting for God*, trans. Emma Craufurd (1951; rpt. New York, 1959), 194.

But we do not really take his measure until we hear the changed man who speaks the last line:

> Then for thy passion—I will do for that—
> Alas, my God, I know not what.
>
> (49–50)

When he finally confronts the meaning of "thy passion," he can only say "alas," not "anon," and gasp out his helplessness—this time not as a general statement ("the tale is told," 8) but as a personal confession of inadequacy ("I know not what," 50) such as we find at the end of "Miserie." That is the first step to his regeneration, if he would only know it. The following poem, "The Reprisall," a pendant that in the Williams manuscript had the title "The Second Thanks-giving," concludes by defining a viable battle strategy for the Christian soldier:

> though I can do nought
> Against thee, in thee I will overcome
> The man, who once against thee fought.
>
> (14–16)

The opposition of "against thee" (heard twice in two lines) and "in thee" makes Herbert's point. All the worthy plans of the speaker were conceived "against thee," and therefore misconceived. A wretch cannot hope to measure with great God. The one "Victorie" ordained for him is to put off, "in" Christ, the old man.

In "Jordan, II" the spiritual high-jumper is a poet—Herbert himself. He wants to clothe God in glory:

> When first my lines of heav'nly joyes made mention,
> Such was their lustre, they did so excell,
> That I sought out quaint words, and trim invention;
> My thoughts began to burnish, sprout, and swell,
> Curling with metaphors a plain intention,
> Decking the sense, as if it were to sell.
>
> (1–6)

"Burnish," "sprout," "swell," "curling," "decking"—there is a positive frenzy of activity here. Yet all this ef-

fort, all these burnished lines, do not affect God much,
are not his aim. The poet is searching for words in
theaters and courts, as it were, when all he need do is to
look up at the sky.

Even as he is "bustling" in this misguided fashion (cf.
"while we were yet sinners," Rom. 5:8), the truth comes
to him in the words of a friend:

> But while I bustled, I might heare a friend
> Whisper, *How wide is all this long pretence!*
> *There is in love a sweetnesse readie penn'd:*
> *Copie out onely that, and save expense.*

(15–18)

Because the friend "enters in mid-line," as Fish puts it,
"we experience exactly the sense of sudden and peremp-
tory intervention the poet recalls." Fish goes on to say
that the friend is advocating "not the plain style, but no
style at all and, in a way, silence. By copying out what is
already there one speaks in the words of another, and
therefore, to the extent that speech is an assertion of self,
does not speak."[54]

But is the friend really whispering, "Sit back in silence
and let God write your lines"? *"Onely"* refers not to
"copie" ("You need *only copy*, a mechanical task equivalent
in effect to silence"), but rather to *"love"* ("Copy out *only
sweet love*, nothing else, certainly not the foolishness you
have been wasting your time on"). The poet is instructed
to change not the task but the object. "Copying" (Gk.
mimesis, Lat. *imitatio*) had long been considered the task of
the artist, but the Christian poet is given a new object: not
Plato's "reality," not Aristotle's "universals," but Christ's
"love." God provides the model, the pattern of Love, just
as he lets down the silk twist from heaven, but it is man's
work to "copie" as it is to "climbe."[55]

It is no wonder, moreover, that the *friend* speaks about

54. Fish, *Self-Consuming Artifacts*, 198, 199.
55. *Climbe:* "Mattens," 20; "The Pearl," 40.

copying *love*. As Tuve has noticed, Christ calls himself man's "friend" in the Gospel of John in the very passage where he enjoins man to imitate his love:[56]

> This is my Commaundement, that ye love one another, as I have loved you.
> Greater love hath no man then this, that a man lay downe his life for his friends.
> Ye are my friends, if you do whatsoever I command you. Henceforth I call you not servants, for the servant knoweth not what his lord doth, but I have called you friends: for all things that I have heard of my Father, I have made knowen unto you.
>
> (John 15:12–15)

Here, then, is the answer to the question raised in "The Thanksgiving": "But how then shall I . . . / Copie thy fair, though bloudie hand?" (15–16). He must "copie out" love, and that he can do only in the spirit of love.

The narrator of "The Holdfast," like that of "The Thanksgiving," wants to establish his own righteousness. Knowing the Law as "strict," he is eager to do what he thinks is required of him:

> I threatned to observe the strict decree
>   Of my deare God with all my power & might.
>   But I was told by one, it could not be;
> Yet I might trust in God to be my light.
> Then will I trust, said I, in him alone.
>   Nay, ev'n to trust in him, was also his:
>   We must confesse that nothing is our own.
> Then I confesse that he my succour is:
> But to have nought is ours, not to confesse
>   That we have nought.
>
> (1–10)

It is Paul's own case—the Paul who boasted himself "an Hebrew of the Hebrewes, as touching the Law, a Pharise: . . . touching the righteousnesse which is in the Law, blamelesse" (Phil. 3:5–6). That, however, was before his conversion:

56. Tuve, "*Caritas*," 309.

But what things were gaine to me, those I counted losse
for Christ. . . . for whom I have suffered the losse of all
things, and doe count them but doung, that I may win
Christ,
And be found in him, not having mine owne righteousnesse, which is of the Law, but that which is through the
faith of Christ, the righteousnesse which is of God by faith.
(Phil. 3:7–9)

In the opening lines the speaker reveals himself a very
Pharisee. The "decree" he speaks of is, of course, the
law of laws: "And thou shalt love the LORD thy God
with all thine heart, and with all thy soule, and with all
thy might" (Deut. 6:5). In the synoptic Gospels, this
commandment is heard in the context of Jesus' encounter with a Pharisee lawyer; Jesus calls it "the first
and great Commandement," one of the two on which
"hang all the Law and the Prophets" (Matt. 22:38, 40). In
the Old Testament the injunction to love God is usually
coupled with a requirement for action on man's part: to
"keepe . . . his Commandements," to "serve him," to
"walke in all his wayes" (Deut. 11:1, 13, 22); the obser-
vance of the commandments is understood to be an expression of love for God. But the speaker's ambition to
serve is a caricature of the Judaic attitude toward the
Law. Though he calls God "deare," he says nothing
about loving the Lord; he forgets about heart and soul,
referring instead to his own "power & might," a revealing redundancy. The bluster of "threatned" alerts us to
what might charitably be called an excess of zeal. In the
lines that follow he tries hard to hold his own, and his
very self-assurance, as in "Redemption," lends an air of
comedy to his failure of understanding.

The Pharisaic speaker is taken to task by an interlocutor, whose lines are punctuated by negatives: "it could
not be"; "Nay, . . . nothing is our own"; "to have nought
is ours, not to confesse / That we have nought." The
teaching is Paul's: "Not that wee are sufficient of our

selves to thinke any thing as of our selves: but our sufficiencie is of God" (2 Cor. 3:5; cf. Eph. 2:8–9, Phil. 2:13,
etc.). But Paul's *not*, in context, is prefaced to the assurance that "our sufficiencie is of God." The interlocutor of
"The Holdfast" is communicating only part of Paul's message. No wonder the narrator feels "much troubled." One
is reminded of Dr. Faustus brooding over a truncated
summary of Christian doctrine, "For the wages of sinne is
death," ignoring the hopeful conclusion of the verse, "but
the gift of God is eternall life" (Rom. 6:23)—and bidding
divinity adieu.

Herbert, however, does not leave the poor creature in
his confusion. Instead, in three emphatic lines, he goes
on to make explicit what the interlocutor has left unsaid,
giving far more than he has taken away:

> I stood amaz'd at this,
> Much troubled, till I heard a friend expresse,
> That all things were more ours by being his.
> What Adam had, and forfeited for all,
> Christ keepeth now, who cannot fail or fall.
>
> (10–14)

Significantly, Herbert puts the good news once again in
the mouth of a *friend:* "All things were more ours by
being his." William James has written about the phenomenon of "self-surrender": by letting go of the "little
private convulsive self," one encounters "that fundamental mystery of religious experience, the satisfaction found
in absolute surrender to the larger power."[57] Fish reduces
the experience of "The Holdfast" to the "humiliati[on]" of

57. William James, *The Varieties of Religious Experience* (1902; rpt.
New York, 1936), 207, 109, 314. James adds that "self-surrender has
been and always must be regarded as the vital turning-point of the
religious life, so far as the religious life is spiritual and no affair of outer
works and ritual and sacraments. One may say that the whole development of Christianity in inwardness has consisted in little more than the
greater and greater emphasis attached to this crisis of self-surrender"
(207).

discovering one's "personal insufficiency."[58] But the poem is not just about "the high cost of dying to the old man."[59] One who is moved to self-surrender does not count the cost.

The paradox that "All things were more ours by being his" is a difficult one, and likely to perplex the speaker, so the friend goes on to explain:

> What Adam had, and forfeited for all,
> Christ keepeth now, who cannot fail or fall.
>
> (13–14)

Here we have in brief the Christian understanding of history: "For as by one mans disobedience many were made sinners: so by the obedience of one, shall many bee made righteous" (Rom. 5:19). Adam failed, Christ keeps; things are different *now*, and *better*. This typological claim is strengthened by a strategic allusion to the Book of Psalms. "Christ keepeth now, who cannot fail or fall" recalls the verse, "Behold, hee that keepeth Israel: shall neither slumber nor sleepe" (Ps. 121:4). The correspondence of Old and New is conveyed by formal similarities: "keepeth" echoes the psalm verse, and the alliteration and consonance of "fail/fall" reinforces the Hebrew parallelism of ideas with a parallelism of sound, as in "slumber/sleepe." That the New surpasses the Old is suggested by subtle differences of phrasing: "now" sets off the present moment from the whole of the past; "cannot" is more emphatic than "shall neither," and "fail or fall" more portentous than "slumber nor sleepe." All this is dogma, but in the poem it is presented as a discovery. When the speaker is brought to an impasse, the truth is given to him again as an unasked gift.

The protagonists of the poems we have just considered come to grace almost despite themselves, and with comparatively little distress. For those who are angry or rebel-

---

58. Fish, *Self-Consuming Artifacts*, 175.
59. I owe this phrase to Virginia Mollenkott.

lious, however, the way to grace winds through a land-scape of pain. In "Affliction, I," "The Crosse" and "The Collar," Herbert is dealing not with the doctrinal question of the inefficacy of works, which admits of a comic treatment, but rather with a problem of the will: the monumental difficulty of putting off the old man. That creature now seems not merely a "poore silly soul" but a "wonder tortur'd in the space / Betwixt this world and that of grace."[60] The narrators (Herbert himself in "Affliction, I" and "The Crosse," and a high-pitched version of Herbert in "The Collar") are too occupied with griefs or grievances to consider the source of their misery, though retrospectively they would acknowledge Paul's diagnosis:

> For the good that I would, I do not: but the evill which I would not, that I doe. . . .
> O wretched man that I am: who shall deliver me from the body of this death?
>
> (Rom. 7:19, 24)

They cross-bias themselves, though they do not know it; but in the end they are, all of them, delivered. For Herbert, as for Paul, the human predicament in its very darkness is the "foil" that sets off grace. If Paul speaks unequivocally of sin and guilt, it is precisely because he is convinced he has found an effective remedy in Christ. Between two sentences of the Epistle to the Romans—"O wretched man that I am" and "Who shall separate us from the love of Christ?" (Rom. 7:24, 8:35)—in the "space betwixt," lies the course of these three "tortur'd" poems. Herbert lets us look long and hard at man's wretchedness, but the purposive drive of his rhetoric is toward the illumination of grace.

"Affliction, I" starts by recalling, with more than a touch of nostalgia, a time of "youth and fierceness" when God's service seemed splendid:

---

60. "Vanitie, II," 1; "Affliction, IV," 5–6.

When first thou didst entice to thee my heart,
  I thought the service brave:
So many joyes I writ down for my part,
  Besides what I might have
Out of my stock of naturall delights,
Augmented with thy gracious benefits.

I looked on thy furniture so fine,
  And made it fine to me:
Thy glorious houshold-stuffe did me entwine,
  And 'tice me unto thee.
Such starres I counted mine: both heav'n and earth
Payd me my wages in a world of mirth.

                                                    (1–12)

The fine furniture that Herbert confesses he found so attractive reminds us of the "glorie" that was Sion. Thus we expect the "now" (55) of the mature man to reflect some sign of growth, of a deepened spirituality, as the fee of all his woes. The first third of the poem might then have been prelude to a statement about coming of age: "When I was a childe, I spake as a childe, I understood as a childe, I thought as a childe: but when I became a man, I put away childish things" (1 Cor. 13:11). Alternatively, as in "The Glance," the speaker might have looked upon the sugared delights of childhood as the pledge of a more promising future. Instead, stuck in a bleak present, he calls the past a loss ("At first thou gav'st," then "thou took'st away" [19, 31]) and the future a blank ("what thou wilt do with me / None of my books will show" [55–56]). "Now" means only "decay," and the peevish heart fixes the blame for its misery on God the betrayer. It is not so easy, after all, to put off the child.

It is only when the speaker announces, "Well, I will change the service and go seek / Some other master out," that he recognizes with a gasp—"Ah my deare God!" (63–65)—what he has threatened. The Old Testament plot of rebellion and return concludes with an Emmaus of recognition: "And their eyes were opened, and they knew him" (Luke 24:31). "Master" is one of a number of words of relationship (the others being "friend" and "father") that figure importantly in the conclusions of these poems of discovery.

We have already spoken about the associations of *master* in "The Odour," where Herbert savors the music of that word: "How sweetly doth *My Master* sound! *My Master!*"[61] We may think of "Affliction, I" as pivoting on *master:* the abrupt reversal in the last couplet is possible only because the word has such unmistakable associations. The speaker recognizes at once the blasphemy implicit in his casual aside, and his whole passionate rant collapses under the weight of implication of that single word. He reminds himself of a relationship that he cannot, would not, will not abandon, and the word "love," missing till then, is spoken twice in a powerful access of emotion:

> Ah my deare God! though I am clean forgot,
> Let me not love thee, if I love thee not.

> (65–66)

As Empson puts it, "he has no worse imprecation than the first part of the line, and it is used to give force to the statement of purpose in the second."[62] The curse he pronounces is Paul's: "If any man love not the Lord Jesus Christ, let him bee Anathema" (1 Cor. 16:22). But now that his eyes have been opened, that curse becomes a blessing in his mouth.

In contrast to "Affliction, I," which starts with a memory of past joys, "The Crosse" is about anguish pure and unalloyed. The detailed history of "Affliction, I" is abridged here into a few accusing lines:

> And then when after much delay,
> Much wrastling, many a combate, this deare end,

---

61. See my discussion of "The Odour" in chap. 1.
62. William Empson, *Seven Types of Ambiguity,* 3d ed. (1953; rpt. Harmondsworth, 1961), 184.

So much desir'd, is giv'n, to take away
My power to serve thee; . . .

(7–10)

Underlying the complaint about giving and taking away is
a verse from Job that is intoned in the Anglican Order for
the Burial of the Dead: "The LORD gave, and the LORD
hath taken away, blessed be the Name of the LORD" (Job
1:21). But the speaker is too angry, for the moment, to
pronounce these (or any) words of acceptance.

His accusation of God is unsparing:

Thou turnest th' edge of all things on me still,
Taking me up to throw me down.

(21–22)

Herbert is paraphrasing a verse from the Psalms, "thou
hast taken me up, and cast me downe" (102:10), which he
understands, as Calvin does, in its most devastating
sense:

For in asmuch as we lift up the things aloft which we mynd to
dashe more hardly ageinst the ground: a violente throwyng
down myght be betokened in such words as these: Thou hast
crushed me sorer with throwing me headlong from aloft, than
if I had bin but shooved down from my standing.[63]

In "Hymne to God my God, in my sicknesse," Donne
takes as the text to his own soul, "Therfore that he may
raise the Lord throws down,"[64] resting his hopes on a
God of comfort. Herbert is imagining, quite the contrary,
a God of pure malice. But even in this diatribe, he keeps
the knife-edge of irony turned against himself. No one
would think of calling "The Crosse" a comic poem, yet
here too we are reminded of the naive speakers of "Redemption" or "The Thanksgiving" or "Jordan, II" by the
grandiosity of "and not onely I, / But all my wealth and

63. Calvin, *Psalmes*, pt. 2, fol. 89ᵥ.
64. John Donne, *Divine Poems,* ed. Helen Gardner (Oxford, 1952;
corr. rpt. 1966), 50, lines 28–30.

familie might combine / To set thy honour up, as our designe" (4–6), or the unabashed self-absorption of "Besides, things sort not to my will" (19). Herbert borrows from Jonah to play Job: even in his affliction he is at times, indeed, a little ridiculous.

In the last stanza, after thirty lines of complaint, the speaker turns suddenly to the God who has cast him down to ask for help:

> Ah my deare Father, ease my smart!
> These contrarieties crush me: these crosse actions
> Doe winde a rope about, and cut my heart.
>
> (31–33)

At this point he can see only as far as his own pain: "crosse actions," like "crosse-bias" in "Affliction, I" (53), is intended as a summary word of complaint. But the word *crosse* inevitably reminds him of a suffering larger than his own, one that encloses and makes sense of it:

> And yet since these thy contradictions
> Are properly a crosse felt by thy Sonne, . . .
>
> (34–35)

As Fish says, "The extraordinary impact of these lines is attributable in large part to the precise ambiguity of the words "thy Sonne.""[65] They refer first of all to Christ, a brother in anguish, who feels even now the "contradictions" that torment the speaker. But the words also refer to the speaker himself, who has been adopted as a "sonne" of God (Gal. 4:5–7, 1 John 3:1), and who has just addressed God as "my deare Father." As a Christian, he knows he must "take up his crosse" (Matt. 16:24) and crucify the old man (Rom. 6:6). These meanings come together—Christ suffering for man, man bearing his suffering in order to conform himself to Christ—and enable him, in an astonishing moment of growth, to take Christ's words as his own:

---

65. Fish, *Self-Consuming Artifacts*, 187.

With but foure words, my words, *Thy will be done.*

(36)

When the old man is put off—made to bear his cross, crucified—the Christian is able to speak the first words of a new language.

These poems about putting off the old man are a series of variations on one of Herbert's central themes: truly to become a Christian means to relive, in one's own body and blood, the difficult passage from the old to the new. To summarize what I have said about this subject, I would like to look at "The Collar," which offers perhaps the best-known portrait of the old man. "Not thriving," like the persona of "Redemption," he has, it seems, already attempted to plead his case before the poem opens. This time there is no answer and he grows impatient. "Shall I be still in suit?" he proclaims loudly, in case Anyone is listening, and with a show of determination rises up "to flee . . . from the presence of the LORD" (Jonah 1:3; cf. Gen. 3:8). It is the primal temptation he faces: "there is fruit, / And thou hast hands." But this naïf is deaf to the implications of his words. As critics have noted, the *thorn* he complains of suggests both Eden and Calvary, and the *wine* and *corn* he longs for are the elements of the Eucharist.[66]

Indeed, the entire first section of the poem is a tissue of double and triple meanings:

> I struck the board, and cry'd, No more.
> I will abroad.
> What? shall I ever sigh and pine?
> My lines and life are *free*; free as the rode,
> Loose as the winde, as large as store.
> Shall I be still in suit?

---

66. Martz, *Poetry of Meditation,* 303; Jeffrey Hart, "Herbert's *The Collar* Re-read," *Boston University Studies in English* 5 (1961), rpt. *Essential Articles,* 453–60; Patrides, ed., *English Poems,* 19; Ilona Bell, "The Double Pleasures of Herbert's 'Collar,' " in *"Too Rich to Clothe the Sunne,"* 77–88.

Have I no *harvest* but a *thorn*
To let me *bloud*, and not restore
What I have *lost* with cordiall *fruit?*
    Sure there was *wine*
Before my sighs did drie it: there was *corn*
    Before my *tears* did drown it.
    Is the yeare onely *lost* to me?
    Have I no bayes to *crown* it?
No flowers, no garlands gay? all blasted?
    All wasted?

(1–16, my italics)

Bloud, tears, and *crown* recall incidents of the Passion
(Luke 22:44, 19:41, Matt. 27:29) as well as biblical "Promises for comfort":[67] the "blood of the new Testament" by
which we are justified (Matt. 26:28, Rom. 5:9); the new
creation when "God shall wipe away all teares" (Rev.
21:4); the "crowne of righteousnesse" laid up for the
faithful (2 Tim. 4:8). *Fruit* and *harvest* have their analogues
in the world of the spirit (Gal. 5:22; Matt. 9:37, 13:39), and
loss and *freedom* find a new meaning in Christ: "For what
is a man profited, if hee shal gaine the whole world, and
lose his owne soule?" (Matt. 16:26); "For whosoever will
save his life, shall lose it: but whosoever will lose his life
for my sake, the same shall save it" (Luke 9:24); "If the
Sonne therfore shall make you free, ye shall be free indeed" (John 8:36). As in "The Sacrifice," where the tor-
mentors of Christ "wish *my bloud on them and theirs*" (107),
not knowing what they say, the symbolic overtones of the
speaker's language expose his ignorance: the double
meanings of his words "aright / Used, and wished" (109–
110) supply the answers to his angry questions, but he is
shouting so loud he can't hear himself. The turn in the
poem is initiated, as in "Redemption," "Jordan, II" and
"The Holdfast," by "one calling":

But as I rav'd and grew more fierce and wilde
    At every word,

67. *A Priest to the Temple, Works,* 228.

Me thoughts I heard one calling, *Child!*
And I reply'd, *My Lord.*

(33–36)

It has been observed that "the caller" is one of the puns
implicit in the title (along with "choler" and various
senses of "collar").[68] The verb *to call* is charged with biblical meaning. One thinks of the calling of Moses and Samuel in the Old Testament (Ex. 3:4, 1 Sam. 3:8) and of the
disciples in the New (Matt. 4:21), of Paul "called to be an
Apostle" and the faithful "called to be Saints" (1 Cor. 1:1–
2). In "The Collar" we find dramatized Jesus' proclama-
tion, "I came not to call the righteous, but sinners to
repentance" (Luke 5:32) and Paul's assurance that God
has "called us with an holy calling, not according to our
workes, but according to his owne purpose and grace"
(2 Tim. 1:9). It is of some significance that the call is heard
(or imagined) while the speaker is at his most rebellious—
"as I rav'd"—just as the whisper of the friend in "Jordan,
II" is heard "while I bustled" (15). Lewalski, describing
the Protestant conception of "calling," points out that the
experience is unexpected, unearned, mysterious, and that
it involves pain as well as promise:

> The *Calling* of the elect Christian involves God's awaken-
> ing in him at whatever time God has appointed and by what-
> ever means . . . such a sense of his desperate sinfulness but
> also of the gospel promises that he is prepared to receive the
> accompanying gifts of effective repentance and saving faith.[69]

The "caller" accomplishes all this by crying "*Child!*"
This one word offers both rebuke and comfort: "You are a
child, not an adult"; "You are my child, not a stranger."
In the Bible *child* can suggest unripeness or confusion:
"Returne ye backsliding children, and I wil heale your
backslidings" (Jer. 3:22); "When I was a childe, I spake as

68. Rickey, *Utmost Art*, 99–101.
69. Lewalski, *Protestant Poetics*, 16.

a childe, . . . but when I became a man, I put away childish things. . . . Brethren, bee not children in understanding" (1 Cor. 13:11, 14:20). But it also implies softness and
suppleness: "Except yee be converted, and become as
little children, yee shall not enter into the kingdome of
heaven" (Matt. 18:3). Israel's beginnings as a people is
remembered in this metaphor: "When Israel was a childe,
then I loved him, and called my sonne out of Egypt"
(Hos. 11:1). Now the Christian is granted the status of
"children of God by faith in Christ Jesus" (Gal. 3:26):

> Ye have received the spirit of adoption, whereby we cry,
> Abba, father.
> The spirit it selfe beareth witnes with our spirit, that we
> are the children of God.
> And if children, then heires, heires of God, and joynt
> heires with Christ.
>
> (Rom. 8:15–17; cf. Gal. 4:5–7)

The word *child* epitomizes the spiritual condition of Herbert's naive personae: as "children in understanding,"
they are deficient, retrograde; as "children of God," they
are received with love in a new order of being.

What we find in "The Collar" is one of the informing
patterns of the Bible, that of rebellion and return. A central motif of the prophetic books is the recalcitrance of
Israel and (depending upon the temperament and outlook
of the prophet) God's readiness to punish or forgive. The
historical books keep repeating the same story: Israel sins,
is punished, returns to God—a cycle endlessly repeated.
Indeed the Old Testament, if one were to reduce it to its
merest outline, would be a record of the recurrent backslidings of Israel. In the biblical view of history we find
the paradigms that govern the movement of so many of
Herbert's poems: man sins and repents; God admonishes
him and bids him welcome. The happy endings of Herbert's poems, then, are not really as "easy" as some
readers might suppose. They are absorbed into the larger
cyclical patterns of the volume, momentary intuitions of

blessedness in a chronicle that is filled with despondency and bitterness of spirit. God's call at the end of "The Collar," with its note of tender reproof, initiates one such moment, charged with possibility.

The poems we have just discussed all have happy endings, in one way or another, but even where Herbert sets the speaker in a comic light, they are not happy poems. These are records of past misery made public. But to what purpose? "That which is past who can recall?" Herbert writes in "The Discharge"; "onely the present is thy part and fee" (10, 21). Why doesn't the new man leave his old self behind and live happily ever after in the redeemed present? Barbara Harman, writing of "The Collar," tries to understand why the speaker should wish "to preserve a story that is otherwise of no use to him at all (it is, after all, obsolete and embarrassing)."[70] The obvious Christian "use" for such a story, however, is to bear witness: "Oh wretched man that I was till Christ entered my life." Indeed the Church's preservation of the Old Testament, which to some Christians has seemed both "obsolete" and "embarrassing," is just such a form of testimony, a witnessing to God's grace.

Why, one must ask in conclusion, are there so many "discoveries" in *The Temple?* One would suppose that in the poems of a convinced Anglican, the servant of a church orderly and "fit" in all its ways, where the religious impulse seems almost domesticated, there would be little room for surprise. Herbert, however, does not often speak with the settled accents of "The Happy Priest" (to use Palmer's unfortunate phrase),[71] content with showing off the furniture of his church. Rather, he writes about the living power of Christianity to resolve the contrarieties of the human condition. And in doing so he gives dramatic shape to a basic truth of human behavior: what we know

70. Harman, *Costly Monuments,* 84.
71. Palmer, ed., *English Works,* III, 1–63.

we do not always remember. We may be sustained by some belief, some large view of life, and still feel it slip from us at a moment of crisis. We keep forgetting what we most profoundly know, and we must struggle to recover what has been lost and found and lost again and again. Thus we recapitulate in our own lives the experiences of the race. The theologian Rudolf Bultmann phrases this truth in specifically Christian terms: "Faith, as the possibility of Christian existence ever to be grasped anew, is a reality only by constantly overcoming the old existence under the Law"; "this existence under grace is never arrived at once and for all but is vital only as it is ever grasped anew."[72]

One of Herbert's great achievements as a religious poet is to reveal the "underside" of faith: the difficulty of holding on to what one most deeply believes. One discovery is emphatically not enough, just as "one creation / Will not suffice": "Except thou make us dayly, we shall spurn / Our own salvation."[73] Herbert believes that Christ is his Redeemer, and that the New Dispensation made possible a new way of being for the believer, but at times even this fundamental belief seems unavailable to him. When he retrieves it, finally, or when it finds him out, it has the power to change his life.

72. Rudolf Bultmann, "The Significance of the Old Testament for the Christian Faith," in *The Old Testament and Christian Faith,* ed. Bernhard W. Anderson (New York, 1963), 15, 22.
73. "Giddinesse," 25–28.

· 4 ·

Talking to Man

CHRISTIAN TEACHING: "LORD, INSTRUCT US"

"Lord Jesu! teach thou me, that I may teach them," Herbert begs in his "Prayer before Sermon."[1] A perpetual student of his own experience, he is always teaching, "first . . . himselfe, and then . . . others."[2] Herbert finds in every sorrow a sermon, in every affliction a lesson to be learned, in his very being here a kind of witness: "I live to shew [God's] power," he writes in "Josephs coat" (13). The ideal parson's house he describes as a kind of school:

> All in his house are either teachers or learners, or both, so that his family is a Schoole of Religion, and they all account, that to teach the ignorant is the greatest almes.[3]

In *The Temple*, which may be justly called "a Schoole of Religion," he is both a "learner," struggling to put off the old man, and a teacher of those in his "house," his "family."

Herbert's explicitly didactic poems are often scanted in anthologies and critical commentaries today, giving us a bowdlerized Herbert congenial to current tastes. Our notions of what belongs in a poem are, to be sure, very different from Herbert's, and many readers confess to picking out the raisins and leaving the pudding. But the didactic impulse is essential to *The Temple*, whether we like

1. "Prayer before Sermon," *Works*, 289.
2. *A Priest to the Temple, Works*, 279, paraphrasing Rom. 2:21.
3. Ibid., *Works*, 240.

it or not. We must come to terms with it, I believe, if only to understand how Herbert differs from us and to avoid the temptation of reading him as a contemporary.

The widely accepted notion that Herbert's "intimate poems" are either "colloquies of the soul with God or self-communings"[4] requires some qualification. *The Temple* includes many lyrics whose concerns are public and general, such as those addressed to personified abstractions, narratives, reports of dialogues, homilies on man's estate and "definition poems."[5] Lyrics addressed to God are not always intimate colloquies: "Faith" is really a celebration of the power of belief; "The Windows" is about the preacher's place in God's temple; "The Quidditie" offers a definition of verse; "Obedience" hopes for "some kinde man" who will hear and respond. And Herbert's "thou" is often directed not only to himself but also to his fellow sinner. "Herbert writes in [some] poems as though he and his soul had yet to make each other's acquaintance," Vendler objects, but his "cold detachment" seems odd only if we assume that he is always communing with himself.[6] The problems attendant on reading every poem as spiritual autobiography may be illustrated by Palmer's unintentionally droll account of "Vanitie, II": "[Herbert] is enticed by a fair-eyed, money-loving woman."[7]

The dividing line between the self and the reader is not a wall but a semipermeable membrane, like the line between self and persona. We may think of Herbert's sensibility as unique, but he would have found that a dubious

---

4. Hutchinson, "Introduction," *Works,* xxxvii.
5. E.g., "The H. Scriptures, II," "Church-musick," "Sunday," "Lent," "The British Church," "Justice, II," "The Priesthood"; "Redemption," "Humilitie," "The World"; "Hope," "Time," "The Holdfast"; "Constancie," "Mortification," "Mans medley," "Dotage"; "Prayer, I," "The H. Scriptures, I."
6. Vendler, *Poetry of Herbert,* 187, 186.
7. Palmer, ed., *English Works,* II, 356.

honor. He saw himself as belonging to a community of believers—one sense of the word *temple*—and did not doubt that what was true of himself would be true of others as well. Hence the prayer "Lord, instruct us" occurs as often in *The Temple* as "Teach me, my God," and is its virtual equivalent.[8] Nor is it possible to separate poems to God from poems to himself and others. Summers recognizes this when he compares the lyrics of "The Church" to "public prayer," directed to God but "delivered in the presence of the congregation."[9] Herbert defines his audience much as Augustine does in *The Confessions:*

> To whom tell I all this? For to thee I tell it not; but before thee relate it to mine own kind, the human kind, even to so small a part of it as may light upon these writings of mine. And to what purpose do I this? Even that both myself and whosoever reads this, may bethink ourselves out of what depths we are to cry unto thee.[10]

It seems to me unprofitable, then, to inquire whether Herbert is addressing himself, other men, or God, for he speaks to all three.

Vendler argues that an "expressive theory of poetry suits *The Temple* best": a poem by Herbert "seems usually to have begun in experience, and aims at recreating or recalling that experience. To approach such private poetry as an exercise in public communication is to misconstrue its emphasis."[11] On the other hand, Fish finds in *The Temple* a "Christian pedagogic design" that is "true to Herbert's own hopes for his verse, hopes that are, in the

8. "Yet Lord, instruct us so to die" ("Mortification," 35), "Yet Lord instruct us to improve our fast" ("Lent," 43); "Teach me thy love to know" ("Mattens," 17), "Teach me, my God and King, / In all things thee to see" ("The Elixir," 1).

9. Summers, *George Herbert*, 104. He also compares them here, with equal validity, to Elizabethan love poems, "addressed to a mistress but circulated in manuscript or published by the poet."

10. Augustine, *Confessions*, I, 71 (bk. II, chap. 3).

11. Vendler, *Poetry of Herbert*, 5.

best sense of the word, rhetorical."[12] That these two opposing views are not in fact mutually exclusive is suggested by one of Walton's anecdotes. Walton has Herbert
describe *The Temple* on his deathbed as an account of his
own sufferings:

> Sir, I pray deliver this little Book to my dear brother *Farrer*,
> and tell him, he shall find in it a picture of the many spiritual
> Conflicts that have past betwixt God and my Soul, before I
> could subject mine to the will of *Jesus my Master*.

He has Herbert go on to say that only its didactic value
would justify publishing the book:

> desire him to read it: and then, if he can think it may turn to
> the advantage of any dejected poor Soul, let it be made pub-
> lick: if not, let him burn it.[13]

Se non è vero, è ben trovato: though this account of Herbert's last words may be pure fabrication, it is consonant
with the spirit of the volume.[14] Herbert's poetry is at once
expressive and didactic, a picture of his own spiritual conflicts offered up as a help to dejected poor souls. Athough
I discuss didactic strategies in this chapter, and expressive

12. Fish, "Catechizing the Reader," 209–10.
13. Walton, *Life*, 314 (italics reversed). Both Vendler and Fish quote
parts of this speech to support their positions. Vendler claims that "to
give 'a picture of . . . many spiritual conflicts' was Herbert's essential
intent, and the notion of a 'dejected poor soul['s]' deriving comfort from
the poems arose only subsequent to composition" (*Poetry of Herbert*, 5).
Fish quotes only the second part of the statement ("Catechizing the
Reader," 210), disregarding the implications of the first part.
14. J. Max Patrick, "Critical Problems in Editing George Herbert's
The Temple, in *The Editor as Critic and the Critic as Editor*, ed. Murray
Krieger (Los Angeles, 1973), 3–40. Patrick observes that "these words
were put into Herbert's mouth more than a third of a century after the
event, by a man who never knew him" (8); "like those Roman historians
who put speeches into the mouths of the men they write about, Walton
was concerned not with literal truth but with that higher truth which is
faithful to character and situation" (10). On Walton's reliability, see
David Novarr, *The Making of Walton's 'Lives'* (Ithaca, 1958), pp. 301–61,
and Charles, *Life of Herbert*.

psalmlike poems in the next, their relation, as I will be pointing out, is more complex than these divisions imply. Herbert's didactic poems frequently begin in an experience and attempt to summon up that experience, while his expressive poems are implicitly didactic, spoken in God's presence for the sake of his fellow men. Indeed, in that very conjunction—the expressive inseparable from the didactic, the expressive in the service of the didactic—we recognize the spirit of Scripture.

If the didactic impulse in *The Temple* owes something to the norms of Renaissance poetry, and to the classical tradition, its primary inspiration, I believe, is scriptural. The Bible, through all its diverse books, is intent on teaching. The Pentateuch is called "Torah" in Hebrew, which literally means "instruction," though it is usually translated "Law." The figure of the teacher is clearly drawn in the wisdom literature and the prophetic books, but even narrative and poetry in the Old Testament have a didactic end in view. In the Gospels Jesus is described as "a teacher come from God," who "taught them as one having authoritie, and not as the Scribes"; when apprehended, he reminds his assailants: "I sate daily with you teaching in the Temple" (John 3:2, Matt. 7:29, 26:55). The writings of John stress the notion of bearing witness, a characteristically Christian form of teaching (John 1:7–8). And the Pauline Epistles, finally, have as their purpose the "edification" or building up of the Church. "Let all things be done unto edifying" (1 Cor. 14:26) is cited in *A Priest to the Temple* as one of "the Apostles two great and admirable Rules"[15]—a rule that applies not only to the parson's church but also to the poet's "Church."

Herbert's explicitly didactic poems are not thought to be among his most attractive works. In some of them we hear the "hectoring tone" of an "unpleasant schoolmaster," "an ill-tempered Herbert not often brought to

15. *A Priest to the Temple, Works,* 246.

view by critics."[16] This severity of tone reflects the moral
rigor of biblical teaching, whether in the sages' ridicule of
folly, the prophets' stinging denunciation of sin, or Jesus'
impatience with those who are dull of hearing. Herbert,
like his master Jesus, is more "tart"[17] than many readers
like to think. If we try to explain away the occasional
harshness of *The Temple*, we are in danger of painting a
pastel Herbert, like the Christ of the greeting cards: flaccid, effeminate, with a damp wispy soulfulness.

On the other hand, it is an exaggeration to say, as Fish
does in *Self-Consuming Artifacts*, that Herbert tries to educate the reader by humiliating him.[18] It seems to me in-
herently unlikely that Herbert would have found humilia-
tion an apt method of education. In *A Priest to the Temple*,
he speaks of "helping and cherishing" the pupil, "making
much even of a word of truth from him," for "instructions seasoned with pleasantnesse, both enter sooner,
and roote deeper." When the parson, in his role as God's
"Sentinell," must administer some correction to those in
his care, he is told to do so "discretely, with mollifying,
and suppling words," practicing the indulgence of a
father toward his child, in imitation of God's own way:
"for thou art Love, and when thou teachest, all are
Scholers." Like the country parson, Herbert usually wins
his audience with "a very loving, and sweet usage of
them."[19] Fish is right in emphasizing the "pedagogic design" of *The Temple*, but in identifying Herbert the poet
with Herbert the catechist, as he does in *The Living
Temple*, he gives us far too narrow a view of Herbert's
didactic practice. Herbert's precisely phrased directions to

16. Vendler, *Poetry of Herbert*, 186, 185. Cf. Earl Miner, *The Metaphysical Mode from Donne to Cowley* (Princeton, 1969), 188–89; Freer, *Music
for a King*, 176–79.
17. "Paradise," 8.
18. Fish, *Self-Consuming Artifacts*, 156 and passim.
19. *A Priest to the Temple, Works*, 256, 268, 252, 250, 233, 262. See
Chana Bloch, " 'Dehumanizing' Herbert," *Seventeenth-Century News* 37
(Spring–Summer 1979): 1–5.

the parson make catechizing merely a preliminary step in
the building of a "spirituall Temple,"[20] and however
broadly Fish interprets its purpose and procedures, it simply does not answer to the enormous variety of Herbert's
poetic means. There is, as we shall see, more than one
way of rhyming the reader to good.

In this chapter I will single out three didactic strategies
that seem to me of particular importance: proverbial sayings, dramatic symbols and homely images. These are
associated primarily with biblical wisdom, prophecy and
the Gospel parables, though they are found to a greater or
lesser degree throughout the Bible. My concern in what
follows, let me make clear, is not with the biblical genres
per se; hence I will have nothing to say about the specula-
tive wisdom in the Book of Job, the mantic voice of the
prophets or narrative style in the parables. I wish to focus
specifically on proverbial sayings, dramatic symbols and
homely images because they embody attitudes and beliefs—about the wisdom of the community, learning
through experience, the humble and the sublime—that lie
at the very heart of Herbert's poems. The didactic strategies I will be discussing have been traced respectively to
the classical epigrammatic tradition, Renaissance emblem
books and popular preaching.[21] Without denying these
influences, I wish to look to the biblical models for a fuller
understanding of how Herbert's poems teach.

PROVERBIAL WISDOM:
"SPEAK PLAINLY AND HOME"

It is certainly true that *The Temple* "refuses to yield a portable truth, or to be contained within a formula."[22] Yet at

20. *A Priest to the Temple, Works,* 255.
21. Robert J. Wickenheiser, "George Herbert and the Epigrammatic
Tradition," *George Herbert Journal* 1 (1977): 39–56; Rosemary Freeman,
English Emblem Books (London, 1948); L. C. Knights, "George Herbert,"
Scrutiny 12 (1944), rpt. *Explorations: Essays in Criticism Mainly on the Literature of the Seventeenth Century* (New York, 1947), 132.
22. Fish, *Self-Consuming Artifacts,* 216.

the same time, Herbert's poems consistently include and make use of such formulas: pithy, aphoristic sayings, like the proverbs of biblical wisdom literature, that express some general truth of human experience. In its impulse to aphorism, the didactic intent of Herbert's poetry openly proclaims itself. These sayings do not pretend to give us Herbert's "teaching" in brief; it would be difficult in any case to summarize in a few words the complexities of experience and perception that Herbert usually brings to a poem. But they are fashioned in such a way that we carry them off and remember them. Compact and sententious, drawn tight by antithesis, alliteration or assonance, they stand out even against the close-grained texture of Herbert's verse.

The presence of "portable wisdom" in *The Temple* is in keeping with some other patterns of style that we have observed. Herbert looks to verses of Scripture for support at moments of stress (*"But thou shalt answer, Lord, for me," "Thou art still my God,"* etc.); he abridges biblical teachings so that they may be more easily held in the mind (*"Love God, and love your neighbour. Watch and pray. / Do as ye would be done unto"*); he appropriates scriptural tags and makes them his own, as "posie" (*"Lesse then the least / Of all Gods mercies"*) or as "tincture" (*"for thy sake"*).[23] In much the same way, he quotes bits of wisdom at himself or at the reader. In his advice to the country parson, Herbert suggests that "sayings of others," like stories, are didactically effective because they may be committed to memory: "for them also men heed, and remember better than exhortations; which though earnest, yet often dy with the Sermon . . . but stories and sayings they will well remember."[24]

23. "The Quip," 8, "The Forerunners," 6; "Divinitie," 17–18; "The Posie," 11–12, "The Elixir," 15. The phrase "for thy sake" in "The Elixir" appears in Matt. 10:39, Rom. 8:36 (Ps. 44:22); cf. 1 Cor. 4:10, 2 Cor. 12:10, Phil. 1:29, etc.
24. *A Priest to the Temple, Works*, 233.

The maxims in *The Temple* are related to biblical wisdom in subjects and attitudes as well as in style. I am speaking here of the practical wisdom of Proverbs and Ecclesiastes, which comprises both "secular" and "pious" maxims, advocating a prudential morality for reasons of enlightened self-interest. Even the so-called "pious" strain reveals a distinctly practical piety: virtue always has one eye on recompense. In this respect, Old Testament wisdom differs materially from the Law and the Prophets, which prescribe absolute standards of morality based on Israel's covenant with God.

The primary form of biblical wisdom is the proverb (Heb. *mashal*), defined in the margin of the Geneva Bible as "a grave and notable sentence, worthie to be kept in memorie,"[25] typically a prudent rule of conduct based on shrewd observation or on the belief in a retributive justice. The *mashal* is poetic in form, and its distinguishing prosodic feature, as with all biblical poetry, is its parallelistic structure.[26] Antithetical parallelism, which teaches by both precept and warning—"A soft answere turneth away wrath: but grievous words stirre up anger" (Prov. 15:1)—is particularly congenial to the sages whose maxims are anthologized in the Book of Proverbs. One of the basic ideas of wisdom is the choice between good and evil, "the way of wisedom" and "the path of the wicked" (Prov. 4:11, 14). The opposition of the righteous and the wicked, the wise and the foolish, the diligent and the slothful, reflects the ingrained tendency of the biblical authors to think by moral contraries, a tendency we have already observed in Herbert.[27] The *mashal*, which is used so often to condemn

---

25. *The Bible* [Geneva] (1560), pt. 1, fol. 267.
26. On parallelism as a structural device in biblical poetry see chap. 5, pp. 288–89.
27. See chap. 3. Note also, for example, the antithesis of *grief* and *vertue* in "The Foil," *death* and *life* in "Vanitie, I," *Life* and *Strife, Salvation* and *Damnation* in "The Water-course"; as well as *Sinne* and *Love* in "The Agonie," and *pleasures* and *sorrows* in "Dotage," where whole stanzas are set in opposition.

excess or deviations from the norm, is itself the formal embodiment of the concept of "rule" or "size." With its economy of phrasing, its use of balance and antithesis, the *mashal* conveys above all the notion of order, proportion, control within limits. The very use of proverbial wisdom implies a certain outlook, a moral stance. The adage, as Rosalie Colie defines it, "sums up a mass of human experience in one charged phrase, demonstrating the community of human experience."[28] When he quotes or echoes proverbial truths, Herbert brings to the immediate moment the accumulated wisdom of generations. He does not pretend to uniqueness but, on the contrary, affirms his relation to his fellows, and in doing so manages to see his own situation in clearer perspective. I think this is part of the attraction Herbert feels for proverb and aphorism, besides his obvious delight in wit, brevity and formal control.

Herbert's two major works of translation (his only other attested translation being the Twenty-third Psalm) are latter-day versions of Proverbs and Ecclesiastes. *Outlandish Proverbs* is a collection of more than a thousand French, Spanish and Italian proverbs very much in the spirit of Solomon's, full of practical shrewdness ("Buy at a faire, but sell at home," "Saint *Luke* was a Saint and a Physitian, yet is dead") and pungent humor ("Looke not for muske in a dogges kennell," "Who spits against heaven, it falls in his face").[29] *A Treatise of Temperance and Sobrietie* is a moral

28. Rosalie L. Colie, *The Resources of Kind: Genre-Theory in the Renaissance*, ed. Barbara K. Lewalski (Berkeley and Los Angeles, 1973), 33.

29. *Outlandish Proverbs*, nos. 160, 1008; 23, 346, *Works*, 321–55. Hutchinson argues convincingly that Herbert "may with some confidence be accounted the collector and the skilful translator of at any rate a considerable part of *Outlandish Proverbs*" ("Commentary," *Works*, 572). It is by no means an easy task to preserve the spirit of proverbs in foreign dress. Terse, pointed, idiomatic, they make severe demands on the translator's ability. Herbert occasionally uses rhyme or alliteration, but for the most part he produces effective English versions by concise phrasing, brisk rhythms and idiomatic turns of speech (cf. nos. 181, 327;

tract by an eighty-three-year-old Italian, Luigi Cornaro, who, having come to wisdom through personal experience, commends to the young a life of "fit measure" and "exact rule."[30] It is not by chance that Herbert translated these two works. They are clearly related to his own poems, notably "The Church-porch."

A lineal descendant of Proverbs,[31] "The Church-porch" celebrates the virtues of prudence, chastity, sobriety and diligence, and offers practical advice based on common human experience: "Truth dwels not in the clouds" (317). Summers recognizes that in some sense "The Church-porch" is " 'pre-Christian,' despite the poem's assumption of baptism and church attendance"; he sees in it an attempt "to put the traditional classical mixture of pleasure and profit to the uses of Christian didactic verse."[32] If "The Church-porch" is "pre-Christian," however, its roots are as much in the Old Testament as in the classical literature. Both in its style ("wisdom compressed in memorable formulations") and in its intended audience ("a

---

215, 485; 121, 207; 49, 568; 261, 818)—the very qualities that are distinctive of his own poems.

30. *A Treatise of Temperance, Works,* 293, 296.

31. Cf. Palmer, ed., *English Works,* II, 3; Patrides, ed., *English Poems,* 9; Carole Kessner, "Entering 'The Church-porch': Herbert and Wisdom Poetry," *George Herbert Journal* 1 (1977): 10–25; Lewalski, *Protestant Poetics,* 67–68; Heather A. R. Asals, *Equivocal Predication: George Herbert's Way to God* (Toronto, 1981), 76–86.

Kessner rules out the Book of Proverbs as a model for "The Church-porch" because "it is simply an unorganized collection of aphorisms with no regard to subject matter" and because "the ethical system it espouses is frequently utilitarian and materialistic—its tone often ironic and skeptical" ("Entering 'The Church-porch,' " 18). Instead she proposes the apocryphal Ecclesiasticus (The Wisdom of Ben Sira), reasoning that the "pious and learned" Herbert would have found in Ben Sira "a kindred spirit" and "a fit model" (19). I am concerned, however, not with the arrangement of the aphorisms but with their form and tone. Ben Sira's solemn adjurations are scarcely like Herbert's brisk salty verses, which are frequently "ironic" and "utilitarian."

32. Joseph H. Summers, ed., *George Herbert: Selected Poetry* (New York, 1967), xxii, xv.

worldly young man of [Herbert's] own class and time"),[33] it resembles the Book of Proverbs. As we can infer from its contents, Proverbs was addressed to wealthy young men who had the means and the leisure for personal indulgence.[34]

"The Church-porch" follows Proverbs in espousing "rule" as the fundamental principle of civilization: "Hee that hath no rule over his owne spirit, is like a citie that is broken downe, and without walles" (25:28). Herbert argues that "rule" in one's person corresponds to order and design in the macrocosm:

> Slight those who say amidst their sickly healths,
> Thou liv'st by rule. What doth not so, but man?
> Houses are built by rule, and common-wealths.
> Entice the trusty sunne, if that thou can,
>   From his Ecliptick line: becken the skie.
>   Who lives by rule then, keeps good companie.
>
> (133–38)

In the human sphere, "rule" means self-control and moderation in eating, drinking, speech—even, it appears, in friendship and charity. Herbert enlarges on some of the major themes of Proverbs: "Wine is a mocker, strong drinke is raging" (20:1); "Be not amongst wine-bibbers; amongst riotous eaters of flesh" (23:20); "Traine up a childe in the way he should goe" (22:6); "Lying lippes are abomination to the LORD" (12:22); "He that hath knowledge, spareth his words" (17:27); "The discretion of a man deferreth his anger: and it is his glory to passe over a transgression" (19:11); "Seest thou a man diligent in his businesse? hee shall stand before kings" (22:29). He touches on a number of subjects not covered in Proverbs (dress, gambling, foreign travel and a few others), but

33. Ibid., xvii, xviii–xix. Charles suggests that "The Church-porch" may have been written for Herbert's younger brother Henry when the latter first went to France (*Life of Herbert*, 84).

34. Robert Gordis, *Koheleth—The Man and His World: A Study of Ecclesiastes*, 3d ed. (New York, 1968), 32.

given the difference in time and milieu, one is surprised at the similarity of tone and emphasis. Perhaps the voice of experience has the same sobering advice for the hot-bloods of every generation.

"The Church-porch," like the Book of Proverbs, is notable for its hardheaded, utilitarian counsels. Good behavior is recommended as the high road to success, while friendship, charity, all the warm and generous motions of the heart, are reined in by a sober expediency. The young man on the way up is directed to be as virtuous as he can manage without undue strain.

The advice about charity is businesslike ("In Almes regard thy means, and others merit," 373) and even calculating ("Think heav'n a better bargain," 374). Although Proverbs reckons on a reward in this life, and "The Church-porch" in the next, both are concerned, one might say, with getting a good return on an investment:

> Hee that hath pity upon the poore, lendeth unto the LORD; and that which he hath given, will he pay him againe.
> (19:17)

> God reckons for him, counts the favour his:
> Write, So much giv'n to God; thou shalt be heard.
>   Let thy almes go before, and keep heav'ns gate
>   Open for thee; or both may come too late.
> (381–84)

Both proclaim friendship a virtue:

> Thine owne friend and thy fathers friend forsake not.
> (27:10)

> Thy friend put in thy bosome: wear his eies
> Still in thy heart, that he may see what's there.
> If cause require, thou art his sacrifice;
> Thy drops of bloud must pay down all his fear.
> (271–74)

Yet both make clear that even friendship has its limits:

> My sonne, if thou bee surety for thy friend, . . . Thou art snared with the words of thy mouth, . . . deliver thy selfe.
> (6:1–3)

Yet be not surety, if thou be a father.

(277)

The married man should not be charitable at the expense of his dependents; the single man should not hazard more than he has: "None is bound / To work for two" (285–86).

Blake writes in his "Proverbs of Hell" that we cannot know what is enough unless we know what is more than enough. Not so, insist the biblical sages: we have no need to test the boundaries because we can learn from the accumulated wisdom of the race. If innocence looks forward to the sweetness of pleasure, then experience remembers its aftertaste. Proverbs warns against wine and women as pleasures that "bite" or turn "bitter":

> Looke not thou upon the wine when it is red, when it giveth his colour in the cup, when it moveth it selfe aright.
> At the last it biteth like a serpent, and stingeth like an adder.

(23:31–32)

> For the lips of a strange woman drop as an hony combe, and her mouth is smoother then oyle.
> But her end is bitter as wormewood, sharpe as a two edged sword.

(5:3–4)

This way of thinking is met with in the poems of "The Church," for example in "The Rose" ("Sweetly there indeed it lies, / But it biteth in the close," 23–24),[35] but it is the prevailing attitude in "The Church-porch," and is summed up once for all in the final stanza: "Look not on pleasures as they come, but go" (458); "If thou do ill; the joy fades, not the pains" (461).

---

35. Cf. "Lent" (where "abstinence" is "sweet" and "fulnesse" produces "Sowre exhalations, . . . Revenging the delight," 19, 22–24), and "Vanitie, II" ("Heark and beware, lest what you now do measure / And write for sweet, prove a most sowre displeasure," 5–6).

Deviations from the norm are held up to ridicule on the knife-points of irony and satire. In "The Church," Herbert's satire is directed against himself—we have already spoken about the persona of the "old man" as a comic version of the self—and the sins he writes about are, for the most part, those he has studied in his own bosom, and at home. "The Church-porch," on the other hand, presents a series of "characters" that one assumes to be very different from their author, among them the lustful man, the drunkard, the idler, the "scraper," the "curious unthrift," the dandy, the "gigler," and the babbler. Here Herbert is working in one vein of biblical wisdom, the satirical vignette. His picture of the slothful man, for example,

> God gave thy soul brave wings; put not those feathers
> Into a bed, to sleep out all ill weathers.
>
> (83–84; cf. 93–96)

should be compared with that of Proverbs for its tone of wry mockery, its humorous exaggeration:

> The slothfull man sayth, There is a lion in the way, a lion is in the streets.
> As the doore turneth upon his hinges: so doeth the slothfull upon his bedde.
> The slothfull hideth his hand in his bosome, it grieveth him to bring it againe to his mouth.
>
> (26:13–15; cf. 6:9–10)

Proverbs is full of contempt for the drunkard:

> Who hath woe? who hath sorrow? who hath contentions? who hath babbling? who hath wounds without cause? who hath rednesse of eyes?
> They that tarry long at the wine, they that goe to seeke mixt wine. . . .
> They have stricken me, shalt thou say, and I was not sicke: they have beaten me, and I felt it not: when shall I awake? I will seeke it yet againe.
>
> (23:29–30, 35)

Herbert too describes the damaging effects of wine as well
as the drinker's impatience to have another glass (25–54)
with a lively sense of the social context in which people
drink more than they should. The satirical vignette is an
effective didactic resource, spelling out in comparative detail what the maxim or proverb teaches in brief; indeed, as
we know, many proverbial sayings are actually condensed versions of fables or cautionary tales. But it is the
proverb itself that is the sage's stock in trade, indispens-
able to pedagogy because it is made to be learned by
heart.

"The Church-porch" is a tissue of proverbial sayings.
Many of these are observations of everyday life: "*He pares
his apple, that will cleanly feed*" (64), "*Slacknesse breeds worms*"
(339), "*A good digestion turneth all to health*" (358). Some
exhibit the satiric wit of the popular proverb: "*Man breaks
the fence, and every ground will plough*" (22), "*Some till their
ground, but let weeds choke their sonne*" (98), "*Kneeling ne're
spoil'd silk stocking*" (407).[36] These are effective vehicles of
teaching not only because they are easily committed to
memory but also because they spring from a world the
reader recognizes as real. The very form—terse, rhythmic,
with the ring of long-acknowledged truths, of wisdom
passed down from generation to generation—carries a certain authority, and does part of the work of persuasion.

"The Church-porch" inevitably suffers from comparison with the poems of "The Church," in the same way
that Polonius' "few precepts" to Laertes, perfectly re-
spectable fatherly advice, are made to seem crude and a
little silly in the face of Hamlet's predicament. The "sweet
youth" to whom "The Church-porch" is addressed is a
mere stripling in virtue. The poem, accordingly, is filled
with those "rules of reason" with which parents "season"
us in our tender years, before the trials of adult life—

---

36. In this section I will italicize all of Herbert's aphorisms for the
sake of clarity.

"afflictions sorted, anguish of all sizes"[37]—help make us what we are. In "Superliminare" Herbert links "The Church-porch" with "The Church," while telling us how they differ: the soul, once the passive object of exhortation ("Thou, whom the former precepts have / Sprinkled and taught, how to behave / Thy self in church," 1–3) is now invited to an active participation in the Christian life ("approach, and taste / The churches mysticall repast," 3–4). But the soul does not sit and eat until the very last line of "The Church." Up until that transcendant moment, it needs to be reminded more than once of the precepts it is supposed to have mastered.

Herbert's critics tend to dismiss "The Church-porch" as irrelevant to the rest of his poetic oeuvre in its concerns, its style and tone. The received view is that "Herbert is a moral poet only in 'The Church Porch,' on the other side of the wall from 'The Church,' which treats the urgent questions of God and man."[38] Even Summers, who stoutly defends "The Church-porch" for the disinclined modern reader, says it "may have served Herbert as a way of . . . purging the immediate didactic impulse" in order to "turn more freely in the other poems to other uses of language in the service of poetry and the worship of God."[39] But teaching in *The Temple* is not restricted to "The Church-porch." "*Turn their eyes hither, who shall make a gain,*" Herbert writes in "The Dedication," which is prefixed to the entire volume. "The Church," like "The Church-porch," is full of examples of Herbert's aphoristic style.[40] My argument is that the habit of aphorism is intimately connected with the didactic impulse, and that it

---

37. "Sinne, I," 4, 2, 6.
38. Halewood, *Poetry of Grace*, 96.
39. Summers, ed., *Selected Poetry*, xxvi.
40. Noted by Patrides in his introduction to *English Poems*, 9: "Herbert's emulation of the Book of Proverbs afforded him the opportunity to indulge in that highly compressed, economic phrasing, whose precise impact on his poems we are yet to study"; cf. Stein, *Herbert's Lyrics*, 14.

manifests itself not only in "The Church-porch" but in "The Church" as well.

On occasion Herbert quotes or paraphrases popular proverbs (e.g., "*Most take all*," "*Wouldst thou both eat thy cake, and have it?*" "*Grasp not at much, for fear thou losest all*," "*That which is past who can recall?*") or alludes to proverbial sayings ("*a nine dayes wonder*," "*rope of sands*," "*breaks the square*").[41] More often he coins maxims that exhibit the brevity and sharpness of the form, presenting in one line or less, in homely concrete language, some truth discovered by observation or experience. Although resembling folk wisdom, these are not strictly "proverbs" because they have never been in common use. On the other hand, they are to be distinguished from *sententiae*, sophisticated and literary in their effect, which depend rather upon the classical and epigrammatic tradition.[42]

In "Charms and Knots," where we have an example of the style embalmed and set on display, Herbert strings together moral and practical observations ("Who shuts his hand, hath lost his gold: / Who opens it, hath it twice told," 5–6; cf. Prov. 11:24) and verses about the duties of a Christian (the poem begins with an exhortation to read the Scriptures). The most one can say of "Charms and Knots" is that it reads like an exercise in composing maxims in octosyllabic couplets. Even as an exercise it is hardly worth a glance; there is not one striking or memorable couplet in the lot. Still, it is significant, I think, that

41. "The Quidditie," 12; "The Size," 18, 38; "The Discharge," 10; "Content," 21; "The Collar," 22; "The Discharge," 32. See Morris P. Tilley, *A Dictionary of the Proverbs in England in the Sixteenth and Seventeenth Centuries* (Ann Arbor, 1950): M 1186 ("Most takes all"), C 15 ("You can't eat your cake and have it too"), M 1295 ("Who too much grasps, the less he holds"), A 192 ("He that will have all loses all"), T 203 ("Things past cannot be recalled"); W 728 ("A wonder lasts but nine days"), R 174 ("to twist a rope of sand"); Hutchinson, "Commentary," *Works*, 528 ("An inche breaketh no square").

42. E.g., "Anagram," and the witty or paradoxical couplets that reinforce the sense of closure at the end of "The Agonie," "Affliction, I," "Artillerie" and "Josephs coat."

Herbert's interest in the *mashal* prompted him to make
such an attempt, just as it moved him to translate and
collect the *Outlandish Proverbs*. Happily, "Charms and
Knots" is not the only evidence of Herbert's fondness for
aphorisms.

Herbert's poetic style is so compressed and rhythmic
that many of his lines have a proverbial ring.[43] This tendency is reinforced at points by antithesis (*"Hard things
are glorious; easie things good cheap"*), rhyme (*"Who wants
the place, where God doth dwell, / Partakes already half of
hell"*), alliteration (*"Hearts have many holes"*) or enumeration (*"Angels must have their joy, / Devils their rod, the sea his
shore, / The windes their stint"*).[44] Herbert's maxims include
sound practical observations of the world in which he
lives:

> *Each beast his cure doth know.*
>
> *A rose, besides his beautie, is a cure.*
>
> *Where are poysons, antidotes are most.*

and the penetrating notations of a man who has made
human nature his study:

> *Cold hands are angrie with the fire, / And mend it still.*
>
> *The distance of the meek / Doth flatter power.*
>
> *What is so shrill as silent tears?*[45]

43. Cf. Knights, "George Herbert," 133.
44. "Providence," 97; "Time," 23–24; "An Offering," 4; "Praise,
III," 21–23.
45. "Good Friday," 19; "Providence," 78, 87; "Church-lock and
key," 5–6; "The Priesthood," 39–40; "The Familie," 20. Some other ex-
amples are:
"*Life is a businesse, not good cheer.*" ("Employment, II," 16)
"*Man is one world, and hath / Another to attend him.*" ("Man," 47–48)
"*We are the trees, whom shaking fastens more.*" ("Affliction, V," 20)
"*Each creature hath a wisdome for his good.*" ("Providence," 61)
"*A single deed is small renown.*" ("The Bunch of Grapes," 12)
"*Faith needs no staffe of flesh.*" ("Divinitie," 27)
"*If blessings were as slow / As mens returns, what would become of fools?*"
   ("An Offering," 1–2)
"*Sweet things traffick when they meet.*" ("The Odour," 27)

Where proverbial wisdom is used as a figure of elaboration, as in most of these instances, it establishes the speaker as a shrewd, seasoned observer, a man of prudence and understanding, who dares to "speak / Plainly and home"[46]—helpful qualities in one who presumes to teach. On occasion it can also comfort (e.g., *"All creatures have their joy: and man hath his"*; *"Ev'n the greatest griefs / May be reliefs"*) and, more often, admonish or restrain (*"Who cannot on his own bed sweetly sleep, / Can on anothers hardly rest"*; *"Till thine own ground"*).[47]

Here I must pause to ask, as the reader may now be asking, how the *mashal*, which belongs to "The Churchporch," finds its way into "The Church." Is it not out of place there? In "Artillerie," as Strier points out, the speaker's very reliance on prudential wisdom (*"From small fires comes oft no small mishap,"* 4) points up the inadequacy of natural reason in the domain of religion.[48] Nonetheless, the *mashal* can be made to serve the purposes of Christian teaching, as Herbert learned from his master, Jesus.

Many of Jesus' sayings in the synoptic Gospels, like those of Old Testament wisdom, appeal to common sense:

Is a candle brought to be put under a bushell? (Mark 4:21)

No man can serve two masters. (Matt. 6:24)

Which of you by taking thought, can adde one cubite unto his stature? (Matt. 6:27)

Can the blinde leade the blinde? (Luke 6:39)

Every tree is knowen by his owne fruit. (Luke 6:44)

Proverbs of this sort are reflections on practical experience that Jesus made to "serve for lights . . . of Heavenly

---

46. "The Church-porch" 217–18.
47. "Mans medley," 3, 31–32; "Content," 3–4, 33.
48. Strier, *Love Known*, 98–99.

Truths";[49] it is their context that gives them a specifically Christian application. Another type of saying, less frequent but more characteristically Christian, demands an entirely new disposition of mind:

> If thine eye offend thee, pluck it out. (Mark 9:47)
>
> Let the dead, bury their dead. (Matt. 8:22)
>
> Whosoever shall lose his life, shall preserve it. (Luke 17:33)
>
> Love your enemies, doe good to them which hate you. (Luke 6:27)

These ideas may be unconventional, but their form is perfectly commonplace: stretching the popular proverb with hyperbole and paradox, Jesus filled it with new wine, relying on its very familiarity to make his radical teachings more readily accessible.

Each of these types has its counterparts in *The Temple*. Consider, first, the ending of "Repentance":

> *Fractures well cur'd make us more strong.*
>
> (36)

This looks like a piece of medicinal lore of the kind that often figures in popular proverbs, for example, "Great paines quickly find ease" or "Hee that goes to bed thirsty riseth healthy."[50] But knowing that "fractures" are a metaphor for the suffering of the sinner punished by God (Herbert is alluding in line 32 to "the bones which thou hast broken," Ps. 51:8), we read the final maxim, in con-

---

49. *A Priest to the Temple, Works,* 257; on Jesus' homely sayings, see my discussion later in this chapter. Recent studies have shown "how a mashal with the profane wisdom of folk-lore as its content was given a religious, indeed a specifically 'Christian' meaning by its absorption into the tradition of the Church," a process which was "particularly active in the metaphorical sayings" (Rudolf Bultmann, *The History of the Synoptic Tradition,* trans. John Marsh, 2d ed. [New York, 1968], 97, 98; see the entire section, "Logia [Jesus as the Teacher of Wisdom]," 69–108). See also William A. Beardslee, "Uses of the Proverb in the Synoptic Gospels," *Interpretation* 24 (1974): 61–73.

50. *Outlandish Proverbs,* nos. 534, 1003, *Works,* 339, 354.

text, as a variation on the *felix culpa* theme, like "Then shall the fall further the flight in me" in "Easter-wings" (10). A more distinctively Christian use of the *mashal* may be seen in "H. Baptisme, II":

> *The growth of flesh is but a blister;*
> *Childhood is health.*
>
> (14–15)

The formal pattern—both the opposed aphorisms and the final equation ("*X* is health")—comes from the Book of Proverbs:

> There is that speaketh like the pearcings of a sword: but the tongue of the wise is health.
>
> (12:18)

> A wicked messenger falleth into mischiefe: but a faithfull ambassadour is health.
>
> (13:17)

The Old Testament sages, however, thought of childhood as a disease that only time and the rod would cure.[51] It was Jesus who glorified childhood: "Suffer the little children to come unto mee, . . . for of such is the kingdome of God" (Mark 10:14). In this instance Herbert, like Jesus, uses the popular proverb as a vehicle for a new kind of teaching, very different in spirit from the sayings in the Book of Proverbs.

The steps by which Herbert makes the *mashal* into an instrument of Christian teaching may be observed in "The Discharge" and "The Size." In the first Herbert assaults the "busie enquiring heart" with a steady barrage of practical wisdom:

> *Let what will fall.* (9)
>
> *That which is past who can recall?* (10)
>
> *Onely the present is thy part and fee.* (21)

---

51. Prov. 13:24, 22:15, 23:13, 29:15.

*Raise not the mudde / Of future depths, but drink the cleare and
good.* (27–28)

Dig not for wo / In times to come. (29–30)

Man and the present fit. (31)

These lines resemble a saying of Christ's—"Take therefore no thought for the morrow" (Matt. 6:34)—which, on
the face of it, is not distinctively "Christian"; Erasmus in
the *Adagia* cites proverbs on the theme *in diem vivere*, "to
live from day to day," by Homer, Cicero, Horace and
others.[52] Christ's rule of conduct, however, is part of the
Sermon on the Mount and is prefaced by the exhortation
"Seeke ye first the kingdome of God" (Matt. 6:33). In the
same way, the maxims quoted above are colored by the
immediate context, with its repeated references to God,
as well as by the allusion in lines 7–8 to the act of self-
surrender to God described in "Obedience."[53] So too,
"The crop is his, for he hath sown" in line 15 sounds like a
country saying; it is the context that identifies "his" as
God's. *"God chains the dog till night"* (46), on the other
hand, is an example of a secular proverb that has been
baptized, or at least dipped in the font, however much it
clings to its origins.

"The Size" goes a good deal further "in the way which
Christ hath gone."[54] The heart that is rebuked here is
greedy for joy on earth. It wants to "enact good cheer"
(16), in Herbert's sardonic phrase; it wants its joy here

52. Margaret M. Phillips, *The 'Adages' of Erasmus* (Cambridge, 1964),
31, 387. Erasmus adds: "This was the life approved by Christ as the
happiest of all lives; he followed it himself and set it before his disciples
for them to follow also" (387).

53. The word *discharge*, Hutchinson notes, is used "for a document
conveying release from an obligation" ("Commentary," *Works*, 528).
Herbert may be referring to the "Deed" in "Obedience" in which his
heart vowed "to passe it self and all it hath to thee" (8). He is probably
thinking too of Eccles. 8:8: "There is no man that hath power over the
spirit to retaine the spirit; neither hath he power in the day of death: and
there is no discharge in that warre."

54. "Lent," 37.

and now, as others appear to have it. Those lucky ones
are glimpsed out of the corner of the eye in stanza 2. They
have their portion of "cloves and nutmegs" in this world,
they "sail" in "cinamon"—spices being associated with
fulfillment in the Song of Songs. "The Size" is about making do with less, accommodating the "greedie heart" to
the "modest and moderate joyes" (1–2) that befit the
Christian. It urges a moral diet to keep the spirit lean and
sinewy. The "long and bonie face" that Herbert describes
in line 33 is, incidentally, like his own face as we know it
from the Robert White drawing.[55]

Old Testament wisdom literature, with no belief in a
life to come, urges man to enjoy within bounds the pleasures of this life.[56] But Herbert's attitude to pleasure is
resolutely ascetic: in other poems he dismisses worldly
joys, calling them a "bubble," a "scourge," "joyes in
jest." "Yet if we rightly measure, / Mans joy and pleasure / rather hereafter, then in present is," he writes.
"There is no pleasure here," but only in heaven, which
promises "delights more true / Then miseries are here!"[57]
In "The Size" Herbert urges self-restraint in this life based
on the assurance of a life to come. The secular proverbs
he quotes (*"Wouldst thou both eat thy cake, and have it?"*18;
"Grasp not at much, for fear thou losest all," 38) as well as
those of his own devising (*"Great joyes are all at once,"* 19;
"A bit / Doth tice us on to hopes of more," 28–29) take on a
specifically Christian meaning because they refer to the
belief in an afterlife. Moreover, the incentives to moderation come from the otherworldly teaching of the Beati-

55. Reproduced as the frontispiece in Palmer's edition of the poems
and Charles' biography, as well as on the cover of the *George Herbert
Journal*. See Charles, *Life of Herbert*, 218–23, for details about this drawing.
56. Cf. Prov. 27:9, Eccles. 5:18, 9:7–9. Among those pleasures are
food, drink, ointment, perfume, friendship and wedded love.
57. "Vanitie, II," 18; "The Rose," 26; "Dotage," 14; "Mans
medley," 4–6; "The Rose," 5; "Dotage," 17–18.

tudes and the example of Jesus' own life—not "it biteth in the close" but rather "thy Saviour sentenc'd joy" (25). Herbert refers the greedy heart to the Gospels: "Blessed are yee that hunger now: for yee shall be filled. . . . for behold, your reward is great in heaven"; "Woe unto you that are full: for yee shall hunger" (Luke 6:21, 23, 25). And he celebrates Jesus' humble way of life in a newly coined aphorism—"*To be in both worlds full / Is more then God was, who was hungrie here*" (13–14)—which is directly opposed to the spirit of Old Testament wisdom literature.

"The Discharge" and "The Size" are about order and rule, about learning to "rightly measure" and to "temper . . . excesse"; when the speaker "swells" beyond his prescribed "size," the voice of wisdom comes as a reproof, a rap on the knuckles.[58] These poems, with their sober counsel, their praise of moderation and scorn of folly, their aphoristic bite, are not out of place in *The Temple;* the attitude that informs them has touched even such a lyric as "The Flower." Herbert's welcome to joy, one of his most expressive lyrics, "The Flower" belongs by right with his psalms of thanksgiving, and I will return to it later in more detail. But I wish to glance at it here because it reveals with especial clarity the function of proverbial wisdom in "The Church."

The poem would seem to exist for the sake of the marvelous sixth stanza:

> And now in age I bud again,
> After so many deaths I live and write;
> I once more smell the dew and rain,
> And relish versing: . . .

$$(36–39)$$

But when we read "The Flower" after poems like "The Size," we are better able to bring into focus its didactic intent. For Herbert, it is not enough to present an experi-

---

58. "Mans medley," 4; "Miserie," 9; "The Flower" ("swelling through store"), 48; "The Size"; "The Rose," 4.

ence; he must draw from it a lesson for himself and others. The need for definition is particularly strong here because the emotion is so intense and unstable. Vendler has pointed out that the poem moves from the "syntactically impersonal" first stanza, which describes a "universally known phenomenon," to the poet's own experience of "renewal and rebirth."[59] But it does not rest in the personal: in the third and seventh stanzas, Herbert circles back to, and ends with, the universal. In these stanzas of generalized reflection, the poet's "I" gives way to the "we" of the human community, which is then supplanted, in the final lines, by the impersonal "who."

Stanza 3 is addressed to the "Lord of power":

> These are thy wonders, Lord of power,
> Killing and quickning, bringing down to hell
> And up to heaven in an houre;
> Making a chiming of a passing-bell.
> We say amisse,
> This or that is:
> Thy word is all, if we could spell.

(15–21)

Here Herbert defines in a pious aphorism the contrast of God's omnipotence and man's helpless confusion: *"Thy word is all, if we could spell."* Although "spell" means "interpret,"[60] the line naturally evokes the image of a child struggling to learn his letters. Returning from "under ground," Herbert knows in part: the problem we face is not our suffering but our inability to grasp its meaning. Because we cannot "spell," we perceive only the terrific "power" that sweeps us up and down again and again. But in stanza 7, contemplating this little spot of earth as if from the felicity of heaven above, he understands that God is a loving schoolmaster:

59. Vendler, *Poetry of Herbert,* 49, 53.
60. Palmer, ed., *English Works,* III, 306, citing "The Temper, I," 16, and "A Dialogue-Antheme," 4; cf. my Introduction, n. 4.

These are thy wonders, Lord of love,
To make us see we are but flowers that glide:
    Which when we once can finde and prove,
Thou hast a garden for us, where to bide.
            Who would be more,
            Swelling through store,
Forfeit their Paradise by their pride.

(43–49)

All the "wonders" (and terrors) the poet has experienced
were designed, he now realizes, "to make us see." What
he has learned is phrased as a statement of general truth:
"We are but flowers that glide."

The final lines of the poem are built on the familiar
antithesis of reward and punishment that we find in
Proverbs: "A faithfull man shall abound with blessings:
but hee that maketh haste to be rich, shall not be innocent" (28:20), and in the paradoxical formulation of Jesus:
"For whosoever exalteth himselfe, shalbe abased: and hee
that humbleth himselfe, shalbe exalted" (Luke 14:11).
These lines reveal that "The Flower," finally, is a poem
about "size." In the light of the last stanza, "shoot[ing]
up fair" and "offring at heav'n" are defined retroactively
as wanting to be more than one's strict size. The heart
that is guilty of hubris will be punished, Herbert says, by
the reversal of fortune that always attends on pride. That
final impersonal antithesis, like the return to strict meter
and rhyme at the end of "The Collar," imposes the order
of necessity upon the heart's confusion. To borrow a
phrase from Barbara Herrnstein Smith, "it yields emotion,
which is not stable, over to wisdom, which is."[61]

And yet the last three lines, coming as they do after the

61. Barbara Herrnstein Smith, *Poetic Closure: A Study of How Poems
End* (Chicago, 1968), 204. In the following two paragraphs I am indebted
to Smith's remarks on the art of the epigrammatist: "He will seem
brusque, cold, uncompromising, arrogant, authoritative, 'authoritarian.'
If we are not put off by his manner, however, we will sense, beneath the
reserved surface, the pressure of the mastered emotion, the guarded
vulnerability" (208–9).

expansive movement of stanza 6, seem severe, brusque, judgmental. The sensation of flowering is so poignant, like moments we have all preserved in memory, that we would like to dwell on it, to relish its pure pleasure. "But it biteth in the close." For Vendler the "homiletical neatness" of the law-and-order ending "is probably a flaw in the poem."[62] Like Vendler I regret the harshness of the final lines, but I must ask: a flaw for whom? For us, perhaps, but not for Herbert. That we dislike "homiletical neatness" reveals above all our angle of divergence from him.

Vendler writes elsewhere about the "peril of generalization for Herbert": "his mind is resolutely unphilosophic and wholly restricted to the private case, a turn of temper perplexing to a poet who wished to address himself to Christians in general."[63] The use Herbert makes of proverbial wisdom, however, argues that his mind is hardly "restricted to the private case." For Herbert the "private case" is but an instance of the "general," and not unique; his many proverbial sayings draw upon, and contribute to, the fund of common human experience. Moreover, his very attraction to the form is revealing. The compression and control of his aphorisms, like the discipline of his patterned stanzas, suggest the importance Herbert attached to the containment of emotion. The impulse to aphorism in *The Temple* testifies that for Herbert a poem is not simply emotion expressed but emotion defined and mastered.

DRAMATIC SYMBOLS: "ASSAY AND TASTE"

Herbert's use of symbol for didactic purposes has so far been most helpfully discussed in relation to the emblem books, in which we find the conjunction of visual image and edifying interpretation. Rosemary Freeman, Rosalie Colie and Barbara Lewalski have all shown the relevance

62. Vendler, *Poetry of Herbert*, 53.
63. Ibid., 151.

of emblems for Herbert's poetry.[64] "Herbert's whole method of accumulating and interpreting images," the "relation between simple, concrete, visible things and moral ideas," the "visual quality" of his images, have been traced to this source.[65] Suggestive though it may be, however, the emblem model is in some ways unsatisfactory. The problem is best defined by Freeman's remarks on the limitations of the form:

> The figures in the emblem books . . . do not move freely and naturally with their own life but are made to move by the author, and to move more for the sake of display than of action. Secondly, this stiffness and lack of freedom in presentation is accompanied by a passion for allegorical detail for its own sake. . . . the details are laboriously enumerated and attached to a figure that is, and remains, lifeless.[66]

"Stiff," "laborious," "lifeless"—while these charges may be brought against a great many emblems, they are hardly true of the poems of *The Temple*. Approaching the subject from a different quarter, I would like to draw some parallels between Herbert's lively way with symbols and that of the prophets, particularly as it finds expression in "prophetic picture and vision" and "prophetic deed or act."[67]

Lewalski, who quotes these terms from a Renaissance handbook of biblical rhetoric, excludes the prophetic literature from consideration in *Protestant Poetics and the Seventeenth-Century Lyric* because "prophecy, though often directed to the mind and heart, is a public mode," and "religious lyric, though often didactic in intention or

64. Rosemary Freeman, *English Emblem Books* (London, 1948), 148–72; Colie, *Resources of Kind*, 32–75; Lewalski, *Protestant Poetics*, 196–206, 212, 308–9.

65. Freeman, *English Emblem Books*, 155–56.

66. Ibid., 21.

67. Lewalski, *Protestant Poetics*, 81–82, quoting from Matthias Flacius [Illyricus], *Clavis Scripturae*, 2 pts. (Basle, 1617), pt. 2, tract 4, "De Tropis et Schematibus Sacrarum Literarum." These are included among "the species of simile."

effect, is a private mode."[68] In talking about Herbert, however, I think we must finally put aside the distinction between public and private, like that between didactic and expressive. What we may call the "biblical mode" encompasses these oppositions; Herbert learned from the Bible to write poems at once public and private, didactic and expressive. As we have seen, he draws upon books of the Bible that are "public" and "didactic," such as Proverbs and Ecclesiastes, and in even so personal and "private" a poem as "The Flower" he shares the wisdom he has gained with those who have been invited into "The Church."

True, Herbert rarely speaks as a prophet. "Church-rents and schismes" and "The Church Militant" are the only poems in which he can be said to assume the prophetic mantle. Still, the dialogue of God and man in his poems, the familiarity with which man addresses God (at times verging on impudence or effrontery), the heavenly voice that intercedes to admonish or explain, the nostalgia for ancient times, the censure of the present state of religion, the yearning to transform human nature, the vision of redemption—all these owe something to the prophets. I wish to focus specifically upon Herbert's dramatic use of symbol, a vehicle of teaching that seems calculated, in Fish's phrase, to "[involve] the reader in his own edification."[69]

Let us begin with the prophetic vision, which has influenced both the emblem book and *The Temple*. Amos is questioned by God about his visions: "And the LORD said unto mee, Amos, what seest thou? And I sayd, a plumb-line. . . . And he said, Amos, what seest thou? And I sayde, A basket of Summer fruite." Jeremiah re-

68. Lewalski, *Protestant Poetics,* 4. On the relation between public and private in *The Temple,* see Claude J. Summers and Ted-Larry Pebworth, "Herbert, Vaughan, and Public Concerns in Private Modes," *George Herbert Journal* 3 (1979–80): 1–21.

69. Fish, *Living Temple,* 27.

ports to God that he sees a branch of an almond tree and a seething pot; Zechariah describes a golden candlestick and a flying scroll to an angel.[70] A number of poems in *The Temple* owe their shape to such encounters. "What do I see / Written above there?" (13–14), Herbert asks himself in "The Method," echoing the question "What seest thou?" that is put to the prophets in each of the episodes just mentioned. "Mark you the floore?" at the beginning of "The Church-floore" recalls the divine imperative "Lift up now thine eyes, and see."[71] In "Love-joy" the narrator sees "a vine drop grapes with J and C / Anneal'd on every bunch" in a church window, and explores its meaning with a stranger who is "standing by" (2–3). In "Love unknown" he tells a "deare Friend" that he "saw a large / And spacious fornace flaming, and thereon / A boyling caldron" (25–27). In each of these examples the prophetic vision, given its dramatic setting, seems to me a truer source for Herbert's poems with their real or implied dialogue than the "stiff" and "lifeless" emblem.

A prophetic symbol is not just a picture but an experience. When the prophet (and the reader with him) is drawn into an action or event, he cannot remain indifferent. Jeremiah, for example, is told to seek out a potter at work:

> Arise and go downe to the potters house, and there I will cause thee to heare my words.
> Then I went downe to the potters house, and behold, hee wrought a worke on the wheeles.
> And the vessell that he made of clay, was marred in the hand of the potter so he made it againe another vessell as seemed good to the potter to make it.
> Then the word of the LORD came to me, saying,
> O house of Israel, cannot I doe with you as this potter, saith the LORD? behold, as the clay is in the potters hand, so are ye in mine hand, O house of Israel.
>
> (Jer.18:2–6)

70. Amos 7:8, 8:2; Jer. 1:11, 13; Zech. 4:2, 5:2.
71. Zech. 5:5, cf. Isa. 51:6, Jer. 13:20, Ezek. 8:5.

In the following chapter the symbol is given a distinctly negative turn. The prophet is commanded to "Goe and get a potters earthen bottell" and to break it to pieces in the sight of the elders, proclaiming, "Thus saith the LORD of hostes, Even so will I breake this people and this citie as one breaketh a potters vessell that cannot bee made whole againe" (19:1–11). In either case the dramatic action lets us experience Power, that is, God's power to create and destroy.

Through symbols of this kind we are instructed in "The Agonie." The meaning of Sin and Love is revealed to whoever will "repair" to Gethsemane and Golgotha, to "assay / And taste":

> Who would know Sinne, let him repair
> Unto Mount Olivet; there shall he see
> A man so wrung with pains, that all his hair,
>   His skinne, his garments bloudie be.
> Sinne is that presse and vice, which forceth pain
> To hunt his cruell food through ev'ry vein.
>
> Who knows not Love, let him assay
> And taste that juice, which on the crosse a pike
> Did set again abroach; then let him say
>   If ever he did taste the like.
> Love is that liquor sweet and most divine,
> Which my God feels as bloud; but I, as wine.
>
>   (7–18)

Herbert, reflecting on the events of the Passion, like Jeremiah contemplating the potter's vessel, finds symbols that are diametrically opposed yet inescapably related: the torture rack of the second stanza, seen from a different perspective, becomes the wine press of the third. He does not circle around his subject with "curious questions and divisions," like the clerics who are mocked in "Divinitie" (12). Instead, he urges us to "taste," to know with more than the mind,[72] as Jeremiah is given to know Power.

---

72. Cf. Strier, *Love Known*, 143, 145, on the "strong stress on individual inner experience in Herbert's poetry," a tendency that is "central to historical Protestantism."

What I am suggesting is that the "direct sensuous apprehension of thought"[73] that we find in *The Temple* has its roots in biblical modes of perception.

It has often been remarked that *davar* in Hebrew means "thing" as well as "word." The word, especially the divine word, has a physical presence in the Bible. The prophets talk about seeing the word, hungering and thirsting for it, eating it. The word can light upon Israel, can go forth and accomplish God's purpose, can act with an almost physical force: "Is not my word like as a fire, saith the LORD? and like a hammer that breaketh the rocke in pieces?" (Jer. 23:29).[74]

The prophets not only see God's word, they ingest it, enact it, body forth its meaning in their lives. In this way we can explain the symbolic acts they are commanded to perform, many of them curious or bizarre, which confirm in public the power and truth of God's word. Hosea takes a "wife of whoredomes"; Isaiah gives his sons odd symbolic names, and goes about "naked and bare foote three yeeres for a signe and wonder"; Jeremiah breaks an earthen flask, wears a wooden yoke on his neck, signs a legal deed to purchase a field; Ezekiel eats a scroll, lays siege to a tile with a battering ram, refuses to mourn the death of his wife.[75] One feels in these actions a bold (not to say desperate) attempt by the prophets to penetrate the spiritual lethargy of their audience.

In one of the least spectacular of symbolic actions, Jeremiah purchases a piece of family property despite the threat of impending exile. He performs the transaction with scrupulous attention to legal custom, weighing out the silver, signing and sealing the deed in the presence of

73. T. S. Eliot, "The Metaphysical Poets," *Selected Essays,* 3d ed. (London, 1951), 286.
74. Cf. Isa. 2:1, Jer. 2:31, Amos 8:11, Jer. 15:16; Isa. 9:8, 55:11.
75. Hos. 1:2; Isa. 7:3, 8:1, 20:3; Jer. 19:1–11, 27, 32:6–15; Ezek. 3:1–3, 4:1–2, 24:15–27.

witnesses, and arranging for its safekeeping, as a sign of hope for himself and for others:

> And I bought the field of Hanameel my uncles sonne, that was in Anathoth, and weighed him the money, even seventeene shekels of silver.
> And I subscribed the evidence, and sealed it, and tooke witnesses, and weighed him the money in the ballances.
> So I tooke the evidence of the purchase, both that which was sealed according to the law and custome, and that which was open.
>
> (Jer. 32:9–11)

Knowing the history of Jeremiah, we can better appreciate "Obedience," where the speaker makes a covenant with God, using the legal terminology of a deed of sale:

> My God, if writings may
> Convey a Lordship any way
> Whither the buyer and the seller please;
> Let it not thee displease,
> If this poore paper do as much as they.
>
> On it my heart doth bleed
> As many lines, as there doth need
> To passe it self and all it hath to thee.
> To which I do agree,
> And here present it as my speciall Deed.
>
> (1–10)

What links Herbert's poem to the prophetic tradition is both the symbolic action, spelled out in some detail, and the impulse to transmit a message to the community of the faithful, to enact before others the truth he has discovered for himself. In "Obedience" Herbert is concerned not just with saving his own soul; in the final stanzas of the poem, we learn that he has performed this act in public, as it were, in order that he might "some other hearts convert":[76]

> He that will passe his land,
> As I have mine, may set his hand

76. "Praise, III," 39.

And heart unto this Deed, when he hath read;
        And make the purchase spread
To both our goods, if he to it will stand.

        How happie were my part,
    If some kinde man would thrust his heart
Into these lines; till in heav'ns Court of Rolls
    They were by winged souls
Entred for both, farre above their desert!

(36–45)

It has been noticed that in "The Match" Henry Vaughan responds to Herbert's symbolic action:

Here I joyn hands, and thrust my stubborn heart
        Into thy *Deed*.

(7–8)

In the Preface to the 1655 edition of *Silex Scintillans*, he calls himself "the least" of Herbert's "many pious *Converts*."[77] This is more than a gallant compliment: Vaughan believes that Herbert's words have literally changed his life. Some biblical scholars speak of "the power of the symbol which acts creatively in history."[78] If one may say so, we have here an instance of a symbol that has acted creatively in literary history.

In the prophetic books, as we have seen, symbols are not "just words": they are made and marred, broken, gazed upon, subscribed in a deed of purchase. They may be, as we shall see, taken up in the hands and presented to others. Jeremiah, for example, is charged to make wooden yokes, wearing one himself, and sending others to the kings of the neighboring Edom, Moab, Ammon, Tyre and Sidon, in order to teach that resistance to Nebuchadnezzar is useless: they must "bring their necke

77. *Works of Henry Vaughan*, ed. L. C. Martin, 2d ed. (Oxford, 1957), 435, 391. Vaughan is probably alluding to Herbert's *"lesse then the least"* ("The Posie").
78. Gerhard Von Rad, *Old Testament Theology*, trans. D. M. G. Stalker, 2 vols. (New York, 1965), II, 97. See Von Rad's very helpful chapter on "The Prophets' Conception of the Word of God," II, 80–98.

under the yoke of the king of Babylon" (27:11). He is challenged by a false prophet, Hananiah, who "tooke the yoke from off the prophet Jeremiahs necke, and brake it" in the presence of the people, proclaiming, "Thus saith the LORD, Even so will I breake the yoke of Nebuchadnezzer" (28:10–11). Jeremiah replies in kind: "Thou hast broken the yokes of wood, but thou shalt make for them yokes of yron" (28:13), and prophesies, forebodingly, that Hananiah will die within the year. In this dramatic encounter—Jeremiah fashions and wears a symbol, Hananiah breaks it, Jeremiah replies with another symbol—the prophet takes a figure of speech and gives it the force of a reality.

We do not readily associate "The Rose" and "Hope"— those courtly, elegant, understated poems—with this piece of public spectacle. Still, there is a parallel worth considering. In "The Rose" a symbol is handed back and forth in a ritual dance of seduction and refusal. Herbert is addressing a tempter who has urged him to "take more pleasure" (1). We have already heard the tempter's speech in "The Quip," where Beautie offers herself—in a rose. There he does not choose to reply (*"But thou shalt answer, Lord, for me,"* 8); here, one poem answering the other, he returns a rose for a rose: "Onely take this gentle rose, / And therein my answer lies" (15–16). The drama of the poem, as in the prophetic incident of the potter's vessel or the wooden yokes, revolves about the changed meaning of the symbol: a rose is a rose is *not* a rose. In "Hope" the protagonists exchange a series of symbolic objects: a watch, a prayer book, an "optick," a vial of tears, a few green ears of grain. Some of these are biblical in origin: "which hope we have as an anker of the soule" (Heb. 6:19), "put my teares into thy bottel" (Ps. 56:8), "thy first fruits, greene eares of corne" (Lev. 2:14); most of them turn up in the emblem books. But the effect of these symbolic objects in "Hope" is quite unlike that of the emblem with its static equivalences. In Herbert's subtle poem of gesture and response, the symbol is warmed into life because of its place in a charged human encounter.

There is no great distance from "The Rose" and "Hope," where symbols are handed back and forth across the table, to poems where Herbert embodies his meaning in a physical shape. "Make thee a poem in the shape of an altar": in "The Altar," "Easter-wings," "Paradise," "A Wreath" and others, Herbert carves out the form of the poem as Jeremiah carved out his wooden yokes, the better to teach us with. These poems have been consistently misunderstood. Although they are no longer ridiculed as in the eighteenth century, they are still regarded by many as frivolous trifles or at best bravura pieces. Herbert undoubtedly saw them very differently. I do not think he was primarily concerned with mastering a technical difficulty; these poems are not formal exercises (as "Charms and Knots" is an exercise in writing maxims) but rather outward and visible signs of inward and spiritual states. If his intention was to make the symbols stick in the memory, his success may be gauged by the fact that readers who recall nothing else of Herbert's often remember him as the author of the shaped poems. But his larger purpose, I think, was to teach like the prophets in a nondiscursive way, to present symbols that the reader could experience in all their constrictions and expansions, their cuttings and crooked windings.

The prophets always insist that what they are speaking about directly concerns their audience. "Do you see this? This means you" lies behind every prophetic utterance. Consider Isaiah's parable of the vineyard: "Now will I sing to my welbeloved, a song of my beloved touching his vineyard" (5:1ff.). This is thought to have been presented in the marketplace under the guise of a minstrel's ballad, a rhetorical device calculated to attract a crowd of listeners. Halfway through the performance, the audience would have recognized that they were hearing something more than a diverting fiction: "I will tell you what I will doe to my Vineyard" (5:5). Finally, Isaiah pronounced the chilling, though not unexpected, application: "The Vineyard of the LORD of hostes is the house of Israel" (5:7). Those words have the force of an existential challenge, like Nathan's "Thou art the man" to King David (2 Sam. 12:7). We can see Herbert working in this fashion in "The Church-floore," where the initial question "Mark you the floore?" holds the reader captive until the speckled and black squares, the gentle rising, and the cement that binds them together are all explained as Christian virtues. The process of interpretation is completed in the surprising last couplet, which, in Summers' words, "makes the poem":[79]

> Blest be the *Architect*, whose art
> Could build so strong in a weak heart.
>
> (19–20)

These lines tell the reader, in effect, "Thou art the floor."

The prophet's task is to communicate not only the symbol but its meaning as well. Interpretation is necessary because signs and symbols are often hard to understand: "Wilt thou not tell us what these things are to us, that thou doest so?" the people ask Ezekiel in bewilderment (24:19). The prophet himself is sometimes puzzled: "Knowest thou not what these be?" Zechariah is asked by an angelic interpreter, and he replies, "No, my Lord" (Zech. 4:13). Even where the prophet knows what he sees, he needs a little help from his Friend:

> Moreover, the word of the LORD came unto me, saying; Jeremiah, what seest thou? And I said, I see a rodde of an almond tree.
> Then said the LORD unto me, Thou hast well seene: for I will hasten my word to performe it.
>
> (Jer. 1:11–12)

79. Summers, *George Herbert*, 125.

Interpretation is provided by God himself or, where prophecy verges on apocalyptic, by an angelic intermediary:

> I Daniel was grieved in my spirit in the midst of my body, and the visions of my head troubled me.
> I came neere unto one of them that stood by, and asked him the truth of all this: so he told mee, and made me know the interpretation of the things.
>
> (Dan. 7:15–16)

The problem of interpretation is central in "Jesu" and "Love-joy," to which I now turn.

In "Jesu" the speaker himself puzzles out the meaning of what he has seen: "I sat me down to spell them, and perceived. . . ." This poem, in which Herbert is literally "spelling a word," brings together two familiar topoi—the broken heart (Ps. 51:17) and the new covenant in the heart (Jer. 31:33)—with a third that we have so far not discussed, the expressive name:

> JESU is in my heart, his sacred name
> Is deeply carved there: but th'other week
> A great affliction broke the little frame,
> Ev'n all to pieces: which I went to seek:
> And first I found the corner, where was *J*,
> After, where *E S*, and next where *U* was graved.
> When I had got these parcels, instantly
> I sat me down to spell them, and perceived
> That to my broken heart he was *I ease you*,
> And to my whole is *J E S U*.

"Jesu" cannot be understood without some notion of the importance attached to the meaning of names in the Bible.

A name is believed to express the very essence of a creature; hence many names of the Old Testament are accompanied by some form of explanation. The frequent popular etymologies are based on a similarity of sound: the name, as one scholar says, is "reduced" to a "series of sounds," which then yields "a greatly intensified meaning."[80] *Abraham*, for example, is understood as "a father of many [nations]" (Heb. *av hamon* [*goyim*], Gen. 17:5) and *Israel* as "he who strives with God" (Heb. *yisra'el*, Gen. 32:28). The actual meanings of these names are beyond recovery, names being among the oldest layers of language, but biblical etymologies are concerned less with linguistic accuracy than with symbolic truth.

It is this symbolic significance, with its potential as an instrument of teaching, that interests the prophets. Hosea names his children *Jezreel* ("God shall sow"), *Lo-ruhamah* ("not pitied") and *Lo-ammi* ("not my people") (Hos. 1:4, 6, 9); Isaiah names his own sons *Shear-jashub* ("a remnant shall return") and *Maher-shalal-hash-baz* ("pillage hastens, plunder speeds") and refers to another child, soon to be born, who will be named *Immanuel* ("God is with us") (Isa. 7:3, 8:3, 7:14). The children carrying these names are to serve as living reminders of the prophet's teaching.

It is not surprising that the name *Jesus* should have been subject to interpretation. Matthew points out the connection between the names *Jesus* and *Joshua* ("God shall save") by way of claiming that the prophecy about *Immanuel* has been fulfilled:[81]

> And she shall bring forth a sonne, and thou shalt call his Name Jesus: for hee shall save his people from their sinnes.
> (Now all this was done, that it might be fulfilled which was spoken of the Lord by the Prophet, saying,

80. Von Rad, *Old Testament Theology*, II, 84. Cf. also Immanuel M. Casanowicz, *Paronomasia in the Old Testament* ([Boston, 1894], facs. rpt. Jerusalem, 1970), 36–40.

81. *Jesus* is the Latin form of *Iesous*, which is the Greek form of the late Hebrew or Aramaic *Yeshua'*. Cf. Donne, *Sermons*, VI, 169: "Others were called *Jesus*, *Josuah* was so, divers others were so; but, in the Scriptures there was never any but Christ called *Immanuel*. Though *Jesus* signifie a Saviour, *Joseph* was able to call this childe *Jesus*, upon a more peculiar reason, . . . because *he should save the people from their sins;* and so, no *Josuah*, no other *Jesus* was a *Jesus*. But the blessed Virgin saw more then this; not only that he should be such a *Jesus* as should save them from their sins, but she saw the manner how, that he should be *Immanuel, God with us,* God and man in one person."

Behold, a Virgin shall be with childe, and shall bring foorth a sonne, and they shall call his name Emmanuel, which being interpreted, is, God with us.) (Matt. 1:21–23)

We are now in a position to understand "Jesu" more fully. The poem is about the interpretation of an expressive name, "broken" after the biblical fashion into its constituent elements, J-ES-U, "I-ease-you." Herbert's pun, playful yet serious, reflects the biblical fascination with names and naming, with etymology as a repository of symbolic truth. The poem seems less trifling, more thoughtful in its claims, when read in the light of its biblical antecedents.

"Love-joy," like "Jesu," finds its meaning in the separable elements of a name. This time the initials *J* and *C* are found to contain a hidden significance. The poem involves what Fish calls an "interpretive drama":[82]

> As on a window late I cast mine eye,
> I saw a vine drop grapes with *J* and *C*
> Anneal'd on every bunch. One standing by
> Ask'd what it meant. I, who am never loth
> To spend my judgement, said, It seem'd to me
> To be the bodie and the letters both
> Of *Joy* and *Charitie*. Sir, you have not miss'd,
> The man reply'd; It figures *JESUS CHRIST.*

The oracular figure "standing by," mysterious and omniscient, is like the angelic intermediary ("one of them that stood by," Dan. 7:16) who interprets for Daniel, and his courteous, "Sir, you have not miss'd" reminds us of "Thou hast well seene" in Jer. 1:12. The speaker's interpretation, given first, refers only to the emotions of the Christian. Paul names "love" and "joy" first among the "fruit of the spirit" (Gal. 5:22); Peter associates these with the believer's feeling for Christ, "whom having not seene, yee loue, in whom though now ye see him not, yet beleeving, ye rejoyce with joy unspeakeable" (1 Pet. 1:8).

82. Fish, *Living Temple*, 34.

The knowing bystander corroborates and extends the speaker's perception: "It figures *JESUS CHRIST.*"

Herbert's title, "Love-joy," adds another piece to the interpretive puzzle, since the initials in the window are not *L* and *J*, as the title leads one to expect, but rather *J* and *C*. What links the title to the poem is the silent equation of "Love" and "Charitie," which would have been of interest to Herbert's contemporaries. The proper translation of the Greek word *agape* was a matter of some controversy in the Reformation. Tyndale tendentiously translated "love" instead of "charity," just as he translated "congregation" instead of "church," "repentance" instead of "penance," "favour" instead of "grace."[83] The Geneva Bible has "love," following Tyndale, but the AV, in the spirit of compromise, has sometimes "love" and sometimes "charitie."[84] In Col. 3:14, for example, where the Geneva Bible translates "put on love, which is the bonde of perfectnes," the AV has "put on charitie." Alluding to this verse in "The Church-floore," Herbert names both together, in the only stanza with two abstract nouns:

> But the sweet cement, which in one sure band
> Ties the whole frame, is *Love*
> And *Charitie.*
>
> (10–12)

I would assume that he does so not just for the sake of the rhyme scheme. To the argument that Herbert was not much given to theological controversy, we may add this small but telling piece of evidence. By using "Love" and "Charitie" together in "The Church-floore" and interchangeably in "Love-joy," Herbert quietly puts to rest

83. J. Isaacs, "The Sixteenth-Century English Versions," in *The Bible in Its Ancient and English Versions*, ed. H. Wheeler Robinson (Oxford, 1940), 159.
84. E.g., *Charitie:* I Cor. 8:1, 13:1–13, 14:1, 16:14, I Peter 4:8; *love:* John 15:9–13, Rom. 5:8, 8:39, Eph. 5:2, 1 John 4:7–21.

a theological issue. Love is Charity, and Charity, Love; and both, the speaker is told, derive ultimately from Christ.

The whole question of interpretation is raised in a different way in "Love unknown." If in "Love-joy" the speaker sees only in part, here he barely sees at all. Literal-minded and obtuse, he is dazzled by great things, as in "Redemption," and he looks upon the numinous with a provincial common sense, as in "Artillerie." He presents himself as the very picture of wronged innocence. Having brought a dish of fruit as a gift to his Lord, with his own heart carefully placed "in the middle" (what could be more considerate? more gracious?), he has been violently attacked, for no reason that he can fathom, by the Lord's servant:

> The servant instantly
> Quitting the fruit, seiz'd on my heart alone,
> And threw it in a font, wherein did fall
> A stream of bloud, which issu'd from the side
> Of a great rock.
>
> (11–15)

All he knows for certain is his pain: "the very wringing yet / Enforceth tears" (17–18). Even after he is told by the interpreter, *"Your heart was foul, I fear"* (18), and he concedes the truth of that judgment, he still seems none the wiser.

In the second episode, he beholds a terrifying sight:

> I saw a large
> And spacious fornace flaming, and thereon
> A boyling caldron, round about whose verge
> Was in great letters set *AFFLICTION*.
>
> (25–28)

The reader may recognize this as a prophetic vision of purification through suffering:

> Behold, I have refined thee, but not with silver; I have chosen thee in the fornace of affliction.
>
> (Isa. 48:10; cf. Ezek. 22:17–22)

Set on a pot, set it on, . . . make it boyle well, . . . Heape
on wood, kindle the fire, consume the flesh, . . . that the
filthinesse of it may be molten in it, that the scum of it may
be consumed.

(Ezek. 24:3, 5, 10–11)

But we cannot expect the speaker to know its meaning.
Gazing upon furnace and caldron, he remarks only their
physical impressiveness: "The greatnesse shew'd the
owner" (29). His first impulse, which he recounts with an
engaging openness, is to offer a propitiatory sacrifice:

> So I went
> To fetch a sacrifice out of my fold,
> Thinking with that, which I did thus present,
> To warm his love, which I did fear grew cold.

(29–32)

That response, however, could not be more inappropriate.
The sacrifice from his fold, like the dish of fruit, is a "vain
oblation," the subject of many a prophetic diatribe:[85]

> To what purpose is the multitude of your sacrifices unto
> me, sayth the LORD? I am full of the burnt offerings of
> rammes, and the fat of fedde beasts, and I delight not in the
> blood of bullockes, or of lambes, or of hee goates. . . .
> Bring no more vaine oblations. . . .
> Wash yee, make you cleane, put away the evill of your
> doings from before mine eyes, cease to doe evill.

(Isa. 1:11, 13, 16).

What is required is the cleansing of the heart, first by
blood from the rock, and then in the scalding pan:

> But as my heart did tender it, the man,
> Who was to take it from me, slipt his hand,
> And threw my heart into the scalding pan;
> My heart, that brought it (do you understand?)
> The offerers heart.

(33–37)

85. E.g., 1 Sam. 15:22, Jer. 6:19–20, 7:21–23, Hos. 6:6, Amos 5:22, Mic. 6:6–8. See also Pss. 50:8–15, 51:16–17, 19.

As he complains of this second attack, the narrator's urgent question ("do you understand?") reveals the depth of his ignorance. He has been complaining about love grown cold to a sympathetic friend, when all the while Love has been showing him "favour" (63). The subject of the poem is Love unknown and the speaker unknowing.

We are not told whether the speaker finally learns from his own experience; the poem ends with the interpreter's gloss, not his response to it. From some of the poems that follow, we can only conclude that he has not yet mastered the lesson. Signs and symbols, though they are meant to teach, are often too difficult for man's meager understanding; indeed, as we have seen, they may be puzzling even to the prophets.

How, then, can one educate a creature who is so slow to learn and so quick to forget? One more didactic strategy remains to be considered, the use of homely imagery, which may be seen in part as a concession to man's limited capacities.

HOMELY IMAGERY: "THIS BOX WE KNOW"

Herbert's homely images are perhaps the most provoking aspect of his art. Generations of readers have wished away his humble "pots" and "boxes" as an embarrassment, unworthy of the master. In earlier centuries these were dismissed as "uncouth," "vulgar" and "gothic,"[86] but they have not fared much better in our own day. Grierson in 1921 noted in *The Temple* the " 'mean' similes which in Dr. Johnson's view were fatal to poetic effect even in Shakespeare." "We have learned not to be so fastidious," he protests, but goes on, coughing politely: "when they are not purified by the passionate heat of the poet's dramatic imagination the effect is a little stuffy."[87]

86. Noted in Hutchinson's account of Herbert's reputation, "Introduction," *Works*, xlvii–xlviii.
87. Herbert J. C. Grierson, ed., *Metaphysical Lyrics and Poems of the Seventeenth Century: Donne to Butler* (1921; rpt. New York, 1959), xliii.

More recently, Mary Ellen Rickey defends Herbert against the critics who "routinely praise him as the master of homely metaphor." Such misconceived praise, she maintains, "is certain to diminish one's respect for *The Temple*" because it nurtures the "image of Herbert as a sweetish singer," undervaluing "his intellectual toughness and his richness of allusion." And Vendler takes exception to the "deliberately rustic treatment" of an "exalted subject" in "almost grossly literal" images. Such "incursions into foreign territory," she writes, "reach out to vocabularies not ordinarily found in verse about divine things."[88]

L. C. Knights, on the other hand, approaches Herbert's homely imagery with genuine sympathy, observing that "its function is sometimes misinterpreted, as though Herbert's experience were somehow *limited* by his interest in the commonplace." Knights compares Herbert to Bunyan, "in whose blend of Biblical language and native idiom the august events of the Bible seem to be transacted in a familiar world, and the humble doings of every day are placed in a context that reveals how momentous they are."[89] Still, the very comparison, apt as it is, raises a new set of difficulties: what reader has ever been troubled by homely images in *The Pilgrim's Progress*?

Here we have a major crux of Herbert criticism. How are we to account for the presence of language that is felt by many readers to be coarse or vulgar in a book of poems that is "one of the most beautiful and finished" in the language?[90] Does it in fact represent a lapse of taste? If we think of it as deliberate, how can we justify it? My own view is that Herbert's use of homely imagery is a didactic strategy, like his proverbial sayings or dramatic symbols, and that we can best come to terms with its

88. Rickey, *Utmost Art*, 149, cf. 176–78; Vendler, *Poetry of Herbert*, 195–96, quoting stanzas 2, 3 and 6 of "Praise, III."
89. Knights, "George Herbert," 134, 138.
90. Vendler, *Poetry of Herbert*, 8.

presence in *The Temple* if we understand its place in the Bible.

First, the English Bible. It can be plausibly argued that in his use of homely images and colloquial expressions Herbert was influenced by the Protestant vernacular translations, which preserved the racy flavor of Tyndale's pioneering version.[91] The Protestant translators were inspired by the evangelical resolve to make the Bible accessible and familiar to the ordinary reader. Tyndale's translation, like Luther's, is remarkable for its simple directness, economy and colloquial vigor. Since each new translation was in essence a revision of the last, substantial portions of Tyndale's work were passed on intact, and he may justly be said to have "fixed, once for all, the style and tone of the English Bible."[92] Although this subject deserves further inquiry, I do not pause to elaborate because I think Herbert had a far more compelling model than that of Tyndale and his successors.

In *A Priest to the Temple*, Herbert associates homely imagery with Scripture, in particular with the parables of Jesus, suggesting that the "knowing of herbs" may be useful "by way of illustration, even as our Saviour made plants and seeds to teach the people":

> first, that by familiar things hee might make his Doctrine slip the more easily into the hearts even of the meanest. Secondly, that labouring people (whom he chiefly considered) might have every where monuments of his Doctrine, remembring in gardens, his mustard-seed, and lillyes; in the field, his seed-corn, and tares; and so not be drowned altogether in the works of their vocation, but sometimes lift up their minds to better things, even in the midst of their pains.[93]

91. Freer makes a similar claim for the influence of the Sternhold-Hopkins Psalter; see my discussion in chap. 5. Leah S. Marcus considers another contemporary influence in "George Herbert and the Anglican Plain Style," in *"Too Rich to Clothe the Sunne,"* 179–93.

92. Alfred W. Pollard, ed., *Records of the English Bible* (London, 1911), 6.

93. *A Priest to the Temple, Works*, 261.

Referring to a number of sayings and parables,[94] Herbert explains that "familiar things" not only make heavenly truths understood, but are themselves the signs of such truths. And in a passage about catechizing, Herbert advocates "illustrating the thing by something else, which [the hearer] knows, making what hee knows to serve him in that which he knows not":

> This is the skill, and doubtlesse the Holy Scripture intends thus much, when it condescends to the naming of a plough, a hatchet, a bushell, leaven, boyes piping and dancing; shewing that things of ordinary use are not only to serve in the way of drudgery, but to be washed, and cleansed, and serve for lights even of Heavenly Truths.[95]

Since his examples come from Jesus' parables and sayings,[96] it would seem that here too Herbert was thinking of Jesus' homely language, though he does not explicitly say so.

In these two passages, Herbert points to the vivid evocation of the everyday world that is characteristic of the parables. Homely imagery is found throughout the Bible, but in the Gospel parables it is especially pronounced and concentrated. The parables set before us, in effect, a picture of everyday life in a provincial village. One is struck by their "immediate realistic authenticity," by the way "deeper dimensions are married to such ordinariness and secularity."[97] Jesus speaks of masters and servants, stewards, tenants and day laborers; judges and

94. The lilies of the field (Matt. 6:28–34) and three parables of the kingdom: the sower, the tares among the wheat, and the mustard-seed (Matt. 13:1–23, 24–30, 31–32). Patrides has some penetrating remarks on Herbert and the parables in his introduction to *English Poems*, 10–11.

95. *A Priest to the Temple, Works*, 256–57.

96. *Plough:* Luke 9:62; *hatchet:* Matt. 3:10 ("axe"); *bushell:* Matt. 5:15; *leaven:* Matt. 16:6–12, 13:33; *boyes:* Matt. 11:16–17 ("children"). Cf. also *plowman* in Isa. 28:23–29; *hatchet* in Isa. 10:15 ("axe"); and *leaven* in 1 Cor. 5:6–8.

97. Amos N. Wilder, *The Language of the Gospel: Early Christian Rhetoric* (New York, 1964), 81, 84.

plaintiffs; fathers and sons, housewives, friends and neighbors; rich man, debtor, beggar and thief. He observes these in the act of sowing and harvesting, fishing and shepherding, building houses and settling disputes, making bread, patching old clothes, sweeping a room, taking a journey, or simply sitting in the marketplace. He finds sermons in birds and lilies, grapes and figs, dogs, swine, serpents and doves. He "condescends to the naming" of such common household objects as candle and candlestick, cup and platter, salt, leaven and wineskins. The parables may be complex and enigmatic, but their language is simple. And, what concerns us here, Jesus uses such language in speaking of matters of the spirit. His homely images characteristically present "heaven in ordinarie."[98]

Jesus employs such imagery even in passages of the highest seriousness. Consider the climax—or is it an anticlimax?—in the parable of the Last Judgment:

> When the Sonne of man shall come in his glory, and all the holy Angels with him, then shall hee sit upon the throne of his glory:
> And before him shall be gathered all nations, and he shall separate them one from another, as a shepheard divideth his sheepe from the goats.
>
> (Matt. 25:31–32)

Or the barnyard simile in Jesus' terrible indictment of Jerusalem:

> O Hierusalem, Hierusalem, thou that killest the Prophets, and stonest them which are sent unto thee, how often would I have gathered thy children together, even as a hen gathereth her chickens under her wings, and yee would not?
>
> (Matt. 23:37)

The abrupt descent from "the throne of his glory" to sheep and goats, from the children of Jerusalem to the hen and her chickens, would have offended an audience

98. "Prayer, I," 11.

skilled in classical rhetoric and sensitive to the demands
of decorum, but Jesus' audience was trained to a different
standard.

It takes a certain effort of the historical imagination to
appreciate the fact that cultivated pagans in late antiquity
considered the style of the Scriptures, in Erich Auerbach's
words, "gross and vulgar, awkward in syntax and choice
of words," "an affront to good taste": "How could the
profoundest of problems, the enlightenment and redemption of mankind, be treated in such barbarous works?"[99]
Even Augustine, a teacher of classical rhetoric before his
conversion, had to overcome his distaste for the style of
Scripture before he could become its apologist. Once he
had learned to appreciate in the Bible a new kind of
beauty, very different from that of the classical models, he
could exclaim, "How accessible to everyone is the style of
Holy Writ, though only a very few can penetrate its
depths! . . . by its lowly speech it summons all men."[100]
Auerbach summarizes Augustine's remarks on the "low
style" of the Scriptures:

> Thus the style of the Scriptures throughout is *humilis*, lowly
> or humble. Even the hidden things *(secreta, recondita)* are set
> forth in a "lowly" vein. But the subject matter, whether
> simple or obscure, is sublime. The lowly, or humble, style is
> the only medium in which such sublime mysteries can be
> brought within the reach of men. . . . Simple, vulgar, and
> crassly realistic words are employed, the syntax is often collo-
> quial and inelegant; but the sublimity of the subject matter
> shines through the lowliness.[101]

99. Erich Auerbach, "Sermo Humilis," in *Literary Language and Its
Public in Late Latin Antiquity and in the Middle Ages,* trans. Ralph Manheim, Bollingen Series, no. 74 (New York, 1965), 45.

100. Ibid., 50. Cf. Augustine, *On Christian Doctrine,* trans. D. W.
Robertson, Jr. (New York, 1958), bk. 4. On Augustine's views about
Christian rhetoric and their importance for Herbert see especially Stein,
Herbert's Lyrics, xviii–xxix, 14–15; Michael P. Gallagher, S. J., "Rhetoric,
Style, and George Herbert," *ELH* 37 (1970): 495–516; and Lewalski, *Prot-
estant Poetics,* 215–18.

101. Auerbach, "Sermo Humilis," 51–52.

Although Auerbach is not specifically concerned with the parables of Jesus, there could be no better description of the effect of their language. It is this effect, I think, that Herbert is striving for, with varying degrees of success.

A great many of Herbert's "homely" images are drawn from the sphere of the well-ordered home in its setting of cultivated nature. They refer to the occupations of house-keeping and "husbandrie," like sweeping or spinning, pruning or weeding, keeping "busie" or getting things "neat" or "clean." The rooms Herbert constructs have windows, floors, a door to knock on, lock and key; they are furnished with bed, rug, curtains, pillow, candle, table, dishes, knives, cabinets, closets, cupboards, chests and boxes. These images explore with endless fascination, at the level of everyday life, one of the controlling ideas of *The Temple:* God dwelling in man and man in God.

The images of the household bring together two prominent strains of New Testament imagery. We have already spoken about Paul's metaphor of the living temple: the "houshold of God," "an habitation of God thorow the Spirit," "Gods husbandry," "Gods building."[102] Herbert elaborates upon Paul's metaphor of the household with concrete particulars of the kind that Jesus uses in the parables, for example, the open door and the shut door, the lit candle, the half-washed cup and platter, the house "emptie, swept, and garnished," the wheat gathered into the barn.[103] To be sure, not all images of this type have a source in the Bible. I am thinking of "blunted knife," "season'd timber," "disorder'd clocks" and "watring pots," or of illustrative comparisons like "as dirtie hands foul all they touch" and "as cold hands are angrie with the fire, / And mend it still."[104] One could say that these

102.   Eph. 2:19–22, 1 Cor. 3:9. See my discussion of *temple* in chap. 3.
103.   Matt. 7:7, 25:10, Luke 11:5–10, 13:25; Matt. 5:15, 23:25, 12:44, 13:30.
104.   "Affliction, I," 33; "Vertue," 14; "Even-song," 24; "Affliction, IV," 10; "Miserie," 37; "Church-lock and key," 5–6.

spring from Herbert's own milieu and stop there, but I think it is truer to add that they are, at the same time, free inventions in the biblical mode, exploring the vein of Jesus' "salt of the earth," "moth and rust," "two Sparrowes solde for a farthing."[105]

Herbert's household imagery presents a picture of the world that man, poor man with his limited understanding, can readily comprehend. God spins "times and seasons"; reason, "like a good huswife," spins "laws and policie"; man spins God's praise. This is a universe of manageable proportions, scaled down to size and fitted out for man's own especial delectation: "The whole is, either our cupboard of food, / Or cabinet of pleasure." Night loses its somber aspect when it is seen as man's well-appointed bedchamber—"The starres have us to bed; / Night draws the curtain, which the sunne withdraws"—or God's ebony box. When Herbert writes, "in this love, more then in bed, I rest," he compares (even while denying the comparison) the security of God's tender protectiveness to a kind of rest that we have all experienced.[106] The description of the transcendental in terms of the simple or homely is intended, in Tuve's phrase, "to make the ineffable more nearly tangible."[107] Man feels more at home in his Father's house when he finds there accustomed furniture.

The frequent images of "home-bred medicines," which reflect Herbert's own "knowledge of simples" ("Elder, camomill, mallowes, comphrey and smallage made into a Poultis, have done great and rare cures"),[108] bring comfort

105. Matt. 5:13, 6:19, 10:29.

106. "Providence," 57; "The Pearl," 4–5; "Praise, III," 3; "Man," 29–30, 31–32; "Even-song," 21, 32.

107. Rosemond Tuve, *Elizabethan and Metaphysical Imagery: Renaissance Poetic and Twentieth-Century Critics* (Chicago, 1947; rpt. 1961), 217.

108. *A Priest to the Temple, Works*, 261–62. The God of the Old Testament is a God who "healeth all thine infirmities" (Ps. 103:3; cf. Ex. 15:26, Isa. 57:18–19, Jer. 30:17, etc.), and Jesus' mission included "healing all maner of sickenesse, and all maner of disease among the people" (Matt. 4:23; cf. 8:5–13, 15:30, Luke 8:43–48, etc.).

down from the clouds. The effects of baptism are compared to a "plaister" (an obsolete form of "plaster"), that is, a pastelike preparation spread on a piece of cloth and applied to a wound:

> In you Redemption measures all my time,
> And spreads the plaister equall to the crime.
> ("H. Baptisme, I," 10–11)

God is both "*Cordiall* and *Corrosive,*" and Christ's blood a "balsome" that "doth both cleanse and close / All sorts of wounds." The Scriptures yield a medicinal "hony" that is "precious for any grief in any part; / To cleare the breast, to mollifie all pain." Repentance is a "purge," a "physick," as is the wine of Holy Communion.[109] These remedies, known to Herbert's first readers by experience, are effective metaphors for the healing of the spirit.

Even disturbing images, given a familiar setting, are not nearly so painful. More than once we find man standing before a closed door, complaining, "Thou shutt'st the doore, and keep'st within." But the silence of a God who lives in a house, with a door on which one can knock, is less frightening than the silence of the infinite spaces, and even on the doorstep Herbert can smile at his own clumsy importunity: "Perpetuall knockings at thy doore, / Tears sullying thy transparent rooms." Death, too, is robbed of its sting when it is seen as having a place in God's mansion. Death is "but a chair," or a servant of God who "sweeps" away the debris of life, and the grave is a comfortable bed, with "pillows" hardly different from those we know.[110] In speaking of the mysteries that are God's, Herbert dwells lovingly on the things of this world; nor does he find it the sign of a mean or limited mind to do so.

---

109. "Sighs and Grones," 28; "An Offering," 19–21; "The H. Scriptures, I," 2–4; "The Rose," 28, 29; "Conscience," 12–15.
110. "Whitsunday," 21; "Gratefulnesse," 13–14; "The Pilgrimage," 36; "The Church-floore," 18; "Death," 24.

The metaphor of the handkerchief at the end of "The Dawning" is a particularly controversial example of Herbert's practice. The final couplet has troubled many readers:

> Arise, arise;
> And with his buriall-linen drie thine eyes:
> Christ left his grave-clothes, that we might, when grief
> Draws tears, or bloud, not want a handkerchief.
>
> (13–16)

Critics speak of the "notorious last two lines" of the poem, dismissing them as a lapse of artistic taste.[111] As Summers points out, however, the word *handkerchief* would not have seemed quite so "trivial" and "ludicrous" to a seventeenth-century reader.[112] We tend to associate handkerchiefs with noses, but Herbert's penultimate clause ("when grief / Draws tears, or bloud") indicates that he was thinking rather of wiping the eyes or staunching a wound. At all events, the conceit of Christ's "handkerchief," conspicuously placed in a context almost devoid of images—it is both the rhyme word in a closed couplet and the final word of the poem—is intended to surprise. It has the effect of rousing the "sad heart" from the lethargy, the indulgence, of grief.

Part of Herbert's originality here consists in attributing to Christ an action that is not in the Gospel account, as in lines 166–67 of "The Sacrifice," where he has Jesus set the crown of thorns on his own head. The Evangelists report only that the graveclothes left behind were interpreted as a sign of the Resurrection, but Herbert turns result into purpose, inventing a motive for this mysterious detail: Christ left his graveclothes deliberately, in

---

111. Vendler, *Poetry of Herbert*, 145; D. J. Enright, "George Herbert and the Devotional Poets," *From Donne to Marvell*, The Pelican Guide to English Literature, ed. Boris Ford, vol. 3 (Harmondsworth, 1956, rev. rpt. 1982), 190.

112. Summers, *George Herbert*, 114.

order to comfort man. In this passage he brings together a number of biblical texts, which Summers enumerates for the reader's benefit: Isaiah's prophecy that "He will swallow up death in victorie, and the Lord GOD wil wipe away teares from off al faces"; the disciples' discovery of Christ's "linnen clothes" in the sepulcher on the morning of the Resurrection; Mary Magdalene's weeping at the sepulcher, where she is comforted by the risen Christ: "Woman, why weepest thou?" Finally, the word *handkerchief* appears in a narrative about a miraculous instance of healing:

> And God wrought speciall miracles by the hands of Paul: So that from his body were brought unto the sicke handkerchiefs or aprons, and the diseases departed from them, and the evill spirits went out of them.
>
> (Acts 19:11–12)

"The 'conceit' was there for the finding," Summers writes, "and it was of the fullest possible significance."[113]

But while these passages explain Herbert's choice of image, they do not account for its striking effect. For that we must look to the homely similes of Jesus' parables. Like what is the kingdom of heaven? Like a grain of mustard seed; like leaven; like a net cast into the sea. How will Christ judge the nations from his throne of glory? "As a shepheard divideth his sheepe from the goats." By analogy, Herbert says that the comfort Christ holds out to the mourning heart is like a handkerchief that wipes away all tears, a handkerchief that has itself been retrieved from the grave. The conceit is not entirely successful; even judged on its own terms, it seems contrived, excogitated. But what is troubling here is the sense of strain, not the lowness of the image.[114]

113. Isa. 25:8 (cf. Rev. 7:17, 21:4); John 20:3–8, 11–16; Summers, *George Herbert*, 115–16.
114. Cf. Tuve, "The Criterion of Decorum," *Elizabethan Imagery*, 192–247. Tuve goes too far, I think, in insisting that the homely imagery in religious poetry of the period does not offer "the least offense to

I would like to turn from the problematic "handkerchief" to a particularly successful example of this type in "Ungratefulnesse." The poem deals, in part, with a problem of epistemology: how can we comprehend the great mysteries of God, the Trinity and the Incarnation? In very different ways, Herbert says, comparing them to "two rare cabinets full of treasure":

> The statelier cabinet is the *Trinitie*,
>> Whose sparkling light accesse denies:
>>> Therefore thou dost not show
>>> This fully to us, till death blow
>>> The dust into our eyes:
> For by that powder thou wilt make us see.
>
> But all thy sweets are packt up in the other;
>> Thy mercies thither flock and flow:
>>> That as the first affrights,
>>> This may allure us with delights;
>>> Because this box we know;
> For we have all of us just such another.
>
> (13–24)

Man cannot contemplate the mystery of the Trinity till after death, for its very brilliance "affrights," "accesse denies." But the mystery of the Incarnation may be fully revealed to us even in our mortal state "because this box we know." That the Incarnation is symbolized by a "box" makes Tuve think of "gilded box-like pictures, conventional reliquary-like representations of the ark of the tabernacle"[115]—associations that seem to me beside the

---

decorum" (223); in her desire to prove critics like Empson wrong, she tends to smooth over any element of shock or surprise in metaphysical poetry. Most of Herbert's low images are decorous according to the definition she presents—"the poet's images must suit the 'cause and purpose he hath in hand'" (192)—though the definition is too broad to be useful in cases of doubt. It is conceivable, for example, that the image of the handkerchief was designed precisely to defy decorum in the service of a higher ideal. Before we can settle such questions, though, I would agree that we need "new knowledge about the exact connotations of particular words to Elizabethans and Jacobeans" (197 n. 4).

115. Tuve, *A Reading*, 141.

point. Herbert chooses the word *box* rather, I would argue, for the sharp contrast of humble and sublime that so perfectly conveys the meaning of the Incarnation. The common word *box* emphasizes what an astonishing event that was: God dwelt in man, in "just such" a body as we all possess. The "box" of the flesh that holds the incarnate Christ, like the "house" or "room" of the heart where God may "lodge," translates the sublime conception of God-in-man into language that invites "accesse," alluring us with "delights." *"This box we know"* may be taken as the paradigm of Herbert's homely images. What "we know" allows us to approach and taste mysteries that are beyond all knowing.

"Do not grudge / To pick out treasures from an earthen pot," Herbert writes in "The Church-porch" (429–30), paraphrasing Paul: "But we have this treasure in earthen vessels, that the excellencie of the power may be of God, and not of us" (2 Cor. 4:7). The "earthen pot" is precisely the opposite of those whited sepulchers in "Dotage" with their worthless or corrupt contents: "guilded emptinesse," "shadows well mounted," "embroider'd lyes," "nothing between two dishes." God's boxes and cabinets, even when they are "rare," are always less valuable than what they contain: man in his original innocence is "a box of jewels," spring "a box where sweets compacted lie," Mary "the cabinet where the jewell lay." This figure reflects a fundamental Christian belief: "God doth often vessels make / Of lowly matter for high uses meet."[116] By impressing on us that, in the world of matter, ordinary pots and boxes may be the vehicles of God's purpose, Herbert makes plain the rationale for his homely imagery. In the world of language, too, what appears to be "low" may become a vessel "for high uses meet."

116. "Dotage," 3–5; "Ungratefulnesse," 7; "Miserie," 68; "Vertue," 10; "To all Angels and Saints," 14; "The Priesthood," 34–35.

We may read that article of faith between the lines of "The Elixir":

> A man that looks on glasse,
>   On it may stay his eye;
> Or if he pleaseth, through it passe,
>   And then the heav'n espie.
>
> All may of thee partake:
>   Nothing can be so mean,
> Which with his tincture (for thy sake)
>   Will not grow bright and clean.
>
> A servant with this clause
>   Makes drudgerie divine:
> Who sweeps a room, as for thy laws,
>   Makes that and th' action fine.

(9–20)

The image of a servant sweeping a room is introduced just when, in Stein's words, Herbert "seems to be preparing for a visionary ascent, with the eye of the mind passing through glass to a vision above the senses."[117] The image is deliberately chosen for its lowliness. It is unlikely that the aristocratic Herbert ever held a broom in his hands, as most of us have; he undoubtedly let his servants do his sweeping for him. But *servant* is one of those words, like *child* or *friend*, that activate a complex of Christian meanings; we have already noted how *serve* does so in "Love, III." The servant reminds us too of the specifically Protestant notion of the dignity of all vocations in the eye of God, a favorite theme of the Reformers. In this light, the servant's "drudgerie" is potentially "divine," something that God can turn to "gold." What Herbert has to say about humble occupations implicitly reflects on the question of style: no metaphor is so "mean" that it cannot be made "bright and clean" when it is used "for thy sake." One thinks of the language of stews and brothels

---

117. Stein, *Herbert's Lyrics*, 202–3.

that, as Herbert tells us in "The Forerunners," he washed with his tears and brought well dressed to church.

I have been arguing that Herbert is greatly influenced by Jesus' example in his use of homely images, and that these are chosen for their effectiveness in teaching the reader, "making what hee knows to serve him in that which he knows not." But homely imagery constitutes only one strand of the "extraordinary range of language within *The Temple*,"[118] and its effect is very different from that in the Gospel parables, where the whole cloth is homespun. In Herbert's courteous, subtle, sophisticated poems, the low imagery—*fodder, blister, plaister, cupboard, cabinet, dish, pillow, chair, handkerchief, wheel, pot, box*— leaps to the eye. We cannot help noticing it, whether with delight or dismay. Perhaps we should think of it as a kind of "counterpoint" to the sophistication and finish of *The Temple*; at the very least it has the effect of engaging the reader's attention, which is the first condition of effective teaching.[119]

Let me conclude, in proper didactic fashion, with a story and a homely illustration—"stories and sayings they will well remember"—that help to explain the place of low language in *The Temple*. Walton tells a pretty tale of Herbert as good Samaritan that, however apocryphal, reveals an essential truth. On the way to Salisbury for a musical gathering, Herbert came upon a poor man whose horse had fallen under its load. Taking off his canonical coat, he helped the man unload and load the horse again, and proceeded on his way. When he reached Salisbury, his musical friends

118. Summers, *George Herbert*, 118.
119. Albert McHarg Hayes, "Counterpoint in Herbert," *Studies in Philology* 35 (1938), rpt. *Essential Articles*, 283–97, used the term "counterpoint" to describe the tension between rhyme schemes and metrical patterns in many of Herbert's poems. He suggested that by this means Herbert introduces a "resistance" not ordinarily present in smoothly melodic verse, which has the effect of disturbing "the reader's inertia" and making him more attentive (287); cf. Tuve, *Elizabethan Imagery*, 211.

began to wonder that Mr. *George Herbert* which us'd to be so trim and clean, came into that company so soyl'd and discompos'd; but he told them the occasion: And when one of the company told him, *He had disparag'd himself by so dirty an employment;* his answer was, *That the thought of what he had done, would prove Musick to him at Midnight; . . . for, if I be bound to pray for all that be in distress, I am sure that I am bound so far as it is in my power to practise what I pray for. . . . I praise God for this occasion:* And now let's tune our Instruments.[120]

Herbert's musical friends have a constricting sense of propriety, while Herbert, usually "so trim and clean," so quick to tune his lute, is ready to dirty his hands to perform a Christian act. In much the same way, I think, he sees his homely images as "an occasion," an opportunity—just as, in his words, "my friend is an occasion, my Table is an occasion, my apparell is an occasion."[121]

But an "occasion" is not always a simple matter. "Nothing is little in Gods service," Herbert writes in *A Priest to the Temple:* "If it once have the honour of that Name, it grows great instantly"—a notion we encountered in "The Elixir." In that poem he offers the example of a servant sweeping a room; here he chooses one almost certainly from his own experience as a country parson:

Wherfore neither disdaineth he to enter into the poorest Cottage, though he even creep into it, and though it smell never so lothsomly.

In that final clause, one can almost see Herbert turning up his noble nose in disdain and then, by force of will, overcoming his resistance: "For both God is there also, and those for whom God dyed."[122] These lines were written by the Herbert who as a young man kept himself "at too great a distance with all his inferiours,"[123] and who as an

120. Walton, *Life*, 305.
121. *A Priest to the Temple, Works*, 265.
122. Ibid., *Works*, 249.
123. Walton, *Life*, 270.

adult labors in poem after poem to make himself into a true Christian against the grain of his natural tendencies. The tension between Herbert's native fastidiousness and his faith is mirrored in his poems as the tension between the urbane, refined surface and the homely imagery he so often introduces, attempting, as poet and teacher, "to do that which Christ did, and after his manner."[124]

124. *A Priest to the Temple, Works,* 225.

· 5 ·

Singing to God

CHRISTIAN PSALMODY: "THE MUSICK
SHALL BE PRAISE"

The epigraph on Herbert's title page—"*In his Temple doth
every man speak of his honour*" (Ps. 29:8)—defines "Temple"
as a place where praises are offered up to God and tells us
in brief what a psalm is. It also suggests that the volume
of poems we have before us may be read as a kind of
psalmody. In the Book of Psalms, as many critics have
observed, Herbert found his poetic voice.[1] His *Temple*
conveys the very spirit of Psalms in its unsparing self-
revelation, its intimate address of God, its pervasive mu-
sicality, its yoking of complaint and praise.

Louis Martz notes that "echoes of the Psalms permeate
the *Temple* in a remarkable variety of ways."[2] Sometimes
these verbal echoes are pointed up by italics, as in examples considered earlier: "*But thou shalt answer, Lord, for
me*," "*My God, My King*," "*Thou art still my God.*"[3] More
often, verses quoted or paraphrased from the Psalms are

1. On Herbert and the Psalms, see Martz, *Poetry of Meditation*, 273–
82; Lewalski, *Protestant Poetics*, 51, 246–47, 300–304; Harold Fisch, *Jerusalem and Albion: The Hebraic Factor in Seventeenth-Century Literature* (London, 1964), 56–62; Heather Asals, "The Voice of George Herbert's 'The
Church,' " *ELH* 36 (1969), rpt. *Essential Articles*, 393–407; Noel Kinnamon, "Notes on the Psalms in Herbert's *The Temple*," *George Herbert
Journal* 4 (1981): 10–29.
2. Martz, *Poetry of Meditation*, 279.
3. "The Quip" (8), Ps. 38:15; "Jordan, I" (15), 5:2, 84:3; "The Forerunners" (6), 31:16, 143:10; see my discussion of these poems in chap. 1.

not set off in any way, and merge indistinguishably with
Herbert's own words: "Bow down thine eare!" "That so
the broken bones may joy," "Taking me up to throw me
down," "thou art the same."[4] The Psalms furnish Herbert
not only with images—God as rock and tower, man as
fruitful tree or broken vessel—but also with some of his
most characteristic motifs: "What is man that thou art
mindfull of him?" "O Lord rebuke mee not in thine indig-
nation," "I wil thanke thee, for thou hast heard me,"
"Who can . . . shew forth all his prayse?"[5] But I will not
multiply examples because I think Herbert's debt to the
Book of Psalms extends far beyond borrowings of this
sort. The Psalms provide him not only with subjects but
also with forms for expressing them. In this chapter I will
be speaking about the generic structures of the Old Testament psalms—hymns, complaints and thanksgivings—
and the ways in which Herbert transforms these into
Christian songs of praise.

Lewalski describes the "Church" as a "New Covenant
psalter, the song-book of the new temple in the heart."
Here, she writes, Herbert "undertakes nothing less than
the task of becoming a Christian psalmist, transposing
(as he indicates in 'Easter') the elements of biblical art
upon a Christian lute resounding in harmony with
Christ's cross."[6] The Book of Psalms lends itself readily
to such adaptation. From the first, it was accorded a
significant role in the worship of the Church because,
more than any other book of the Old Testament, it invited Christian interpretation. Jesus himself quoted from
it in his ministry, applied its words to his own sorrows

4. "Longing" (21), Pss. 31:2, 86:1; "Repentance" (32), 51:8; "The
Crosse" (22), 102:10; "Whitsunday" (25), 102:27.

5. *Rock*, Ps. 31:3, etc.; *tower*, 61:3; *tree*, 1:3; *broken vessel*, 31:14. The
motifs cited come from Pss. 8:4 ("Man," "Mattens," "Obedience"), 6:1
("Sighs and Grones," "Complaining," "Discipline"), 118:21 ("Praise,
II," "Praise, III"), and 106:2 ("Antiphon, II," "Providence").

6. Lewalski, *Protestant Poetics*, 246, 316.

and let it speak for him on the cross.[7] Beginning with the apostles, Christians saw in the Psalms a prophecy of, and a witness to, Christ's suffering and exaltation. And in the sixteenth and seventeenth centuries, Protestants discerned in it the very image of their own spiritual lives. Calvin, for example, called it a mirror of the soul: "a man shalnot find any affection in himselfe, wherof the Image appeereth not in this glasse."[8] Later in this chapter, when I speak about the faith of the psalmist, it will be clear why this book of the Bible is especially compatible with Protestant theology.

One measure of the interest in the Psalms in our period is the sheer number of attempts to bring them over into English verse.[9] These include translations of selected psalms by Wyatt, Surrey, Bacon and Milton, and verse paraphrases of the entire book by Robert Crowley (1549), Matthew Parker, Archbishop of Canterbury (c. 1567), Henry Ainsworth (1612) and George Wither (1632). By far the most ambitious and interesting verse paraphrase, and the only one that has any bearing on Herbert's style, is that begun by Sir Philip Sidney and completed after his death by his sister Mary Herbert, the Countess of Pembroke.[10] Although this version was not published until 1823, it circulated widely in manuscript. Donne paid tribute to the Sidney psalter in a poem: "They tell us *why*, and teach us *how* to sing."[11] And it is reasonable to suppose that Her-

7. Matt. 5:5 (Ps. 37:11), Matt. 21:16 (Ps. 8:2), Matt. 21:42 (Ps. 118:22–23), Matt. 22:44 (Ps. 110:1); John 13:18 (Ps. 41:9), John 15:25 (Ps. 69:4); Matt. 27:46 (Ps. 22:1), Luke 23:46 (Ps. 31:6).
8. Calvin, *Psalmes*, sig. *[vi$_v$].
9. On psalm translations in the period see Lily B. Campbell, *Divine Poetry and Drama in Sixteenth-Century England* (Berkeley and Los Angeles, 1959), 27–54; Hallett Smith, "English Metrical Psalms in the Sixteenth Century and their Literary Significance," *Huntington Library Quarterly* 9 (1946): 249–71; and Freer, *Music for a King*.
10. *The Poems of Sir Philip Sidney*, ed. William A. Ringler, Jr. (Oxford, 1962), 265–337; references to Sidney's psalms are to this edition. For the Countess's psalms see *The Psalms of Sir Philip Sidney and the Countess of Pembroke*, ed. J. C. A. Rathmell (New York, 1963).
11. Donne, "Upon the translation of the Psalmes by Sir Philip Sydney, and the Countesse of Pembroke his Sister," *Divine Poems*, 34.

bert, who was related to the Sidneys, saw it too, perhaps in that "very elegantly written" copy, "curiously bound in crimson velvet," which Aubrey noted in the library at Wilton.[12] Martz calls Sidney's psalms "the closest approximation to the poetry of Herbert's *Temple* that can be found anywhere in preceding English poetry": with their "simplicity of phrasing," their "frequent 'wit' and constant metrical ingenuity," they represent an "attempt to bring the art of Elizabethan lyric into the service of psalmody."[13] Coburn Freer treats this subject in some detail in *Music for a King*, comparing the "lyric grace" of Herbert's poems with that of Sidney's psalms, and their "muscular logic" with that of "the Countess at her best."[14]

The Sidney psalter is a literary influence of a familiar sort; that is, Sidney and the Countess, by their example, open up to Herbert a new vein of prosodic possibility. But we must remember that for Herbert the Book of Psalms is not simply a "literary" work: Herbert would have encountered the Psalms first of all in a liturgical or devotional context. He would have heard choral settings of the prose Prayer Book psalms at Westminster, Cambridge and Salisbury, and the congregational singing of the metrical psalms in his rustic parish at Bemerton.[15] And probably at home too, for domestic psalm singing was almost a

12. Dick, ed., *Aubrey's Brief Lives*, 139.
13. Martz, *Poetry of Meditation*, 273, 278. Cf. Summers, *George Herbert*, 148, 229 nn. 9-10; Lewalski, *Protestant Poetics*, 241–44.
14. Freer, *Music for a King*, 75; cf. 72–108.
15. Since the rubrics in the Prayer Book did not specify what kind of music was to be employed, different kinds of services evolved in cathedrals and parish churches of the seventeenth century, reflecting the ecclesiastical divisions of the time. In cathedrals, college chapels and the chapel royal, the prose psalms were sung to harmonized chants and performed on festal days in elaborate settings, while metrical psalms were sung unaccompanied by the entire congregation. In parish churches without organ or choir, where the prose psalms would have been simply read aloud, the congregational singing of the metrical psalms became a focal point of the service. See Edmund H. Fellowes, *English Cathedral Music*, 5th ed., rev. J. A. Westrup (London, 1969); Peter Le Huray, *Music and the Reformation in England, 1549–1660* (1967;

national pastime in Reformation England. Donne remembers, in the funeral sermon on Lady Danvers, that Herbert's family was accustomed to singing psalms together on Sunday evenings.[16] Herbert probably played and sang psalms with his musical circle in Salisbury; he may even have composed some settings himself.

The best-known collection of metrical versions, used by Anglican and Puritan alike until the end of the seventeenth century, was that of Sternhold and Hopkins; indeed, the "Old Version," as it came to be called, was one of the most popular books of the time. Although Herbert no doubt knew it well, the clumsy texts of the Old Version, with their strained rhymes and bumbling meters, have very limited implications for *The Temple*. These were literal paraphrases, fitted as conveniently as possible to a handful of popular tunes; that their aesthetic qualities do not stand up under scrutiny is no surprise. One cannot speak of a stylistic debt here, as one can in the case of the Sidney psalter, and Freer's attempt to do so is not at all convincing. Herbert's deliberate awkwardnesses, which work in very controlled and subtle ways, owe nothing at all to the inadvertent crudity of the metrical psalms. Although on infrequent occasions Herbert fails as the Old Version fails, through a lack of control, the latter can hardly be called a model. Even Herbert nods: in poetry where rhymes and fixed meters are the norm, not every choice of a rhyme word or stress pattern will be equally successful. There is no need to explain away infelicities as so many niceties of style; the better part of charity, it seems to me, is to record a failure rather than to construct an ingenious apology to dignify it. When he approaches

corr. ed. Cambridge, 1978); Nicholas Temperley, *The Music of the English Parish Church*, 2 vols. (Cambridge, 1979); Peter Le Huray, "Anglican Chant," and Nicholas Temperley, "Psalms, Metrical: England," in *The New Grove Dictionary of Music and Musicians*, ed. Stanley Sadie (London, 1980), I, 430–31; XV, 358–71.

16. Donne, *Sermons*, VIII, 86.

the Psalms through the awkward paraphrases of Stern-hold and Hopkins, Freer does not do justice to Herbert's debt to these great lyric poems.[17]

Through his work on the Old Version, however, Freer reminds us of the liturgical context in which Herbert experienced the Psalms. This helps to clarify a number of points that should be considered here: the prominence of music in *The Temple*, the nature of Herbert's audience and the apparently random arrangement of the volume. Let me begin with the first and most obvious.[18]

Musical images abound in *The Temple*; some poems were intended to be sung, and many lend themselves to musical settings.[19] It is now taken for granted that the "image of the poet-divine playing and singing in secluded retirement" lies behind many of Herbert's musical conceits,[20] but equally true, and less present to our minds

17. Central to Freer's argument is the question of intention. He assumes that, since Herbert has shown himself to be a master of prosody, he cannot have written a faulty line unless for a strategic purpose; any awkwardness or flatness must therefore be deliberate. Thus Freer seeks out examples of apparent clumsiness and declares them intentional and mimetic in function, taking "poetic failure as a metaphor for spiritual failure" (*Music for a King*, 35). There are a number of poems that lend themselves to this kind of reading ("Deniall" and "The Collar" are the best known), and Freer extends this category to some degree, but much of the time he is stretching a tenuous point.

18. On Herbert and music, see Summers' very helpful chapter in *George Herbert*, 156–70; John Hollander, *The Untuning of the Sky: Ideas of Music in English Poetry, 1500–1700* (Princeton, 1961), 288–94; Amy M. Charles, "George Herbert: Priest, Poet, Musician," *Journal of the Viola Da Gamba Society of America* 4 (1967), rpt. *Essential Articles*, 249–57; Stein, *Herbert's Lyrics*, 110–16; Louise Schleiner, "Herbert's 'Divine and Moral Songs': Song-Text Features in *The Temple* and Their Importance for Herbert's Poetic Idiom," Ph.D. diss. (Brown University, 1973).

19. Charles, *Life of Herbert*, 166, thinks Herbert may have sung some of his own settings at his regular "Musick-meeting" in Salisbury, accompanying himself on the lute. Louise Schleiner lists the settings by Jenkins, Lawes, Wilson, Playford, Blow and Purcell that have come to light ("Seventeenth-Century Settings of Herbert: Purcell's 'Longing,'" in "*Too Rich to Clothe the Sunne*," 198–99). Five of these are transcribed in C. A. Patrides, ed., *George Herbert: The Critical Heritage* (London, 1983), 357–73.

20. Hollander, *Untuning of the Sky*, 288.

today, is the image of the churchman and amateur musician listening to, singing, and playing psalms with others in church and at home. Herbert's two poems about music are in fact praises of church music, and both refer to the Psalms.[21] Many of Herbert's references to music evoke the Psalms. An obvious example, noted by John Hollander, is the "prolific use of 'singing' for 'prayer,' or communication with God generally."[22] "To sing thee," "to sing thy name," "to sing thy praise," "to sing thy victories" and the like echo formulaic phrases from the Psalms.[23] When Herbert writes, "My musick shall finde thee, and ev'ry string / Shall have his attribute to sing," or "musick for a King," or "the musick shall be praise," he is associating music with the praise of God in the manner of the psalmist.[24] That Christmas, Easter and Whitsunday are feast days for which the Proper Psalms were set to music suggests why the poems of those titles are associated with song.[25] We shall encounter other examples in the course of this chapter. In short, the generalization that Herbert's poems move toward "not the plain style, but no style at all and, in a way, silence"[26] does not take into account the

21. "Church-musick" alludes in a phrase (*"God help poore Kings"*) to a common psalm trope; see n. 48. The Latin epigram "De Musicâ Sacrâ" calls the Psalms "holy banquets! O soothing / Oil of the spirit! Flakes of heaven, falling / Droplets of a better world!" (*Musae Responsoriae, Works*, 394, lines 33–36; trans. in Mark McCloskey and Paul R. Murphy, *The Latin Poetry of George Herbert: A Bilingual Edition* [Athens, Ohio, 1965], 35).

22. Hollander, *Untuning of the Sky*, 288.

23. E.g., "Praise, II," 10; "The Dedication," 4; "Love, I," 13; "Easter-wings," 9; cf. Pss. 59:16–17, 61:8, 66:1, 144:9, etc.

24. "The Thanksgiving," 39–40; "Sion," 24; "Dooms-day," 30. Cf. Pss. 33:1–3; 47:6–7; 95:1–2, etc.

25. Summers, *George Herbert*, 157. The Proper Psalms for Christmas, Easter and Whitsunday are listed in Blunt, ed., *Annotated Book of Common Prayer*, 114, and John E. Booty, ed., *The Book of Common Prayer, 1559*, (Charlottesville, 1976), 32–33. Herbert wrote poems for these three festivals, two of which, as Tuve notes, draw on the Proper Psalms: "Easter" quotes directly from Ps. 57:9, and "Whitsunday" refers to Ps. 68:13 (*A Reading*, 145, 157). He wrote no poem for Ascension Day, the only other feast for which Proper Psalms were assigned prior to 1662.

26. Fish, *Self-Consuming Artifacts*, 199.

extent to which his work has been influenced by the psalm mode. I would argue rather that *The Temple* reveals Herbert's intense commitment to all the forms of human discourse, and that his hymns, complaints and thanksgivings in particular aspire not to silence but to song.

Herbert's experience of the Psalms has some bearing, too, on the vexed question of his intended audience. We have already touched on the critical debate about whether he is communing privately with God or writing with a reader in mind. Summers points beyond these constricting alternatives when he compares Herbert's poems to "public prayer": "Unlike the sermon, the prayer was addressed to God rather than to the congregation, yet it was delivered in the presence of the congregation, and the listeners must understand and join their silent prayers with the spoken one."[27] The liturgical and devotional use of the Psalms offers an illuminating analogy that may be set alongside Summers'. More than any other part of the Bible, the Psalms are meant to be used. Hooker defends the frequent repetition of the Psalms in church in precisely these terms: "The praises of God in the mouths of his saints are not so restrained to their own particular, but that others may both conveniently and fruitfully use them."[28] Like the Psalms, I would suggest, the poems of *The Temple* give expression to the poet's own grief and joy, and at the same time are directed to a community of readers who may "conveniently and fruitfully use them." Indeed, if we take account of the psalm model, we will understand more clearly why these alternatives are not mutually exclusive.

Finally, we should consider the order—or rather, the lack of order—of the Psalms. A few clusters are united by form or theme—the Psalms of Ascents, the Hallelujah

27. Summers, *George Herbert*, 104.
28. Richard Hooker, *Of the Laws of Ecclesiastical Polity*, 2 vols., Everyman's Library (London, 1907), bk. 5, sect. xl.

Psalms, the final rousing series of hymns—but for the most part one moves unpredictably from hymn to complaint to thanksgiving.[29] The haphazard arrangement of the Psalms is given a kind of authority—one could say consecrated—by the liturgical practice of the Church of England. In preparing the Prayer Book, Cranmer might conceivably have selected psalms for matins and evensong corresponding to the themes of the daily lessons. Instead, the Book of Common Prayer stipulates that the Psalms are to be read through once every month, and provides a table dividing them between matins and evensong for a typical month of thirty days, rectifying the earlier situation in which, as the Preface notes, "a fewe of them have beene daily saide, and oft repeated, and the rest utterly omitted."[30] As a result, what the churchgoer hears repeated each month—what Herbert heard hundreds of times, and repeated himself, as priest—is a sequence without a predictable pattern. "My God, my God, . . . why hast thou forsaken mee?" (Ps. 22), for example, is followed by "The Lord is my shepheard" (Ps. 23) on the fourth evening of every month, and "Truely God is loving unto Israel" (Ps. 73) by "O God, wherefore art thou absent from us so long?" (Ps. 74) on the fourteenth. One can see how, month after month and year after year, the apparent disorder of the Psalms might be-

29. This unstructured arrangement, George Wither suggests, citing ancient authority, is best suited to the operations of the Holy Ghost. The Church is a kind of "shop wherein the holy Ghost polisheth and maketh us fit to adorne the Cittie and House of God," and the Psalms are "as it were Tooles to frame us." Just as it would be foolish for the workman in a carver's shop to have his tools "placed orderly in a rowe by him: for he is not so to use them; but now a fine Instrument, anone a ruder, and then a finer againe, according to the fashion and necessity of the Worke," so the Holy Ghost, working upon the varied temperaments of men, "hath therefore disposed these his Instruments in such manner as you see, and directeth us to them, according to our severall necessities" (George Wither, *A Preparation to the Psalter* [1619], Publications of the Spenser Society, no. 37 [Manchester, 1884], 51–52).
30. *Booke of Common Prayer* (1604), sig. B.

gin to seem a significant order, one that reflects the inevitable "deaths" and "returns" of the spirit.

The implications for Herbert's poems are obvious. There is no clearly defined principle of organization in *The Temple.* Some transitions seem to be carefully planned, such as the dying fall of "Longing" followed by the upbeat "Away despair! my gracious Lord doth heare" of "The Bag," or the anguish of spirit in "The Crosse" followed by the miraculous recovery of "The Flower." And there are a few thematic groupings, such as the poems about church furniture, the Easter sequence, and the final group of poems on the Last Things. But a good many poems that might have been brought together are instead distributed at intervals throughout the volume. What are we to make of this? Helen White sees the volume as only "partially organized" owing to Herbert's poor health in his final years and his premature death. Summers, on the other hand, speaks of the "fluctuations between sorrow and joy, doubt and assurance" as evidence of Herbert's "psychological realism," his "understanding of the 'giddie' state of man," and Lewalski refers the arrangement of *The Temple* to the Protestant view of the spiritual life as an "uneven, uneasy, and essentially episodic sequence of trials, temptations, failures, successes, backslidings, until the end of life crowns all."[31] I believe that the random order of *The Temple* is deliberate, and that even if he had lived to revise the volume, Herbert would not have imposed on it a more systematic arrangement. If he regarded his poems as a kind of psalmody, it is entirely possible that he intended the "fluctuations between sorrow and joy, doubt and assurance" as analogous to the order of the Book of Psalms.[32]

Because of its organization, we cannot usefully talk

31. White, *Metaphysical Poets,* 162; Summers, *George Herbert,* 87; Lewalski, *Protestant Poetics,* 192.
32. Freer, *Music for a King,* 40, makes this same point.

about the Book of Psalms as a sequence. Hence commentators usually classify the hundred fifty psalms by formal types. In Herbert's day, as Lewalski notes, some found warrant for a threefold division in Paul's "bee filled with the Spirit: Speaking to your selves, in Psalmes, and Hymnes, and Spirituall songs" (Eph. 5:18–19).[33] I will not be using these rubrics in the following pages both because they do not refer to generic types in the Book of Psalms and because the terms are too vague and similar to make useful categories. As Calvin puts it: "Songs, Psalmes and Hymnes . . . differ nothing at all one from another: and therefore I neede not too buzie my selfe in setting foorth any curious distinction of them."[34] Other classifications pose their own difficulties. George Wither's survey of types—"Sometimes his *Odes* are heroicall, sometime tragicall, sometime pastorall, sometime satyricall"[35]—sounds more Greek than Hebrew. Donne helpfully divides the Psalms into "those of Praise, and those of Prayer," prayer being "deprecatory" or "postulatory,"[36] but this grouping fails to distinguish between two related forms of praise.

A more workable approach, for the purposes of this study, is adumbrated by Thomas Ravenscroft in the preface to his collection of harmonized psalm tunes, *The Whole Booke of Psalmes* (1621). Herbert is likely to have used Ravenscroft's *Psalmes* in his church at Bemerton, in his musical circle at Salisbury, and in private worship in his own family; according to an authority, "the book lasted long in the estimation of well-educated musicians, and had much influence."[37] Ravenscroft recommends that "*Psalmes* of

33. Lewalski, *Protestant Poetics*, 45; cf. 300.
34. Calvin, *Sermons upon Ephesians*, fol. 271ᵥ. If any distinction was intended, it is presumably that between evangelical canticles, Old Testament psalms and various kinds of new Christian compositions. Cf. Hedley, *Christian Worship*, 106.
35. Wither, *Preparation to the Psalter*, 77.
36. Donne, *Sermons*, V, 315; II, 144; cited in Lewalski, *Protestant Poetics*, 48.
37. Temperley, *Music of the English Parish Church*, 73.

Rejoycing be *sung* with a *loude voice,* a *swift* and *jocund measure,"* that *"Psalmes* of *Tribulation* be *sung* with a *low voice* and *long measure,"* and that *"Psalmes* of *Thankesgiving* be *sung* with a *voice indifferent,* neither too *loud,* nor too *soft,* and with a *measure* neither too *swift* nor too *slow."*[38] This threefold division corresponds in the main to what biblical scholars today call hymns, complaints and thanksgivings. The *hymn* is defined as a formal celebration of God's attributes or his great works in history and nature; the *complaint,* an urgent prayer for help, and the *thanksgiving,* a song of praise in gratitude for a particular benefit.[39] It should be noted that many psalms show features of more than one type, and that within each category the conventional elements do not occur in a fixed order but combine in a variety of ways.

I have chosen to employ this classification for a number of reasons. First, it is commonly accepted by scholars in our own day as reflecting the three major types in the Book of Psalms. Second, it was clearly anticipated in Herbert's day, whether in Ravenscroft's directions for psalm-singing or (as we shall see) in Calvin's astute commentar-

38. Thomas Ravenscroft, *The Whole Booke of Psalmes* (London, 1621), sig. [vi] (italics reversed). The edition with Ravenscroft's preface is unfortunately not in the Wing collection, but it is available in a number of rare book collections, among them the Chapin Library at Williams College. This passage is cited in Le Huray, *Music and the Reformation,* 382–83.
39. The generic features of the hymns, complaints and thanksgivings of the Hebrew Psalms were first described systematically in the pioneer work of the German scholar Hermann Gunkel, who grouped them on formal grounds. A convenient synopsis in English may be found in Gunkel's *The Psalms: A Form-Critical Introduction,* trans. Thomas M. Horner (Philadelphia, 1967). Gunkel's classifications furnish the basis for much subsequent work on the Psalms. See for example Sigmund Mowinckel, *The Psalms in Israel's Worship,* trans. D. R. Ap-Thomas, 2 vols. (Oxford, 1962); Otto Eissfeldt, *The Old Testament: An Introduction,* trans. Peter Ackroyd (New York, 1965); or Ernst Sellin (rev. Georg Fohrer), *Introduction to the Old Testament,* trans. David E. Green (Nashville, 1968). I will not be concerned here with generic types that have no bearing on *The Temple,* such as royal psalms, songs of Zion or songs of Yahweh's enthronement.

ies, which define so precisely the characteristics of each type. Finally, and most important, it brings into focus three groups of lyrics in *The Temple:* poems of celebration that glorify God, poems of affliction that end in faith, and poems of thanksgiving that rejoice in pain overcome. In what follows I will begin by considering the generic features of biblical hymns, complaints and thanksgivings, and then turn to Herbert's imaginative transformations, which are truly "new creations in the psalmic mode."[40]

HYMNS: "LET ALL THE WORLD SING"

The hymns of the Book of Psalms generally begin with an invitation to "praise the Lord" (the Hebrew word *Hallelujah* means just that) or to "sing" his praises, often specifying an instrumental accompaniment—trumpet, lute, harp, cymbals, strings and pipe in Psalm 150. The invocation is followed by an enthusiastic account of the motives for praise: God's power and majesty, mercy and faithfulness, or his wondrous deeds in history and nature. The hymn is pure praise, with no petitional element; its purpose is to glorify God before all the world, and its mood is one of jubilant adoration. Calvin writes that "the cheef study wherein it becommeth the righttuouse to be occupyed, is to publishe among men the rightuousnes, goodnes, and mightynes of God"; thus "it is meete that they should streine themselves with all their harts too sing his prayses."[41] The best examples of the hymn are Psalms 146–50 at the end of the Book of Psalms, which culminates in the sweeping Hallelujah, "Let every thing that hath breath: prayse the Lord" (150:6).[42]

---

40. Lewalski, *Protestant Poetics,* 51.
41. Calvin, *Psalmes,* pt. 1, fol. 122.
42. Other representative examples are Pss. 33, 47, 96, 98, 103, 104, 105, 135 and 136. For a discussion of this type, see Gunkel, *Psalms,* 10–13, 30–31, and Mowinckel, *Psalms in Israel's Worship,* I, 81–105.

Only a few poems in *The Temple* represent the hymn in its pure form. We naturally think first of the two "Antiphons," the only poems of Herbert's that are scored for chorus; both are clearly intended to be sung.[43] "Antiphon, I" imitates the psalms that were repeated daily at matins and evensong—the *Venite exultemus domino, Jubilate Deo, Cantate domino* and *Deus misereatur*[44]—all exhortations to joyful worship. Its opening lines and refrain—"Let all the world in ev'ry corner sing, / *My God and King*"—echo these rousing Old Testament "Psalmes of Rejoycing":

> O come, let us sing unto the Lord: let us heartily rejoyce in the strength of our salvation.
> Let us come before his presence with thanksgiving: and shewe our selves glad in him with Psalmes.
> For the Lord is a great God: and a great King above all gods.
> In his hand are all the corners of the earth.
> (Ps. 95:1–4)

> O bee joyfull in the Lord (all you lands:) serve the Lord with gladnesse, and come before his presence with a song.
> (Ps. 100:1; cf. 98:5)

> Let the people praise thee, O God: yea, let all the people praise thee.
> (Ps. 67:3, 5)

And the first stanza of the poem recalls the canticles of matins, the *Te Deum* ("All the earth doeth worship thee: . . . To thee all Angels crie alowde") and the *Benedicite* ("O ye heavens, blesse ye the Lord: . . . O let the earth blesse the Lord").[45]

---

43. The first, as Hutchinson notes (*Works*, 53n), is quoted in full in the preface of J. Playford's *Psalms and Hymns in solemn musick* (1671). According to Schleiner, "Antiphon, II" seems to have been sung in the seventeenth century to a preexisting tune; the setting is not extant ("Purcell's 'Longing,'" 198, 206 n. 7).
44. Matins: Pss. 95, 100; evensong: Pss. 98, 67.
45. *Booke of Common Prayer* (1604), sigs. C2v, [C5v], [C8]; C3v, C4–C4v.

In this light we can understand why Herbert writes "The church with psalms must shout" in line 9. The verb is justified both by the nature of the Old Testament hymn and by the Reformation practice of congregational psalm singing. The psalmist's hymns are the noisiest of biblical lyrics, characterized by a mood of unrestrained celebration. On this point the AV is more faithful to the spirit of the Hebrew: where the Prayer Book has "be joyfull" or "shewe our selves glad," the AV translates "make a joyfull noise" (100:1, 95:2); "sing . . . with the voice of melodie" becomes "shoute . . . with the voyce of triumph" (47:1). The Vulgate's *jubilare,* with its connotations of "to halloo, shout, huzza, to shout for joy" (*OED,* "jubilate"), exactly renders the force of the Hebrew (verbal root *rwʿ*). "Shouting" is probably an apt characterization, moreover, of the unaccompanied congregational psalm singing that is the hallmark of the Reformation; earlier, singing in church had been reserved to priest, clerk and choir, with their knowledge of Latin and their specialized training in chant or polyphony. It is interesting that Herbert chose to include "Antiphon, I," which is not found in the Williams manuscript, among the first group of poems in *The Temple.* In doing so he introduces, early in the volume, an image of communal worship that remains present to our minds even as we read the more inward and personal lyrics.

Up to line 10, the poem appears to be an imitation of an Old Testament hymn. But the final couplet, which completes the antithesis of "church" and "heart"—"But above all, the heart / Must bear the longest part"—summons up the temple topos and reminds us that this is after all a Christian psalm, written for a temple whose frame and fabric is within. At the same time, "Antiphon, I" tells us that the heart does not sing solo; its song is always heard against a chorus of many voices.

In "Antiphon, II," that chorus is made up of men and angels. At the end of "Man" (the poem immediately preceding), Herbert pairs men with the forces of nature as "both [God's] servants." He might have composed an antiphon using just those voices, as in Psalm 98, where men make a joyful noise with harps and trumpets, and the waters roar their reply. But an antiphon of men and angels lends itself better to Christian praise. Vendler observes that the poem needs music "to flesh it out," imagining a musical setting, "in which presumably the angels would sing up high, the men down low, and the chorus would blend the two."[46] This insight should affect the way we judge the poem; there is no point in measuring it against poems of a very different sort, in which the words alone must carry the burden of meaning.

"Antiphon, II" may be quoted in full as an example of the hymn. The opening lines issue the call to praise on heaven and earth:

> *Chor.* Praised be the God of love,
>   *Men.* Here below,
>   *Angels.* And here above:
>
>   (1–2)

The main body of the poem enumerates the motive for praise, God's saving deeds in history. Every string has its attribute to sing:

> *Cho.* Who hath dealt his mercies so,
>   *Ang.* To his friend,
>   *Men.* And to his foe;
>
> *Cho.* That both grace and glorie tend
>   *Ang.* Us of old,
>   *Men.* And us in th'end.
>
> *Cho.* The great shepherd of the fold
>   *Ang.* Us did make,
>   *Men.* For us was sold.
>
> *Cho.* He our foes in pieces brake;
>   *Ang.* Him we touch;
>   *Men.* And him we take.
>
>   (3–15)

46. Vendler, *Poetry of Herbert*, 209–10.

The lines that follow deduce man's obligation to praise, repeating the psalm formula (e.g., 106:2) that man's praises are by nature inadequate:

> *Cho.* Wherefore since that he is such,
>   *Ang.* We adore,
>   *Men.* And we do crouch.
> *Cho.* Lord, thy praises should be more.
>   *Men.* We have none,
>   *Ang.* And we no store.
>
>   (16–21)

And the concluding couplet sings Hallelujah:

> *Cho.* Praised be the God alone,
>   Who hath made of two folds one.
>
>   (22–23)

Many of the hymns in the Book of Psalms refer to Israel's history of salvation, and especially to the Exodus.[47] Herbert baptizes the Old Testament form by making the specific focus of praise the Redemption, which is the antitype of the Exodus; by referring to the Eucharist; and by speaking of the "God of love" (a phrase he introduces as well in his version of "The 23d Psalme").

"He our foes in pieces brake" (13), however, conjures up the Lord of hosts, mighty in battle, who "smote great Kings . . . and slewe mightie Kings" (136:17–18). This theme is sounded in the Proper Psalms for Whitsunday matins: "For loe, the kings of the earth . . . marveiled to see such things: they were astonied, and suddenly cast downe. Feare came there upon them, and sorow" (48:3–5); "Kings with their armies did flee and were discomfited: . . . the Almighty scattered kings for their sake" (68:12, 14) and announced prophetically on Christmas: "The Lord . . . shall wound even Kings in the day of his wrath" (110:5) and on Easter: "The Kings of the earth stand by . . . against the Lord. . . . Thou shalt bruse them

47. Cf. Pss. 78, 105, 106, 135, 136.

with a rod of yron: and breake them in pieces like a potters vessel" (2:2, 9). This last verse is apparently the source of Herbert's image.[48] In "Antiphon, II," Herbert is celebrating not only God's love but his power as well.

In the first half of the poem, Herbert uses the antiphonal form to point up a series of oppositions. The dimeter lines here are in antithetical parallelism: *below/above; friend/foe; of old/in th'end; make/was sold.* But the paradox that God has dealt mercifully with "his foe" (this can only be man, if the angels are God's "friends") suggests what is to come; as Herbert writes in "Miserie," God's love does not suffer "those / Who would, to be [his] foes" (29–30). Once Christ's work of redemption is announced ("The great shepherd . . . For us was sold"), the human voices join the angels in speaking of "our foes" in line 13, marking a change in the poem's direction and pointing toward its resolution. From this moment the opposed voices begin to draw together, and the short lines are in synonymous parallelism: *touch/take; adore/crouch; none/no store.* In the end, there is so little difference between what the men and angels are saying that there is no longer any reason for them to speak by turns. Thus where the form of the poem leads us to expect two final short lines in antiphony, Herbert has the men and angels join together in line 23, their harmony symbolically making "of two folds one." As so often, Herbert finds poetic means to give a palpable shape to theological truths. In the final line, by replacing antiphony with harmony, he presents the reconciliation of oppositions as a new Christian theme for celebration.

48. Since the Proper Psalms were frequently set to music, we can understand why Herbert would say "God help poore Kings" in a poem called "Church-musick." Tuve refers us to verse 8 ("To binde their kings in chaines") of the "music-filled" Ps. 149, which "held an imposing place" in the (Latin) liturgy, to explain this line, "for which no one has ever found an explanation" (A Reading, 180–81). But the topos is common enough, especially in the psalms that would have been sung on Anglican feast days, so that we need not be puzzled by this allusion.

Although "Easter" is a far more complex and interesting poem, it is illuminating to read it alongside the two "Antiphons" since it belongs to the same genre. Like many hymns, it begins with a formal summons to praise, naming both the mode (the singer's instruments) and the motive (God's saving deeds). The stirring invocation comes from Psalm 57, one of the Proper Psalms for Easter matins:

> My heart is fixed, O God, my heart is fixed: I will sing and give praise.
> Awake up my glory, awake Lute and Harpe: I my selfe will awake right earely.
> I wil give thanks unto thee, O Lord, among the people: and I wil sing unto thee among the nations.
> (57:8–10; cf. 108:1–3).

The poem starts with the biblical image of rising early to praise:

> Rise heart; thy Lord is risen. Sing his praise
> Without delayes,
> Who takes thee by the hand, that thou likewise
> With him mayst rise:
> That, as his death calcined thee to dust,
> His life may make thee gold, and much more, just.
>
> (1–6)

Herbert makes of the biblical sequence of verbs, *awake, awake, I will awake* (57:9), a new Christian sequence: *rise* heart, thy Lord *is risen*, thou *mayst rise*. He is using *rise* in three different senses here: wake up; Christ has been resurrected from the dead; you may be reborn to a new life of the spirit. Christ's resurrection raises the human heart to new possibilities of action.

In the second stanza, Herbert develops the Old Testament image of the lute in explicitly Christian terms:

> Awake, my lute, and struggle for thy part
> With all thy art.
> The crosse taught all wood to resound his name,
> Who bore the same.

His stretched sinews taught all strings, what key
Is best to celebrate this most high day.

(7–12)

In referring to the "lute," Herbert again draws upon the familiar Prayer Book Psalter (the AV translates the Hebrew *nevel* as "psaltery").[49] Herbert's lute does not wake and sing spontaneously; it must "struggle" with all its "art." Christ is the singing master of the soul: "His stretched sinews taught all strings, what key / Is best to celebrate this most high day." Here, then, is a new theme for celebration: not the Lord who "our foes in pieces brake" but one who himself was broken, his crucifixion a musical offering that man must labor to copy out.

The final stanza is the most explicitly musical:

Consort both heart and lute, and twist a song
                Pleasant and long:
Or, since all musick is but three parts vied,
                And multiplied,
O let thy blessed Spirit bear a part,
And make up our defects with his sweet art.

(13–18)

"Consort" and "bear a part" may have been suggested by the Countess of Pembroke's translation of Psalm 57:

---

49. The lute is named in seven of the Prayer Book Psalms: 33:2, 57:9, 81:2, 92:3, 108:2, 144:9, 150:3. Elizabeth Stambler, "The Unity of Herbert's 'Temple,'" *Cross-Currents* 10 (1960): 262, incorrectly assumes that "for David's psaltery (Ps. 57:8), Herbert substitutes the lute, the accompanying instrument of the ayre, the love song." But no "substitution" was involved. Stambler quotes from the AV, not recognizing Herbert's primary dependence on the Prayer Book Psalter. While the lute is generally associated with secular music, it was also used to accompany domestic psalm singing (cf. Le Huray, *Music and the Reformation,* 382; Rathmell, ed., *Psalms of Sidney,* xxvii). Herbert addresses his lute in a devotional context again in his "Prayer before Sermon": "Blessed be the God of Heaven and Earth! . . . Awake therefore, my Lute, and my Viol! awake all my powers to glorifie thee!" (*Works,* 289).

Wake my tongue, my lute awake,
Thou my harp the consort make,
My self will beare a part.

(34–36)[50]

"My self" is the climactic term here, as in the Hebrew.
But Herbert substitutes a new image: in the third stanza,
by design, the Holy Spirit "bear[s] a part" in the "consort." Herbert has recreated "awake Lute" as a Christian
hymn: man's "awaking" is a spiritual rebirth made possible by Christ's resurrection; his "lute" is taught and
tuned by Christ; the Holy Spirit joins the song to make
the music better.

If in the "Antiphons" and "Easter" Herbert celebrates
the God of History, in "Providence" and "Man" his subject is the God of Nature. His model in "Providence" is
Psalm 104, a Whitsun Proper Psalm that reviews the
works of Creation and God's bountiful provision for his
creatures. We are meant to hear the stately music of the
psalm as we read the "countrey-aires"[51] that are Herbert's
variations on it.

Psalm 104 starts and ends with a formal encomium in
which the psalmist addresses himself: "Praise the Lord,
O my soule"; "O my soule, praise the Lord" (104:1, 35).
In Herbert's poem this feature is developed at considerable length, seven stanzas in the beginning and three at
the end—that is, almost one-quarter of the poem—ex-
pounding the propriety of praise. To praise God is only
"right" and "just": man should "pay the rent" since he
receives the benefits (4, 27). He who fails to praise, on the
other hand, is guilty of far more than an act of omission;
he "robs a thousand" and "commit[s] a world of sinne"
(19–20).

50. Rathmell, ed., *Psalms of Sidney*, 132. See Noel J. Kinnamon, "A
Note on Herbert's 'Easter' and the Sidneian Psalms," *George Herbert
Journal* 1 (1978): 45–46.
51. "Gratefulnesse," 23.

In the major part of the poem, Herbert praises "the wonderfull providence and thrift of the great householder of the world," to borrow a phrase from *A Priest to the Temple*.[52] Calvin had used the same image in his commentary on Psalm 104, writing that God is "a forecasting householder and foster father towards all living things."[53] "Providence" speaks about the creation of the sea and the dry land, wind and rain, night and day:

> When th' earth was dry, thou mad'st a sea of wet:
> When that lay gather'd, thou didst broach the mountains.
> (113–14; cf. Ps. 104:6, 8)

> Thou hast made poore sand
> Check the proud sea, ev'n when it swells and gathers.
> (47–48; cf. Ps. 104:9; Jer.5:22)

> When yet some places could no moisture get,
> The windes grew gard'ners, and the clouds good fountains.
> (115–16; cf. Ps. 104:10–13)

> How finely dost thou times and seasons spin,
> And make a twist checker'd with night and day!
> (57–58; cf. Ps. 104:19–20)

But the most important theme of the poem is the provision of food for man and beast:

> Thy cupboard serves the world: the meat is set,
> Where all may reach: no beast but knows his feed.
> (49–50; cf. Ps. 104:14, 27)

Herbert gives these wonders a local habitation, imagining the primeval acts of creation in a familiar, domesticated English setting.[54] Thus we have God spinning a "twist" of night and day (57–58) or dispensing provisions from a well-stocked "cupboard" (49–50); and we have the "gard'ners" and "fountains" of the English country estate

52. *A Priest to the Temple, Works*, 241.
53. Calvin, *Psalmes*, pt. 2, fol. 102ᵥ.
54. See chap. 4 on Herbert's homely imagery.

(116). Where Psalm 104 speaks of wild asses, wild goats and lions, Herbert speaks of pigeons, bees and sheep; where it has cedars of Lebanon and fir trees, Herbert has herbs and roses; and where it considers the semimythical Leviathan, Herbert speculates about the crocodile and elephant, drawing upon the pseudoscientific lore of his day:

> Most things move th' under-jaw; the Crocodile not.
> Most things sleep lying; th' Elephant leans or stands.
>
> (139–40)

In such transmutations, one recognizes the impulse to make the mythic proofs of God's providence more imaginable, closer to home—an impulse that is felt especially in the vernacular Protestant translations of the Bible. In Luther's idiomatic German version, it has been said, "Judea was transplanted to Saxony, and the road from Jericho to Jerusalem ran through the Thuringian forest."[55] In "Providence," one might say, that road runs from Wilton to Bemerton.

Predictably, Herbert does not allude to those verses of the psalm that present a majestic God clothing himself with light, spreading out the heavens, walking on the wings of the wind, laying the earth's foundations, rebuking the waters with the voice of his thunder (104:2–7), nor the image that Rudolf Otto cites as a *locus classicus* of the numinous: "The earth shall tremble at the look of him: if he do but touch the hils, they shall smoke" (104:32).[56] The psalmist's comprehensive vision includes creatures—wild asses, wild goats, lions, the Leviathan (104:11, 18, 21, 26)—that are in no way serviceable to man. These animals, like those enumerated in Job 39–41, are in Otto's phrase the very "negation of purposiveness." They convey "the downright stupendousness, the wellnigh daemonic and wholly incomprehensible character of the eternal creative power; how, incalculable and 'wholly other', it mocks at all

55. Bainton, *Here I Stand*, 329.
56. Rudolf Otto, *The Idea of the Holy*, trans. John W. Harvey, 2d ed. (Oxford, 1950), 183.

254 · *Spelling the Word*

conceiving."[57] Such images are remote from Herbert's characteristic concerns. Though he takes his epigraph (*"In his Temple doth every man speak of his honour")* from Psalm 29, which describes God's terrifying power revealed in a thunderstorm, he does not borrow its images of daemonic power, just as he avoids those of Psalm 104.

In "Providence," indeed, his subject is the very "purposiveness" of nature. What he describes is a benign order, sensible and perspicuous; he wants to impress on us not only how rich and abundant this world is, but also how sensibly and "sweetly" disposed. He uses the adverb "sweetly," one of his favorites, three times in this poem—a word that is unimaginable in Old Testament accounts of the ordering of the cosmos, though it occurs in the apocryphal Wisdom of Solomon: "Wisdome reacheth from one ende to another mightily: and sweetly doeth she order all things" (8:1). Herbert's purview is restricted to the world where man is comfortably the master, gardening, mining, quarrying marble, cutting down trees, engaging in foreign commerce. His elaborations of the psalm material are all in the mode of homely wisdom, like that of the farmer's almanac:

> Most herbs that grow in brooks, are hot and dry.
> Cold fruits warm kernells help against the winde.
> The lemmons juice and rinde cure mutually.
> The whey of milk doth loose, the milk doth binde.
>
> (129–32)

Nothing could be further from the realm of the numinous.

Typically, Herbert's imitations are more carefully structured than their biblical models, but "Providence" is an exception. For a poem in praise of order, it has a surprisingly casual organization. Psalm 104 follows in a general

---

57. Ibid., 79, 80.

way the account in Genesis, referring in turn to the creation of light, the heavens and the earth, vegetation, sun
and moon, and animal life, but in "Providence" Herbert
moves, apparently without plan, from seasons to pigeons, from poisons to the sea, from the wonders of Creation to the wonders of the coconut:

> The Indian nut alone
> Is clothing, meat and trencher, drink and can,
> Boat, cable, sail and needle, all in one.
>
> (126–28)

He surveys the phenomena without discrimination in a
tone of rapt wonder, precisely the tone of his model: "O
Lord, how manifold are thy works: in wisedom hast thou
made them all, the earth is full of thy riches" (104:24). He
pauses to ponder the miracle of a ship's passage in the
sea (89–90), echoing the psalmist's awed "There goe the
ships" (104:26). "Nothing wears clothes, but Man" (109),
he exclaims, giving that discovery equal weight with
"thou mad'st a sea" (113). The elephant that stands (or
leans) at the end of Herbert's bestiary is hardly the crown
of Creation, just one more curiosity in a random compen-
dium. The lack of a logical progression is as deliberate in
"Providence," I think, as it is in the larger structure of
"The Church," though it has a different justification.
With an appreciative sweep that takes in great and small
alike, Herbert sings God's "even praise":

> Thou art in small things great, not small in any:
> Thy even praise can neither rise, nor fall.
> Thou art in all things one, in each thing many:
> For thou art infinite in one and all.
>
> (41–44)

But if all God's creatures are equal, some are more
equal than others. In the Psalms, the heavens declare the
glory of God; the valleys laugh and sing; the floods clap
their hands; and trees, beasts and birds praise God with-

out man's good offices.[58] Herbert, however, presents a picture of a "mute" creation, wholly dependent on man to be its voice:

> Beasts fain would sing; birds dittie to their notes;
> Trees would be tuning on their native lute
> To thy renown: but all their hands and throats
> Are brought to Man, while they are lame and mute.
>
> (9–12)

Only man uses fire, "to show his heav'nly breed" (111), and neither water nor wind can stop him:

> The sea, which seems to stop the traveller,
> Is by a ship the speedier passage made.
> The windes, who think they rule the mariner,
> Are rul'd by him, and taught to serve his trade.
>
> (89–92)

There is no hint here of man's fallen nature. When Herbert marvels that "nothing wears clothes, but Man," he does not reflect on man's first disobedience but rather on his superiority to the animals—one more instance of God's bountiful providence.

Of all the creatures, indeed, none reveals God's glory in quite such dazzling clarity as man. As Calvin writes:

> And assuredly allthowgh that in the whole order of Nature ther appeereth most large matter of GODS prayse: yet notwithstanding bycawse wee bee more moved with the thinges that wee feele in ourselves, David (not withowt good cause) dooth purposely commend gods speciall grace towardes mankynd, bycause it is the most bryght mirrour wherin we may behold his glorie.[59]

This is the subject of "Man." Hebert's theme, and his handling of it, recall Psalm 8, a Proper Psalm for Ascension Day, which celebrates man's conferred greatness: "What is man that thou art mindfull of him: . . . Thou

58. Pss. 19:1, 65:14 [AV: "shout for joy"], 98:9, 148:9–10.
59. Calvin, *Psalmes*, pt. 1, fol. 22.

makest him to have dominion of the workes of thy handes: and thou hast put all things in subjection under his feet" (8:4, 6). The psalm begins and ends with praise of God: "O Lord our governour: how excellent is thy Name in all the world!" (8:1, 9). Calvin's commentary on Psalm 8 is a helpful gloss on "Man":

> Howbeeit, it behoveth the readers to bee heedful in marking the purpose of the Prophet: namely that by this comparison he enlargeth the wonderfull goodnesse of God: bycawse it is a woonder that the creator of Heaven (whose hygh glorye ravisheth us up too the admiration thereof,) submitteth himselfe so lowe, as too vowtsafe too take uppon him the care of mankynd.[60]

The hero of Herbert's "Man," its title notwithstanding, is God, to whom the poem is addressed. God is the "builder" in the exemplum that frames the poem; the revision of "no man builds" in the Williams manuscript to "none doth build" (2) was perhaps intended to make this clear. The poem's theme, summed up in lines 47–48— "Man is one world, and hath / Another to attend him"—is prefaced, significantly, by the exclamation, "Oh mightie love!" The point is not that man is splendid, but that God has made him so. In stanza 5 Herbert focuses explicitly on the providence of the great householder:

> For us the windes do blow,
> The earth doth rest, heav'n move, and fountains flow.
> Nothing we see, but means our good.
>
> (25–27)

He does so also in the seventh stanza, which sounds very much like "Providence":

---

60. Ibid., pt. 1, fol. 23ᵥ. The introductory material to Ps. 8 in the Geneva Bible reads: *"The Prophet considering the excellent liberalitie and fatherlie providence of God towards man, whome he made, as it were a god over all his workes, doeth not onely give great thankes, but is astonished with the admiration of the same, as one nothing able to compasse suche great mercies."* So too the AV superscription: "Gods glory is magnified by his workes, and by his love to man."

> Each thing is full of dutie:
> Waters united are our navigation;
> Distinguished, our habitation;
> Below, our drink; above, our meat;
> Both are our cleanlinesse. Hath one such beautie?
> Then how are all things neat?
>
> (37–42)

Here Herbert's eye is clearly on the Creator, not the creature. But even the stanzas that consider man's attributes are implicitly praises of God. Man's physical perfections ("all symmetrie, / Full of proportions," 13–14) reflect on the artistry of the Maker. Parrots learn to squawk from man, because God has given him speech; man succeeds in catching his prey because God has put all the creatures under his dominion (11–12, 19–20). The muted suggestion of man's failings (he "should be" more than a beast, just as he should "take notice" of his great retinue, 9, 44) serves only to underscore what God has done for him.

Recently some readers have suggested that this tribute to man must have been intended ironically, because a fallen creature can hardly merit such acclaim. Fish explains it as "merely a strategy made necessary by the absence of the very qualities it rehearses," a rhetorical "ploy" designed to persuade God to dwell in man. If the reader understands it literally, Fish argues, "the revelation of the final stanza will be a rebuke to his presumption."[61] But if the reader is not taken in by the speaker's "ploy," are we to believe that God will be? Moreover, the last stanza of the poem, far from being a reversal, builds upon the preceding stanzas (it opens with the words "Since then"). It is true that, as Strier says, the poem "does not . . . state the case correctly from the Reformation point of view, the point of view from which most of the lyrics in 'The Church' are written."[62] But Herbert is a poet, not a theologian, and *The Temple*, deeply

61. Fish, *Living Temple*, 85–86.
62. Richard Strier, "Ironic Humanism in *The Temple*," in *"Too Rich to Clothe the Sunne,"* 39.

concerned though it is with the issues of Protestant theology, does not strive for the logical consistency of the *Institutes*. The poems of *The Temple* answer one another like a series of antiphonal voices: if the final lines of this poem "reduce man" to the level of nature,[63] the very next poem, "Antiphon, II," as we have seen, has him singing Hallelujah with the angels. I think Herbert avoids any mention of man's failings here not as a ploy to win over God but rather because, as in "Providence," he is writing a hymn in C major—formal, ceremonious praise—without modulations to the minor.

All the poems I have grouped together as "hymns" are modeled upon, or inspired by, psalms that had a prominent place in the liturgy. The "Antiphons" recall psalms sung at matins or evensong; "Easter," "Providence" and "Man," the Proper Psalms sung on feast days. Their speaker is a representative Christian—"I here present / For me and all my fellows praise to thee," Herbert says in "Providence" (25–26)—and their purpose unalloyed celebration. They do not admit the problematic; by design they give us no glimpse of personal experience. The "faithful tracing of the interior disposition of the unique individual soul," for Vendler Herbert's most distinctive achievement, is not their object. Most readers today find the hymns less appealing than Herbert's more complex lyrics. Vendler, for example, remarks that "Providence" and "Man" are "not, on the whole, good enough to solicit or reward sustained attention: they versify what they mean, . . . but they rarely contain those crosscurrents of powerful feeling that vex and freshen Herbert's best poetry."[64]

Why, then, one must ask, would a poet capable of writing "The Crosse" and "The Flower" wish to write

63. Ibid., 38. As Heather Asals writes in another context, "We do the man a serious wrong if we do not allow him to change his mind" (*Equivocal Predication*, 125 n. 42).
64. Vendler, *Poetry of Herbert*, 197, 180.

"Providence" and "Man"? Why would he choose to include the "Antiphons" in *The Temple?* Stein is right in saying that Herbert's "view of the providential order does not permit him to be fascinated only by the difficult."[65] The poems we have just discussed are essential to his design; their very presence in *The Temple* makes it the kind of "place" it is, and subtly affects our understanding even of poems like "The Crosse" and "The Flower," with which we feel more at home. T. S. Eliot's much-quoted dictum that Herbert's poetry is "definitely an *oeuvre*, to be studied entire"[66] should be recalled in this context. Herbert's formal ceremonial voice, like his didactic impulse, lies at the very heart of his difference from us. Only by respecting that difference, as I have said before, can we avoid the error of reading him as a contemporary.

I should add, however, that the hymn is far less important in *The Temple* than it is in the Psalms. One is not surprised to discover that Herbert wrote only a handful of hymns, or that *The Temple* does not end, like the Book of Psalms, with a series of hymns for chorus and orchestra, but instead with the intimate dialogue of "Love, III." Of the psalm types that Herbert imitates, the hymn is by definition the most impersonal. Both thanksgivings and laments offer Herbert a more congenial form, incorporating hymnlike praises into a complex subjective structure, a first-person account based on concrete experience. They consider the fortunes of men from opposed vantage points: "There is but joy and grief; / If either will convert us, we are thine." They take notice, as the hymns do not,

---

65. Stein, *Herbert's Lyrics*, 103. Many of my observations in the following pages are in agreement with points made by Stein in his chapter on "Complaint, Praise, and Love," 85–135, though our frame of reference differs: his "chief interest," as he says, "is not in the contributions of genre and tradition" (85); mine is.

66. T. S. Eliot, "George Herbert," *Spectator* 148 (1932), rpt. Patrides, ed., *Critical Heritage*, 334.

of the checkered nature of human existence in which joys
may be brought "to *weep*" and griefs "to *sing*."[67]
In "Bitter-sweet" Herbert refers this state of affairs to
God:[68]

> Ah my deare angrie Lord,
> Since thou dost love, yet strike;
> Cast down, yet help afford;
> Sure I will do the like.
>
> I will complain, yet praise;
> I will bewail, approve:
> And all my sowre-sweet dayes
> I will lament, and love.

Although God's actions seem contradictory and puzzling, Herbert insists that he will not be daunted: he will
respond, with all the passion of his nature, to God's
wounding and healing. Reading "Bitter-sweet," one understands why *The Temple* is not a book of hymns. Herbert's poems, with their intense fluctuating emotions,
their sudden shifts from joy to despair, from anguish to
relief, more often find models in the psalmist's complaints and thanksgivings.

COMPLAINTS: "LORD, I FALL, YET CALL"

"I will complain, yet praise": here we have a capsule definition of the biblical psalms of complaint. Suffering is their
subject—a suffering left out of account in the hymns, but
here felt as acutely present. The complaint has a double
purpose: to move God to compassion, and to bring relief to
the speaker's burdened heart.[69] As Calvin writes:

---

67. "Affliction, V," 13–14; "Josephs coat," 14.

68. Cf. Hos. 6:1: "Hee hath torne, and hee will heale us: he hath
smitten, and he will binde us up."

69. Gunkel, *Psalms,* 34. Examples of this type are Psalms 6, 13, 22,
31, 69 and 143; some of the complaints are known as "Penitential
Psalms" (6, 32, 38, 51, 102, 130, 143) or "Passion Psalms" (2, 22, 38, 59,
69, 88). For a discussion of the complaint, see Gunkel, *Psalms,* 19–22,
33–36; Mowinckel, *Psalms in Israel's Worship,* II, 1–25. Although Gun-

> to thentent he may move god to succor him, he setteth forth
> the grevousnes of his misery and greef with many com-
> plaints: not for that there needeth reasons to perswade god,
> but bycause he giveth the faithfull leave to deale familiarly
> with him, that they may disburthen themselves of theyr
> care.[70]

This is the most passionate of the psalm types: the speaker is literally pleading for his life. Typically he re-counts his suffering in hyperbolic images that refer to the grief of the body, and argues with an obstinate logic that God should save him. Desperate as he sounds, he claims he is certain that his prayers will be heard: "I am com-plaining right now," he tells us, "but I expect to praise." These three elements—the hyperbolic account of distress, the argument with God and the certainty of a hearing—furnish the substance of Herbert's complaints as well.

Herbert's picture of suffering differs in some respects from that of the psalmist. First of all, he recognizes that his true "foes" are within the mind and the peevish heart. Furthermore, as a "Christian David," he believes that Christ's Passion eclipses all human pain. For this reason his complaints follow "The Sacrifice," which is spoken in Christ's voice; we are meant to hear the music of Her-bert's groans over the ground bass of Christ's repeated "Was ever grief like mine?" Finally, Herbert believes that the Passion gives dignity and purpose to human suffer-ing—to suffer is to be like Christ—and that Christ enters into man's ordeal "to guide and govern it to [his] relief."[71] Thus while the psalmist wishes to be free of the rack, Herbert struggles to embrace it; while the psalmist keeps counting his groans, Herbert confesses that his hard heart

---

kel's term "Klagelied" is commonly rendered "lament," "complaint" is a more accurate translation; "lament" should be reserved for elegiac poems like David's dirge over Saul and Jonathan (2 Sam. 1:17–27) or the poems in the Book of Lamentations. (Professor Moshe Greenberg of the Hebrew University, Jerusalem, pointed this out to me.)
  70. Calvin, *Psalmes*, pt. 1, fol. 113v.
  71. "Affliction, III," 3.

can scarcely groan enough. Even granting these qualifications, however, it is remarkable how closely Herbert's poems of tribulation follow the conventions of the biblical psalms of complaint.

Grief is set forth in the Psalms with anatomical specificity. The heart is melted like wax, smitten or withered; the eye is consumed with weeping; the throat is dry, the knees weak; the belly cleaves to the ground; the bones are out of joint, broken or burnt.[72] This systematic listing of the parts of the body belongs to the psalmist's account of grief, just as the map of the beloved's body belongs to the topography of love in the Song of Songs. Biblical psychology associates the parts of the body with mental or spiritual functions. The heart, for example, is considered the seat of understanding; the soul, of the emotions; the kidneys, of the conscience; and even the bones are capable of affect.[73] The tendency to enumeration is reinforced by the demands of parallelism, the main prosodic device of biblical poetry, in which the second line repeats, with subtle variations, the thought of the first; for example, "There is no health in my flesh, because of thy displeasure: neither is there any rest in my bones by reason of my sinne" (Ps. 38:3). "Look how I suffer," the psalmist cries, or, more accurately, "Look how you make me suffer."

Herbert can be a master of understatement, but he practices little restraint when his subject is his suffering. With all the self-dramatization of the psalmist, he dwells on his symptoms, often in parallel clauses: "my head doth burn, my heart is sick" ("Home," 1); "One ague dwelleth in my bones, / Another in my soul" ("The

---

72. Pss. 22:14, 102:4; 31:10; 69:3, 109:23; 44:25; 22:14, 51:8, 102:3. See Lewalski, *Protestant Poetics*, 87–88, 306–7, on the biblical metaphor of sin as sickness.

73. Hans Walter Wolff, *Anthropology of the Old Testament*, trans. Margaret Kohl (Philadelphia, 1974), 17, 46–51, 65, 67.

Crosse," 13–14); "Bitterness fills our bowels; all our hearts / Pine, and decay" ("Repentance," 27–28). In "Complaining" he asks:

> Am I all throat or eye,
>   To weep or crie?
> Have I no parts but those of grief?
>
> (13–15)

In "Deniall" he enumerates the "parts" of grief—heart, breast, knees, tongue and soul—and in the first two stanzas of "Longing" he presents a very catalogue of woe:

> With sick and famisht eyes,
> With doubling knees and weary bones,
>   To thee my cries,
>   To thee my grones,
> To thee my sighs, my tears ascend:
>   No end?
>
>   My throat, my soul is hoarse;
> My heart is wither'd like a ground
>   Which thou dost curse.
>   My thoughts turn round,
> And make me giddie; Lord, I fall,
>   Yet call.
>
> (1–12)

If we are unconvinced by such stereotyped formulas today, it is because we like to believe that every unhappy man is unhappy in his own way.

Now, Herbert is perfectly capable of reporting what ails him, as for example in "Affliction, I":

> Whereas my birth and spirit rather took
>   The way that takes the town;
> Thou didst betray me to a lingring book,
>   And wrap me in a gown.
>
> (37–40)

But two stanzas earlier we find a passage of formulaic complaint that reads just like a quotation from the Psalms:

    Sicknesses cleave my bones;
Consuming agues dwell in ev'ry vein,
    And tune my breath to grones.

                    (26–28)[74]

If he can write with precision about the personal configurations of his grief, why should Herbert so often choose
to echo the psalmist's formulas? We can best answer this
question if we consider why believers, historically, have
been drawn to recite the Psalms in distress. As I pointed
out earlier, the poems in the Book of Psalms are meant to
be used. To recite, to quote, to echo the Psalms is to
associate oneself with the community of believers, to declare, in effect, "I am suffering as others have suffered
before me; as all men suffer." There is some comfort in
recognizing that one's pain is, after all, not unique. That
the Psalms were incorporated into the canon of Scripture,
and that they assumed such a central place in the devo-
tions of Jews and Christians, is in part owing to what we
may call their therapeutic effectiveness. I think Herbert is
attracted to the psalmist's formulas for this very reason:
the vehicle of complaint in itself affords a kind of healing,
a measure of detachment from the toils of the self.

    Having unpacked his woes, the psalmist typically pre-
sents the arguments by which he hopes to move God—a
God with very human instincts—to a favorable response.
He invokes God's honor: "for thy names sake" (143:11).
He intimates darkly that God will not have his due praise
if the speaker is silenced: "Shall the dust give thankes
unto thee?" (30:10). He reminds God of his promises:
"Looke upon the covenant" (74:21). And he harps on his
own frailty: "I am desolate and in miserie" (25:15); "I am
helplesse and poore" (109:21); "Oh remember how short
my time is" (89:46). The God of the Psalms seems particularly accessible to such discourse—even when he is angry.

---

74. Hutchinson ("Commentary," *Works,* 491) notes that these lines
are set off from the rest of the poem by the use of the present tense.

The many anthropomorphisms (probably more than in any other book of the Bible) make him seem almost human. He has eyes, a nose, a mouth, hands, fingers and, most important, he has ears. The very notion of man addressing God, after all, presupposes a God who listens. One can reason with him, cajole him, beat one's breast in his presence, lay bare one's soul. This is the very essence of the biblical complaint. "Lord, I fall, / Yet call," Herbert writes in "Longing" (11–12). It is the act of turning *to* God in pain that gives the complaint its legitimacy.

In Herbert's poems we hear the voice of the psalmist, charged with urgency, boldness and dialectical verve, wheedling or coaxing, stubbornly remonstrating with God in the face of despair, daring "to assault thee, and besiege thy doore" ("The Storm," 12).[75] It is obvious why Herbert should be attracted by this aspect of the biblical complaint. In "Decay" he recalls with some nostalgia the "sweet" old days when Abraham dared to put the case for Sodom and when God's "power could not / Encounter Moses strong complaints and mone" (1, 3–4). "I would parley fain," he writes in "Artillerie" (27), wishing to establish the same terms of intimacy in his own relationship with God. Like the psalmist he mixes complaint with expostulation. Even poems that have been labeled " 'pure' lament[s]"—"Sighs and Grones," "Home" and "Longing"[76]—incorporate an argumentative strain.

In *The Temple* this feature of the Psalms coincides with what is commonly called the rhetorical mode of metaphysical poetry. One is impressed by the variety and ingenuity of the strategies used by the speaker to advance

---

75. Cf. Stein, *Herbert's Lyrics*, 129: "Man's love . . . is privileged to address God boldly. The music of feeling, even as untransformed complaint, enjoys an access that God will not deny, though it interferes with celestial harmonies." Strier adds that "this rudeness is not an offense to God": "What God demands from the regenerate is not seemliness but sincerity" (*Love Known*, 187, 177).
76. Stein, *Herbert's Lyrics*, 87.

his own interests. One procedure is to remind God of who he is:

> Wilt thou meet arms with man, that thou dost stretch
> A crumme of dust from heav'n to hell?
> Will great God measure with a wretch?
> Shall he thy stature spell?
>
> ("The Temper, I," 13–16)

"Thou onely art / The mightie God, but I a sillie worm," Herbert pleads; or "Thou art the Lord of glorie; . . . but I a silly flie"; or simply "Thou art God."[77] This is hardly disinterested praise, and it may be offered up through gritted teeth, but it is praise nonetheless. Herbert has more in reserve, however, and like the psalmist he knows how to drive a bargain:

> To write a verse or two is all the praise,
> That I can raise:
> Mend my estate in any wayes,
> Thou shalt have more.
>
> ("Praise, I," 1–4)

"Let me not languish . . . barren to thy praise, / As is the dust," he begs, echoing Psalm 30:10. "O give me quick-nesse, that I may with mirth / Praise thee brim-full!" "How should I praise thee, Lord!" he exclaims, offering a monument more lasting than bronze.[78]

With a shrewd sense of purpose, Herbert summons up God's great works. "Yet Lord restore thine image," he begs the God of Creation. "And shall the dew out-strip thy Dove?" he challenges the God of Nature. "Remember that thou once didst write in stone," he pleads with the God of history, turning the calamity of his own hard heart into a divine opportunity.[79] He appeals to God's self-interest: "Let not their plot / Kill them and me, / And also thee." He

77. "Sighs and Grones," 4–5; "Complaining," 6, 8; "Discipline," 31.
78. "Employment, I," 13–15; "Dulnesse," 3–4; "The Temper, I," 1.
79. "The Sinner," 12; "Grace," 10; "The Sinner," 14.

lectures God on his attributes: "Thou art both *Judge* and *Saviour*, *feast* and *rod*, / *Cordiall* and *Corrosive*." And he commends to God the quality of mercy: "Love will do the deed."[80]

"Discipline," the source of this last line, is almost wholly given over to such persuasions. If in "Sighs and Grones" Herbert pleads guilty, here he begins by calling to witness his good behavior. He is, by his own testimony, well intentioned, he lives by the book and he shows some small signs of progress:

> For my hearts desire
> Unto thine is bent:
>   I aspire
> To a full consent.
>
> Not a word or look
> I affect to own,
>   But by book,
> And thy book alone.
>
> Though I fail, I weep:
> Though I halt in pace,
>   Yet I creep
> To the throne of grace.
>
>   (5–16)

Having exhausted his defense, he turns to remind the plaintiff of his immense resources:

> Then let wrath remove;
> Love will do the deed:
>   For with love
> Stonie hearts will bleed.
>
> Love is swift of foot;
> Love's a man of warre,
>   And can shoot,
> And can hit from farre.

---

80. "Affliction, IV," 19–21; "Sighs and Grones," 27–28; "Discipline," 18.

Who can scape his bow?
That which wrought on thee,
   Brought thee low,
Needs must work on me.

            (17–28)

"The absurdity of preaching this sermon to God is evident," writes Vendler; "as though God did not know that
Love 'can shoot, / And can hit.' "[81] Indeed the very posture of argument in all these poems may be called
absurd—"See how thy beggar works on thee / By art,"[82]
Herbert allows, recognizing how it must look to God.
And yet it is never suppressed. Man is permitted to say
his piece; and God, for his part, listens. The unashamed
pleading in the complaints is one measure of the intimacy
and assurance Herbert feels in his relationship with God.
 We find a more extended example of Herbert's argumentative rhetoric in "Longing." Vendler's description of
the poem shows its dependence on the psalms of complaint:

> The childish repetition of "heare, heare," the repeated poign-
> ant self-descriptions, the persistence in demand in spite of all
> seemliness, are the qualities that make Herbert, in this vein,
> one of our most accurate poets of expostulation, pain, outcry,
> wounded hopes, and strategems of emotion.

And the mixture of "reasoned logic" and "hectic implor-
ing" that she points out is equally true to the psalm
model.[83] The poem cannot be considered a pure lament
because its every rift is loaded with argument.
 "The only meane too persever," Calvin writes, "is
when being furnished with Gods promises, wee appeale
untoo him."[84] Herbert insists that God must help because
his very nature demands it:

81. Vendler, *Poetry of Herbert*, 245.
82. "Gratefulnesse," 3–4.
83. Vendler, *Poetry of Herbert*, 265, 262.
84. Calvin, *Psalmes*, pt. 1, fol. 152v.

> From thee all pitie flows.
> Mothers are kinde, because thou art,
> And dost dispose
> To them a part:
> Their infants, them; and they suck thee
> More free.

(13–18)

He assails God with emphatic statements and incredulous questions:

> To thee help appertains.
> Hast thou left all things to their course,
> And laid the reins
> Upon the horse?
> Is all lockt? hath a sinners plea
> No key?

(43–48)

He implores the Creator: "*Shall he that made the eare, / Not heare?*" (35–36; cf. Ps. 94:9). He summons up the Redemption: "Lord, didst thou leave thy throne, / Not to relieve?" (61–62). And he puts his trust in the promises of Scripture: "But now both sinne is dead, / And all thy promises live and bide" (67–68). In this light, Purcell's setting of the poem is revealing in its very omissions. As Joseph Summers and Louise Schleiner have noted, Purcell does not set the "meditative" or "reflective" stanzas (3 and 8–13) because he is "interested only in the effect of piteous desperation": "Thus his text presents an unreserved, uninterrupted cry for mercy."[85] Purcell makes of "Longing" a song in one key, like "Grief," but Herbert's poem has all the complexity of tone, the mixture of weeping and expostulation, that we find in the "Psalmes of Tribulation."

Despite its importunity, "Longing" remains a desolate affair, ending on an uncharacteristically low note:

---

85. Summers, *George Herbert*, 234 n. 28; Schleiner, "Purcell's 'Longing,' " 203–5; cf. Patrides, ed., *Critical Heritage*, 370–73.

> Pluck out thy dart,
> And heal my troubled breast which cryes,
> Which dyes.
>
> (82–84)

While there is hope of healing in this prayer, there is also a depth of misery that is relieved only in the following poem, "The Bag": "Away despair! my gracious Lord doth heare." The assurance that God "doth heare" comes as if in answer to the plea for a hearing in "Longing," where the word "heare" is repeated, with increasing vehemence, six times. But only rarely is the expression of faith put off to another poem; typically, even in his most dispirited complaints, Herbert manages to arrive at an affirmative resolution.

In "Easter-wings" the movement from sorrow to affirmation is given a memorable graphic form. When the speaker looks back on the punishments God has imposed for his sins, the lines begin to grow "most thinne." But at the middle of each stanza, feeling himself consumed with sorrow, he turns to God and the lines expand to form wings, as if his prayer had released the energies that make flight possible. The shape of the poem, as it narrows and widens on the page, impresses itself on us as the paradigm of the spiritual life. Herbert learns that wings are fashioned stroke by stroke from the privations and triumphs of the spirit. As Stein puts it, he refuses "to languish passively among the abysses that his complaints discover. He may be overwhelmed but he makes remarkable recoveries—if not in one poem, then in another. . . . The mark of his feeling that he is understood comes as a release, often sudden, from the tensions of the effort he has been making."[86] Tuve gives us the reason: "Herbert is so entirely convinced and aware of a boundless love received from the one he loves that this is a *datum* in the

---

86. Stein, *Herbert's Lyrics*, 96, 109.

most unhappy, the most tormented of the poems."[87] And White sees how prominent this movement is in *The Temple:* "Even the most disheartened of his poems ends with the steady reassurance of the presence of his God. He may not be able to see the light behind the darkness of the immediate moment, but he never long falters in his confidence that it is really there. That confidence . . . is the most persistent and central thing in Herbert's religious consciousness and the source of the peculiar power of his verse."[88]

These critics might be describing what is perhaps the most striking feature of the Psalm complaints, "the poet's 'certainty of a hearing,' . . . an expression of his confidence that his prayer will be heard."[89] The psalmist believes that estrangement from God, however painful, is only temporary; after all, God has responded to his prayers in the past. He "grounds this confidence," Donne preaches, "upon an undeceivable Rocke, upon Gods seale, *God hath heard me, therefore God will heare mee*": "upon no premises doth any conclusion follow, so logically, so sincerely, so powerfully, so imperiously, so undeniably, as upon this, *The Lord hath, and therefore the Lord will.*"[90]

Even the most despairing of psalms usually include some expression of assurance. Given the anguish of the complaint, this is bound to seem abrupt and unmotivated. One example will stand for many. Psalm 13 begins, "How

87. Tuve, "*Caritas*," 311.
88. White, *Metaphysical Poets,* 177.
89. Gunkel, *Psalms,* 14–15. The German *Erhörung* means "a favorable hearing," "the granting of [one's request]," and the *Gewissheit der Erhörung,* "the certainty of God's responding to one's entreaty." This is the action Herbert refers to in "Praise, II," 5–6: "Thou hast granted my request. / Thou hast heard me." See Friedrich Heiler, *Prayer: A Study in the History and Psychology of Religion,* trans. and ed. Samuel McComb (New York, 1932), 259–65, on the way in which the very process of prayer generates assurance.
90. Donne, *Sermons,* VI, 51, 39 (on Ps. 6:9).

long wilt thou forget me (O Lord) for ever: how long wilt thou hide thy face from me?" and ends, just a few verses later, "But my trust is in thy mercie: and my heart is joyfull in thy salvation. I will sing of the Lord, because he hath dealt so lovingly with me: yea, I will praise the Name of the Lord most Highest" (Ps. 13:1, 5–6).[91]

What happens in the speaker's mind, purging away confusion, anger and dread, and filling him with new courage? Calvin sees exemplified here the power of faith. In his commentary on the Psalms, he writes eloquently of David as an example to all believers:

> So David (so farre as might be conjectured by the very matter) seemed to himself to be forsaken of God. And yit therwithal, by the lyght of faith shyning before him, the eyes of his mynd perced even unto Gods grace although the same were hidden. Therefore when he sawe no where any peece of good hope: so farre foorth as the capacitie of mans reason could extend: by compulsion of greefe he cryeth out, that God regards him not, and yit by the selfsame complaint he witnesseth himselfe to be lifted up higher by fayth, . . . or else how should he direct his syghings and prayers unto him?[92]

It should now be clear why this book, of all the books of the Old Testament, was so appealing to the Reformers: in the Psalms we can discern the motions of a living faith.

When Herbert shows us how faith works, he does so in the very accents of the psalmist. "Assurance," which offers a particularly clear example, begins in exasperated self-torment. The speaker's "foes" are given their proper name here: "spitefull bitter thought," "bitterly spitefull

---

91. The refrains of "The Quip" and "The Forerunners" are expressions of certainty of precisely this type. Ps. 38 begins, "Put me not to rebuke (O Lord) in thine anger: . . . For thine arrowes sticke fast in me: and thy hand presseth me sore." But the psalmist finds grounds for hope: "For in thee, O Lord, have I put my trust: thou shalt answere for me, O Lord my God" (38:1–2, 15). "I am cleane forgotten, as a dead man out of minde" in Ps. 31 is followed almost at once by "But my hope hath beene in thee, O Lorde: I have said, Thou art my God" (31:14, 16).

92. Calvin, *Psalmes*, pt. 1, fol. 41.

thought." There is no escape, it seems, from the enemy within; in the first three stanzas of the poem we are very far from the assurance of the title:

> O spitefull bitter thought!
> Bitterly spitefull thought! Couldst thou invent
> So high a torture? Is such poyson bought?
> Doubtlesse, but in the way of punishment.
>> When wit contrives to meet with thee,
>> No such rank poyson can there be.
>
> Thou said'st but even now,
> That all was not so fair, as I conceiv'd,
> Betwixt my God and me; that I allow
> And coin large hopes, but that I was deceiv'd:
>> Either the league was broke, or neare it;
>> And, that I had great cause to fear it.
>
> And what to this? what more
> Could poyson, if it had a tongue, expresse?
> What is thy aim? wouldst thou unlock the doore
> To cold despairs, and gnawing pensivenesse?
>> Wouldst thou raise devils? I see, I know,
>> I writ thy purpose long ago.
>
> (1–18)

Then suddenly the speaker brightens ("But I will to my Father," 19), turning to God with the confidence of a child who knows that his father is powerful and that he himself is loved. In the act of turning the eyes of the mind, he is lifted up by faith. He is, as he admits, utterly powerless in his own defense, but even this thought cannot depress him once he looks past the toils of the self to the one true source of hope and comfort:

> Wherefore if thou canst fail,
> Then can thy truth and I: but while rocks stand,
> And rivers stirre, thou canst not shrink or quail:
> Yea, when both rocks and all things shall disband,
>> Then shalt thou be my rock and tower,
>> And make their ruine praise thy power.
>
> (31–36)

Our own century, with its deeply ingrained skepticism, is suspicious of happy endings, and not only in Herbert's poems. We tend to assume that (as Brecht put it) in real life the King's messengers very seldom come riding. But to believe in a God of Redemption is to believe in the possibility that one may be saved. "Rock" and "tower" are ancient images of defense: "O set me up upon the rocke that is higher then I: for thou hast bene my hope, and a strong tower for me against the enemie" (Ps. 61:3). Having gained that height, the speaker can look down upon the "spitefull bitter thought" that so tormented him—now it seems merely a harmless "foolish thought" (37)—and give it a taste of its own mockery.

In "Affliction, IV" the speaker is even more battered and helpless to begin with, and the hope of recovery beyond the pale of belief:

> Broken in pieces all asunder,
>   Lord, hunt me not,
>   A thing forgot,
> Once a poore creature, now a wonder,
>   A wonder tortur'd in the space
>   Betwixt this world and that of grace.
>
>   (1–6)

Some of these images come from the Psalms: "I am cleane forgotten, . . . I am become like a broken vessell" (31:14); "I am as a wonder unto many" (71:7 AV). Again he is the victim of his own mutinous "attendants"; the "spitefull bitter thought" of "Assurance" is a whole "case of knives" (7) now, wounding heart and soul. In desperation he turns to God for help, making it a matter of self-interest for God to intervene on his behalf:

> Oh help, my God! let not their plot
>   Kill them and me,
>   And also thee,
> Who art my life: dissolve the knot,
>   As the sunne scatters by his light
>   All the rebellions of the night.
>
>   (19–24)

Then in the final stanza, still addressing God, the speaker looks into the future. What he sees is not at all like the present, certainly not what we would expect a "broken" "tortur'd" man to imagine for himself. After the anguish of the first three stanzas and the piercing "Oh help, my God!" of the fourth, we are hardly prepared for his tone of assurance:

> Then shall those powers, which work for grief,
>> Enter thy pay,
>> And day by day
> Labour thy praise, and my relief;
>> With care and courage building me,
>> Till I reach heav'n, and much more, thee.

(25–30)

In calm, measured phrases he pronounces that he can actually see himself made whole again; his "Then shall . . . " bespeaks absolute belief. The poem concludes, like many psalms, with a vow that the speaker's redirected powers will henceforth "labour thy praise." The image of "building" is implicitly contrasted with "broken in pieces" of the first line. "Building me, / Till I reach heav'n" (29–30), with its reminiscence of Babel, might sound almost blasphemous. But the speaker is not an arrogant man trying to overreach God; he is a broken man who, through faith, has become a tower. The following poem, "Man," calls that tower a "stately habitation" for God the builder to dwell in.

"Repentance" moves toward the same kind of resolution. The title and opening lines ("Lord, I confesse my sinne is great; / Great is my sinne") suggest that this will be a poem of searching self-scrutiny, a penitential psalm, but in fact the confession is rather perfunctory: "I do confesse / My foolishnesse; / My God, accept of my confession" (16–18). All the energy of the first four stanzas goes into expostulation, rising to a pitch of personal urgency with the word "die": "For if thou stay, / I and this day, / As we did rise, we die together" (22–24). Finally, in the penultimate stanza, the speaker makes the necessary connection between his suffering and his sin, paraphrasing

Psalm 39:12: "When thou with rebukes doest chasten man for sinne, thou makest his beautie to consume away":

> When thou for sinne rebukest man,
> Forthwith he waxeth wo and wan:
> Bitternesse fills our bowels; all our hearts
> Pine, and decay,
> And drop away,
> And carrie with them th' other parts.
>
> (25–30)

The poem to this point is filled with self-pity, fear of punishment and the memory of past suffering. In the final stanza, however, every line breathes assurance:

> But thou wilt sinne and grief destroy;
> That so the broken bones may joy,
> And tune together in a well-set song,
> Full of his praises,
> Who dead men raises.
> Fractures well cur'd make us more strong.
>
> (31–36)

Like the psalmist, Herbert subdues his sorrow with an anticipatory song of praise. The peculiar image of the bones comes from Psalm 51:8: "Thou shalt make me heare of joy and gladnes: that the bones which thou hast broken may rejoyce." "But thou wilt" has the bedrock conviction of "Then shall" in "Affliction, IV." The turnabout from misery to affirmation takes up three stanzas in "Assurance" and one in "Affliction, IV"; here it is marked by a single word: "But."

That transition is more abrupt still in "Deniall," with not even a stanza break to signal a change of direction. The speaker gestures dramatically at heart, breast, knees, tongue and soul as if to say, "This is what I suffer because you have refused me a hearing." He charges God with damages to his poetry as well:

> When my devotions could not pierce
> Thy silent eares;
> Then was my heart broken, as was my verse:

My breast was full of fears
And disorder:
(1–5)

The speaker's broken heart is held up for God to see in the unrhymed, limping line that concludes each of the first five stanzas. This prosodic "deniall" strikes the ear forcibly, particularly because every page of the volume proclaims Herbert's skill in versification.

The final stanza begins as a desperate entreaty:

O cheer and tune my heartlesse breast,
Deferre no time;
(26–27)

but God's grace is so intensely imagined and so confidently anticipated by the speaker that his faith makes him whole:

That so thy favours granting my request,
They and my minde may chime,
And mend my ryme.
(28–30)

His suit is granted even as he speaks; his rhyme is mended, and the firm cadence of the last line is, in its own way, a form of praise. Here the psalmist's expression of certainty has been absorbed into the very pulsebeat of Herbert's prosody.

Herbert refers to the experience we have just considered in some other poems. "While I grieve, / Thou com'st and dost relieve" in "A Parodie" (29–30) tells only part of the story. "Prayer, II" gives us a truer account:

If I but lift mine eyes, my suit is made:
Thou canst no more not heare, then thou canst die.
(5–6)

Herbert's complaints, for all their bitterness, are typically not just a grieving but a lifting of the eyes. That motion initiates the mood of certainty in which these poems come to rest.

And not only these poems. The psalmist's "certainty of a hearing," I would suggest, is one of the distinguishing marks of "The Church," prompting the impulse to recovery and praise that governs the apparently random arrangement of the volume. Because of that certainty, "Longing" is followed by "The Bag," and "The Crosse" by "The Flower"; and the entire sequence of lyrics that begins in "The Altar" with tears and a broken heart concludes with God's unconditional welcome to man in "Love, III." These are some of the ways in which Herbert makes good the promise of "Bitter-sweet":

> I will complain, yet praise;
> I will bewail, approve:
> And all my sowre-sweet dayes
> I will lament, and love.
>
> (5–8)

L. C. Knights has written that Herbert's poetry "does not . . . simply *express* conflict; it is consciously and steadily directed towards resolution and integration."[93] I would add that resolution and integration are made possible for Herbert only on the ground of faith. Whether he reads out the inventory of pain, or presents the arguments why he should be saved, or sings in the dark about how he expects to praise, Herbert is laboring—in God's presence—to overcome the isolation and inertia of suffering. Like the psalmist he is convinced that God is listening. For that reason he is determined to order his complaints so that love will always have the last word.

THANKSGIVINGS: "THOU HAST HEARD ME"

The biblical psalm of thanksgiving is a species of the hymn, in gratitude for a particular benefit, presenting the testimony of someone who has himself personally experi-

93. Knights, "George Herbert," 138.

enced God's mercy.[94] At its center is an experience of
suffering—enclosed, mastered, overcome—just as a comedy contains within itself a potential tragedy. Pain, felt as
acutely present in the complaint, is recalled here from the
high ground of deliverance. The complaint, as we have
seen, is by its very nature provisional, focused on the
pain of the moment, looking to the future for relief, with
quick glances to the past for reassurance. Since it contains, in its "certainty of a hearing," the germ of a thanksgiving, we may think of the complaint as an incomplete
thanksgiving, and the thanksgiving as a complaint recol-
lected in gratitude. Northrop Frye's remarks on the Christian view of tragedy are pertinent here:

> Christianity . . . sees tragedy as an episode in the divine
> comedy, the larger scheme of redemption and resurrection.
> The sense of tragedy as a prelude to comedy seems almost
> inseparable from anything explicitly Christian.[95]

In this sense the thanksgiving, in which suffering is swal-
lowed up in victory, is the more "Christian" form.

The Old Testament psalm of thanksgiving, with its
amalgam of testimony and praise, is easily adapted to
Christian purposes, and the deliverance wrought by
Christ, with its consequences for both the community and
the life of each believer, provides the ideal subject for
thanksgiving. We find examples of Christian thanksgivings in the *Magnificat* of Mary: "My soule doth magnifie
the Lord. . . . For hee hath regarded: the lowlinesse of his
handmaiden"; the *Benedictus* of Zacharius: "Blessed be the
Lord God of Israel: for hee hath visited and redeemed his
people"; and the *Nunc dimittis* of Simeon: "For mine eyes
have seene: thy salvation."[96] These thanksgivings became

94. Examples of this type are Pss. 18, 23, 30, 34, 73, 116, 118 and
138. For a discussion of the thanksgiving see Gunkel, *Psalms*, 17–19, 32–
33; and Mowinckel, *Psalms in Israel's Worship*, II, 26–30, 31–43.
95. Frye, *Anatomy of Criticism*, 215.
96. *Booke of Common Prayer* (1604), sigs. [C7], [C5], [C7$_v$]; cf. Luke
1:46–55, 1:67–79, 2:28–32.

part of the daily liturgy, and like the hymns mentioned earlier, were familiar through repetition at matins and evensong.

Of the psalm types we have considered, the thanksgiving is most directly concerned with edification. The Hebrew word "to give thanks" (verbal root *ydh*) also means "to confess." One recovers one's breath in order to praise and tell: "I will not die, but live: and declare the workes of the Lord" (Ps. 118:17). The psalmist testifies publicly, "in the great Congregation," "in the presence of all [God's] people," in order that others may benefit from his experience: "O come hither and hearken all ye that feare God: and I will tell you what he hath done for my soule."[97] The salvation of the individual concerns the entire community of believers:

> I waited patiently for the Lord: and he enclined unto me, and heard my calling.
> He brought mee also out of the horrible pit, out of the myre and clay: and set my feete upon the rocke, and ordered my goings.
> And he hath put a new song in my mouth: even a thanksgiving unto our God.
> Many shall see it, and feare: and shall put their trust in the Lord.
>
> (Ps. 40:1–4)

Calvin comments on this passage:

> He extendeth yit further the frute of the help that he had felt: namely, that it shalbee an instruction too manye, too wayt for the lyke. And surely Gods will is, that the benefites which he bestoweth uppon any one of the faythfull, should bee recordes of his goodnesse towardes them all, that one of them beeing assured by the example of an other, should not doubt but that the same grace is set foorth for them all.[98]

In this respect the thanksgiving psalm resembles the biblical wisdom literature discussed in the preceding chapter,

97. Pss. 22:25, 116:13, 66:14.
98. Calvin, *Psalmes*, pt. 1, fol. 158.

where the sage refers to his own experience as a warrant for the truth of his teaching.

We may think of *The Temple* as a psalm of thanksgiving writ large. The superscription from Psalm 29 on the title page tells us that in his Temple Herbert means to speak of God's honor. In "The Dedication" he presents his "first fruits" as a thank-offering:

> Lord, my first fruits present themselves to thee;
> Yet not mine neither: for from thee they came,
> And must return.
>
> (1–3)

echoing a Deuteronomic liturgy of thanksgiving: "And now behold, I have brought the first fruits of the land, which thou, O LORD, hast given mee" (Deut. 26:10). Herbert's deathbed instructions to Ferrar about his "little Book," as recorded in Walton, describe the volume as a confession of past trials offered up for the edification of others. The note of thanksgiving is loud and clear in *The Temple*, even despite the great number of complaints, as one would expect of a poet who begs God for "a thankfull heart":

> Not thankfull, when it pleaseth me;
> As if thy blessings had spare days:
> But such a heart, whose pulse may be
> Thy praise.
>
> ("Gratefulnesse," 27, 29–32)

That Herbert is aware of the problematics of thanking God is apparent in "An Offering." It is not enough to bring a gift to God in return for his blessings. That gift must be pure:

> Come, bring thy gift. If blessings were as slow
> As mens returns, what would become of fools?
> What hast thou there? a heart? but is it pure?
> Search well and see; for hearts have many holes.
>
> (1–4)

The offerer's gift and the psalm that is put into his hands ("let thy hymne be this," 24) reflect the cultic setting of the Old Testament psalm of thanksgiving as it has been reconstructed by biblical scholars. Let me cite one hypothesis:

> Probably before the sacrificial act itself (116.17ff. [AV]) . . . the offerer would appear with the "cup of salvation" in his hand and empty the wine as a drink-offering upon the altar, while calling on the name of Yahweh (116.13); then the song of thanksgiving would follow, either sung by himself or by one of the temple servants.[99]

The sample "hymne" that the speaker provides in the second part of "An Offering" is like the "song of thanksgiving" that would have accompanied a thank-offering in the ancient Temple:

> Since my sadnesse
> Into gladnesse
> Lord thou dost convert,
> O accept
> What thou hast kept,
> As thy due desert.
>
> (25–30)

The Book of Psalms is an anthology of "prepared statements" of just this sort for the offerer's use.

We know, however, by the third line of the poem ("What hast thou there? a heart?") that the speaker is not referring to the drink offerings and burnt offerings of the Old Testament. The spiritualization of sacrifice occurs even in the Psalms: "For thou desirest no sacrifice, els would I give it thee: but thou delightest not in burnt offerings. The sacrifice of God is a troubled spirit: a broken and contrite heart, O God, shalt thou not despise" (51:16–17).[100] But the New Testament, as we have seen,

99. Mowinckel, *Psalms in Israel's Worship,* II, 31. Cf. Ps. 66:12: "I wil go into thine house with burnt offrings: and will pay thee my vowes which I promised with my lips, and spake with my mouth when I was in trouble."

100. Cf. Pss. 50:13–15, 69:31–32, 141:2. See Moshe Greenberg, "On the Refinement of the Conception of Prayer in Hebrew Scriptures," *Association for Jewish Studies Review* 1 (1976): 78–81.

with its reinterpretation of the meaning of *temple,* gives fresh emphasis to the notion of the "sacrifice of praise" (Heb. 13:15). It is characteristic of Herbert to summon up the ancient rite of thank-offerings as a way of impressing upon the reader the obligations of the Christian. As in the typological poems, Herbert does not content himself with merely asserting the superiority of the New over the Old. If the New Dispensation is more perfect, he believes, it is also more demanding. Before the offerer can presume to bring his gift, he must purify it in the healing "balsome" of Christ: "seek no repose, / Untill thou finde and use it to thy good: / Then bring thy gift" (19, 22–24).

Herbert explores this subject again in "Obedience" and "The Thanksgiving." The first we have spoken about as a poem of symbolic action, but Herbert's "speciall Deed" (10) written in heart's blood may also be construed as an offering of thanksgiving. Moved by Christ's "strange love to all our good," he resigns up his heart to be governed "as thy love shall sway" (27, 19). The legal deed of conveyance is a way of "publishing" the grace he has tasted, in Calvin's phrase, so that other men may be stirred to praise. His "Deed," like the sacrifice of a heart as a "gift" to God in "An Offering," is a Christian antitype of the material sacrifices of the ancient Temple. Here he insists that it is not a gift but rather a "purchase" effected by Christ ("know ye not that your body is the Temple of the holy Ghost . . . and ye are not your owne? For yee are bought with a price," 1 Cor. 6:19–20), firmly marking its distance from the Old Testament type:

> Where in the Deed there was an intimation
> Of a gift or donation,
> Lord, let it now by way of purchase go.
>
> (33–35)

In "The Thanksgiving," finally, we hear the speaker naming the works he intends to perform in gratitude for God's love. One of these is to write psalms of praise, the very poems we are now reading: "My musick shall finde thee, and ev'ry string / Shall have his attribute to sing" (39–40). Although most of his proposed offerings seem good enough on paper, we sense from their very multiplicity that they are insufficient to the object. In the last line of the poem the speaker himself recognizes that no action of his can ever adequately render thanks:

> Then for thy passion—I will do for that—
> Alas, my God, I know not what.
>
> (49–50)

His inarticulate gasp is in fact a true gesture of thanksgiving, a Christian answer to the ritual sacrifices of the Old Testament.

The presence of such poems in *The Temple* does not mean that Herbert would choose silence as the only seemly response to God. To declare the impossibility of praise is, to be sure, a customary form of praise, familiar to every reader of secular love poetry. Here the problem is compounded by the fact that it is literally impossible to praise God enough. Yet man is not dispensed from praising. Augustine writes, "For God, although nothing worthy may be spoken of Him, has accepted the tribute of the human voice and wished us to take joy in praising Him with our words."[101] And Calvin, commenting on "Who can . . . shew forth all his prayse?" (Ps. 106:2), teaches that

> no man living, how much so ever he employ all his study and endever to set forth Gods prayses, is able to goe through with so noble a matter, whose infinitenesse overwhelmeth all our witts. . . . But the best comfort too harten us withall, is that wee knowe howsoever abilitie faile us, the prayses which we offer from our hart, do please God.[102]

Man's psalms, whatever their defects, are God's "portion":

101. Augustine, *On Christian Doctrine*, 11.
102. Calvin, *Psalmes*, pt. 2, fol. 112ᵥ

So our clay hearts, ev'n when we crouch
To sing thy praises, make them lesse divine.
Yet either this,
Or none, thy portion is.

("Miserie," 39–42)

Herbert believes that God doth not crave less praise, but
more. And that is precisely what he promises in two of
the three poems entitled "Praise," where we can hardly
miss the emphatic position of the word "more," used as a
recurrent rhyme throughout the poem:

To write a verse or two is all the praise,
That I can raise:
Mend my estate in any wayes,
Thou shalt have more.

("Praise, I," 1–4)

Lord, I will mean and speak thy praise,
Thy praise alone.
My busie heart shall spin it all my dayes:
And when it stops for want of store,
Then will I wring it with a sigh or grone,
That thou mayst yet have more.

("Praise, III," 1–6)

Although Herbert's thanksgivings are less in number
than his complaints, they exhibit a greater diversity, and
for good reason. If in the complaints Herbert cries out to
God from the confines of suffering, in the thanksgivings
he gives scope to his sense of enlargement. By nature he
is a grateful soul, and wherever he turns his eye he finds
something to praise.

We can better appreciate the imaginative adaptations of
"Church-musick," "Josephs coat," "Even-song," "Paradise" and "The Flower" if we begin with the poems that
come closest in style and temper to the Old Testament
thanksgiving. In "Praise, II," more than in any other
poem, Herbert not only summons up the psalmist's
themes but also attempts to reproduce the formal patterns
of his verse:

King of Glorie, King of Peace,
      I will love thee:
And that love may never cease,
      I will move thee.

Thou hast granted my request,
      Thou hast heard me:
Thou didst note my working breast,
      Thou hast spar'd me.

Wherefore with my utmost art
      I will sing thee,
And the cream of all my heart
      I will bring thee.

Though my sinnes against me cried,
      Thou didst cleare me;
And alone, when they replied,
      Thou didst heare me.

Sev'n whole dayes, not one in seven,
      I will praise thee.
In my heart, though not in heaven,
      I can raise thee.

Thou grew'st soft and moist with tears,
      Thou relentedst:
And when Justice call'd for fears,
      Thou dissentedst.

Small it is, in this poore sort
      To enroll thee:
Ev'n eternitie is too short
      To extoll thee.

Martz is right in saying that the poem is "not so much an imitation of any one psalm, as a blending of motifs from many psalms of praise: a resemblance reinforced here, as elsewhere, by the persistent parallelism of the phrasing."[103] These are the central motifs of each of the seven stanzas:

I will love thee (O Lord). (18:1)

I wil thanke thee, for thou hast heard me. (118:21)

I will sing a new song unto thee. (144:9)

103. Martz, Poetry of Meditation, 280.

He hath not dealt with us after our sinnes. (103:10)

Seven times a day doe I prayse thee. (119:164)

Yea, he delivered me out of all my fear. (34:4)

Who can . . . shew forth all his prayse? (106:2)

In certain details one can see the Christian psalmist at work transposing his materials. The account of sin and deliverance, for example, has a distinctly Protestant ring. And "Thou grew'st soft and moist with tears" in line 21 is a more poignant statement of divine compassion than one finds in the Old Testament. The God of the psalmist is "ful of compassion and mercy: long suffering, plenteous in goodnes and trueth" and the God of Jeremiah says that his "bowels are troubled" for Ephraim, but in the Gospels we actually see Christ weeping.[104] To Herbert this is an important motive for thanksgiving; in his "Prayer before Sermon" he singles it out to represent Jesus' life on earth ("He took flesh, he wept, he died").[105] But these are questions of nuance. Taken as a whole, "Praise, II," like "Antiphon, I" and "Longing," stays very close to its Old Testament models.

Biblical poetry is notable for its compactness and concision: each verse contains no more than a few words, and no unessential word; the highly inflected Hebrew eliminates the need for the accumulation of particles to which we are accustomed in English. Herbert reproduces this effect in "Praise, II," paring down his lines to convey the stripped simplicity of the Hebrew. At the same time, the parallelistic structure of biblical verse satisfies a contrary impulse to elaboration. The "characteristic movement of

104. Ps. 86:15, Jer. 31:20, Luke 19:41, John 11:35. Cf. Donne's comment on John 11:35: "Christ made it an argument of his being man, to weepe, for though the lineaments of mans bodie, eyes and eares, hands and feet, be ascribed to God in the Scriptures, though the affections of mans mind be ascribed to him, (even sorrow, nay Repentance it selfe, is attributed to God) I doe not remember that ever God is said to have wept: It is for man" (*Sermons*, IV, 331).

105. "Prayer before Sermon," *Works*, 288.

meaning" in parallelism, Robert Alter writes, "is one of heightening or intensification . . . , of focusing, specification, concretization, even what could be called dramatization."[106] In the Hebrew, where there is no rhyme and the meter is not strictly bound by fixed patterns of quantity or stress, the parallel lines are related semantically:

> I will alway give thankes unto the Lord: his praise shalbe ever in my mouth.
>
> (Ps. 34:1)
>
> I sought the Lord, and he heard me: yea, he delivered me out of all my feare.
>
> (Ps. 34:4)

In "Praise, II" Herbert calls upon the resources of English poetry (rhyme, meter and fixed stanza forms) to create a parallelism of sound as well. The rhyme words that come at the end of parallel lines extend and explain one another: to "love" God is to "move" him; if God chooses to "heare" man, he will "cleare" him; to "sing" is to "bring" an offering, and so forth. As in the Hebrew, differences in meaning are conveyed by minimal means, a single word, or even a single letter: "I will praise thee" / "I can raise thee."

Some critics have been puzzled that Herbert proclaims his intention to offer his "utmost art," the "cream of all [his] heart," in a poem so frugal and withheld. I do not think he deliberately "occludes all his own gifts by assuming a very limited voice," or that he intended the "constriction" here "to point out the poverty of his craft."[107]

106. Robert Alter, "The Dynamics of Parallelism," *Hebrew University Studies in Literature* (Spring 1983): 92; cf. James L. Kugel, *The Idea of Biblical Poetry: Parallelism and Its History* (New Haven, 1981), 8. Ruth ApRoberts defines "synonymous parallelism" as essentially static rather than dynamic in "Old Testament Poetry: The Translatable Structure," *PMLA* 92 (1977): 987–1004.

107. Vendler, *Poetry of Herbert*, 163; Freer, *Music for a King*, 203. Freer seems to think that writing enjambed lines involves greater "craft" than writing end-stopped lines—an assumption Herbert would not have shared.

Or indeed that a poem's "tight confinement" within a strict form, here or elsewhere, is intended "to induce in us . . . a realization that mere man-made poetry, like other human structures, is inadequate to lead us to God."[108] It seems to me rather that Herbert has set himself the task of working within the formal limitations of biblical poetry, and is attempting to imitate both the characteristic spareness and the parallel structure of the Hebrew. The "ceremonial stiffness"[109] of "Praise, II" is best explained in terms of its probable liturgical purpose. The stanzas are arranged in an alternating pattern of statement and response ("I will," "Thou hast") that suggests it was meant to be sung antiphonally—perhaps, as in "Antiphon, II," with alternating choirs that join together at the end; the parallel syntactic patterns and end-stopping answer the needs of musical performance. Whether or not one likes the poem is ultimately a matter of taste (T. S. Eliot speaks of its "masterly simplicity"),[110] but even without liking it one can see that as an imitation of a biblical psalm it is technically a tour de force.

It is certainly more successful than another imitation of an Old Testament thanksgiving, the second part of "An Offering" ("Since my sadnesse / Into gladnesse / Lord thou dost convert," 25–27). Few readers will be moved to praise the "masterly simplicity" of that song. Herbert marshals the standard tropes in clipped parallel lines—the relief from sorrow, the grateful offering to God, the inadequacy of praise. The underlying fourteeners suggest that this too may have been intended for congregational singing. In "An Offering" Herbert contents himself with

108. Robert Higbie, "Images of Enclosure in George Herbert's *The Temple*," *Texas Studies in Language and Literature* 15 (1974), rpt. *Essential Articles*, 269.

109. Freer, *Music for a King*, 203.

110. T. S. Eliot, *George Herbert*, Writers and Their Works, no. 152 (London, 1962), 33–34.

simulating an Old Testament psalm,[111] barely attempting to give it a Christian complexion. It is rare to find him merely copying his models; more often, certainly in his most characteristic work, he succeeds in transforming them. In the poems we shall consider next, one feels that Herbert is not merely imitating a biblical form but speaking through it.

This is true even in "The 23d Psalme," where Herbert, though bound by the demands of the text, makes his own voice distinctly heard. It is entirely appropriate that his only authenticated translation from the Book of Psalms should be a psalm of thanksgiving.[112] Why did he translate just this psalm? It is certainly among the most familiar, but others who tried their hand at metrical versions (including Wyatt, Surrey and Bacon) did not attempt it.[113] Herbert probably chose the Twenty-third Psalm because of its neat, compact structure, because it lends itself so readily to Christian interpretation and because it embodies themes of central importance to him: God's bountiful providence as master and host and man's enduring

111. Freer (*Music for a King*, 176–78) is troubled by the "pointless elaboration" of the song, which he describes as "spare in form." He postulates a surly persona in the first section, whose rough impatience calls forth a "flaccid" response in the second, and then suggests that the whole poem may be a "piece of extended self-satire." There is no need for this elaborate critical detour; the "spare" yet "repetitive" form is best seen as an attempt (however unsuccessful) to imitate biblical parallelism.

112. Hutchinson presents, under the rubric of "Doubtful Poems," metrical paraphrases of Psalms 1–7 (*Works*, 214–222), but as he says, "the evidence for assigning them to [Herbert] is happily slender" ("Commentary," *Works*, 554–55). In "The 23d Psalme" Hutchinson sees the influence of the AV in "want," "gently passe" (lit. "still waters"), "in my enemies sight" and "runnes"; of the Prayer Book in "convert"; and of the two metrical versions in Sternhold-Hopkins. "And he that doth me feed" and "the tender grasse" appear in the version by W. W. (William Whittingham); "And brought my mind in frame" in the one by Thomas Sternhold ("Commentary," *Works*, 537).

113. Wyatt translated Psalms 6, 32, 38, 51, 102, 130 and 143 (the "Penitential Psalms"); Surrey, Psalms 8, 55, 73 and 88; and Bacon, Psalms 1, 12, 90, 104, 126, 137 and 149.

gratefulness. When he departs from the sense of the original, it is to expand on the implications of these themes, turning an Old Testament thanksgiving into a Christian love poem:

> The God of love my shepherd is,
>   And he that doth me feed:
> While he is mine, and I am his,
>   What can I want or need?
>
> He leads me to the tender grasse,
>   Where I both feed and rest;
> Then to the streams that gently passe:
>   In both I have the best.
>
> Or if I stray, he doth convert
>   And bring my minde in frame:
> And all this not for my desert,
>   But for his holy name.
>
> Yea, in deaths shadie black abode
>   Well may I walk, not fear:
> For thou art with me; and thy rod
>   To guide, thy staffe to bear.
>
> Nay, thou dost make me sit and dine,
>   Ev'n in my enemies sight:
> My head with oyl, my cup with wine
>   Runnes over day and night.
>
> Surely thy sweet and wondrous love
>   Shall measure all my dayes;
> And as it never shall remove,
>   So neither shall my praise.

Some expansion is inevitable in translating the compressed, highly inflected Hebrew into English: the four words of the first verse—*Yahweh ro'i lo ehsar*—become nine words even in the spare translation of the AV. Herbert turns that verse into a quatrain of twenty-seven words. It is not simply the need for metrical filler that moves him to render "The Lord" as "The God *of love.*" The versions in Sternhold-Hopkins have "The Lord is *onely* my support" and "My shepheard is the *living* Lord," while Sidney has "The lord *the lord* my shepheard is" (my italics). Herbert adds "love" to the final stanza as well: "thy sweet and wondrous love" in line 21 is based on the Hebrew *ḥesed* ("kindness, loving-kindness"), translated "mercy" in the Prayer Book and the AV; the versions in Sternhold-Hopkins have "grace" and "favour," and Sidney, "mercy."[114] Herbert alone has chosen to make explicit the love that is implied by *ḥesed* and that informs every line of the psalm.

Herbert's hymns speak about God's love from an adoring distance: "Praised be the God of love," "We all acknowledge both thy power and love," "Oh mightie love!" and his complaints yearn for it, half in despair: "My love, my sweetnesse, heare!" "My Lord, my Love," "Love will do the deed."[115] But his thanksgivings speak with gratitude of an actual experience of love, and love is the keynote of this interpretive paraphrase. In the first stanza of "The 23d Psalme," Herbert brings together "The Lord is my shepheard" with John's abstract definition "God is love" (1 John 4:8) and words of mutuality and fulfillment from the Song of Songs—"My beloved is mine, and I am his" (2:16)—in a configuration distinctly his own. Here again we see how collation is involved in the process of composition. These three biblical passages comment on one another, and in their new-found relation make palpable the meaning of God's love.

Shepherd is one of those biblical words that have gathered enormous significance in the course of literary history. David, assumed to be the author of the Psalms, was himself a shepherd, and the metaphor in Hebrew is one step closer to physical reality: the verb *rbṣ* ("to lie down") is usually applied to animals, while the "paths" of righteousness and the shadowy "valley" retain the sugges-

114. Thomas Sternhold, W. Whittingham, J. Hopkins and others, *The Whole booke of Psalmes* (London, 1602), fols. 70–71; Ringler, ed., *Poems of Sidney*, 301. The Countess's revision (ibid.) has the free translation "food."

115. "Antiphon, II," 1, "Providence," 29, "Man," 47; "Longing," 79, "The Search," 2, "Discipline," 18.

tion of actual places. Where the image of the shepherd appears in Christian translations, it inevitably carries the connotations of Christ as Good Shepherd (John 10:1–16; cf. Matt. 18:12–14). Calvin writes that "God oftentimes in the Scripture usurpeth the name, and putteth uppon himself the persone of a shepherd: it is no slight token of his tender love towards us. For seing it is a lowly and homely maner of speech: it must nedes be that he is singularly welminded towardes us, that disdeyneth not to embace himself so much for our sake."[116] It is this train of associations that prompts "tender" and "gently" as well as "God of love" and "sweet and wondrous love."

Some other additions to the text may be considered more briefly. "Or if I stray" and "not for my desert" in stanza 3, which speak of man's waywardness and inadequacy before God, are introduced to point up by contrast the subject of the last two stanzas: the miracle of God's love. None of the translations offers a precedent for the forceful "Nay, thou dost make me sit and dine" in the fifth stanza. "Thou shalt prepare a table before mee" in the Prayer Book Psalter is a literal rendering of the Hebrew, which means "to provide food" (Ps. 23:5; cf. 78:20). The emphatic "make me," together with "sit and dine," recalls the ending of "Love, III": "You must sit down, sayes Love, and taste my meat: / So I did sit and eat." The image of God as host and man as guest, with its implied reference to communion, links the two poems; by introducing the word *wine*, not found in earlier translations, Herbert makes the reference explicit. And where every other translation concludes with the image of the Temple ("I will dwell in the house of the Lord for ever," 23:6), Herbert speaks of the activity proper to that place. His final words, "my praise," give the human act of thanksgiving its full dignity. The poem that Herbert has fash-

116. Calvin, *Psalmes*, pt. 1, fol. 85ᵥ. See Lewalski, *Protestant Poetics*, 96–97, on the metaphor of shepherd and sheep.

ioned from the Twenty-third Psalm moves from praise of
God to self-denigration to a grateful acknowledgment of
God's bounty and ends with the image of man, elevated
by God's intimate regard, responding in love to God.

How do we evaluate such a lyric? Certainly no one will
want to claim it as one of Herbert's more distinguished
achievements. On the other hand, to call it "a very disap-
pointing performance for this virtuoso of stanzaic patterns"[117] is to miss the point: Herbert could hardly have
used a more elaborate stanza in a version intended for
public singing.[118] It appears at its worst when we read it, as
we can hardly help doing, with the familiar cadences of the
AV in mind. By rights we should measure it against other
translations intended for the same purpose. When we
compare it, for example, with the Twenty-third Psalm in
the Bay Psalm Book ("The Lord to mee a shepheard is, /

---

117. Norman S. Grabo, "How Bad is the Bay Psalm Book?" *Papers of
the Michigan Academy of Science, Arts, and Letters* 46 (1961): 612.

118. Herbert prefers more intricate stanza forms, and he might
have followed the example of Sidney, who used a complex stanza form
($a^4b^3b^2a^4c^3c^2$) for his translation. That he chose Common Meter instead
suggests that he intended the psalm to be sung. Hallett Smith speculates that Common Meter, the jogging 4.3.4.3 stanza of the Sternhold-
Hopkins Old Version, gained currency for metrical translations of the
Psalms because of its "simplicity, regularity, and emphatic beat,"
which made it easy to memorize and thus suitable for congregational
singing ("English Metrical Psalms," 254–55). Even Herbert, with his
celebrated metrical felicity, does not avoid the pitfalls of Common Meter, in part because he is bound by the sense of a given text. Smith
says that in the Old Version "the translator trying to get the sense of
the original was inclined to compress in the four-beat line and to pad
in the three-beat line"; in Sternhold's psalms "the shorter lines are
noticeably the weaker, and it is there, of course, that the translator is
fumbling for his rhyme" (265). A glance at lines 4, 8, 14, 16 and 20 will
reveal what Smith means. Such phrases as "want or need" and "walk,
not fear" are obvious illustrations; only "day and night" may be justified because of its biblical currency. Freer (*Music for a King*, 134–35)
suggests, unconvincingly, that the "deliberate awkwardness" of "The
23d Psalme" is intended to "clarify the pattern of humility that Herbert
has introduced into his materials," and that "the logic of the psalm, as
Herbert has paraphrased it, is to be found in the strained passages."

Want therefore shall not I"), we begin to appreciate its modest virtues.

With "Praise, II" and "The 23d Psalme" as a point of reference, I would like to look now, in conclusion, at six poems that adapt the Old Testament thanksgiving in a variety of ways. In "Praise, III," which is closest to its model, Herbert marvels that the God of the Universe, who is busy on such a grand scale, still has time to attend to him. "When George Herbert calls," as Strier writes, "God drops everything":[119]

> Thousands of things do thee employ
> In ruling all
> This spacious globe: Angels must have their joy,
> Devils their rod, the sea his shore,
> The windes their stint: and yet when I did call,
> Thou heardst my call, and more.
>
> (19–24)

As in the Old Testament thanksgiving, Herbert turns to share with "other hearts" the fruit of his own experience of redemption:

> Wherefore I sing. Yet since my heart,
> Though press'd, runnes thin;
> O that I might some other hearts convert,
> And so take up at use good store:
> That to thy chest there might be coming in
> Both all my praise, and more!
>
> (37–42)

This much is traditional. But Herbert makes it clear that he is speaking as a Christian and an Englishman. In stanzas 5 and 6, as we noticed earlier, he transforms the "bottle" image of Psalm 56:8, stretching his materials to Christian specifications: where the psalmist insists on how much he has wept, Herbert concedes that he has not wept enough and rejoices that Christ's "tear" more than supplies what is lacking.[120] And his song of praise bears the accents of rustic English speech, notably in the honest kersey words of stanza 3:

> But when thou dost on businesse blow,
> It hangs, it clogs:
> Not all the teams of Albion in a row
> Can hale or draw it out of doore.
> Legs are but stumps, and Pharaohs wheels but logs,
> And struggling hinders more.
>
> (13–18)

"Church-musick" and "Josephs coat" further extend the range of the thanksgiving by searching out subjects not found in the Book of Psalms. In "Church-musick" Herbert blesses God's music, which offers him relief from the anguish of body and soul:

> Sweetest of sweets, I thank you: when displeasure
> Did through my bodie wound my minde,
> You took me thence, and in your house of pleasure
> A daintie lodging me assign'd.
>
> Now I in you without a bodie move,
> Rising and falling with your wings:
> We both together sweetly live and love,
> Yet say sometimes, *God help poore Kings.*
>
> Comfort, I'le die; for if you poste from me,
> Sure I shall do so, and much more:
> But if I travell in your companie,
> You know the way to heavens doore.

Here we have all the elements of the thanksgiving—affliction in retrospect, the sense of present relish, the welling up of appreciation—though Herbert's poem is addressed not to God but to the music that brings him to God.

It is his own music that he is grateful for in "Josephs coat." If "Church-musick" is airborne, disembodied, suffused with pleasure (past suffering has come to seem

---

120. On "bottle," see my discussion of Herbert's transformations in chap. 2.

merely "displeasure"), "Josephs coat" is written on the rack of present pain. The poem is crowded with words for "grief" (that word alone occurs three times):

> Wounded I sing, tormented I indite,
> Thrown down I fall into a bed, and rest:
> Sorrow hath chang'd its note: such is his will,
> Who changeth all things, as him pleaseth best.
> For well he knows, if but one grief and smart
> Among my many had his full career,
> Sure it would carrie with it ev'n my heart,
> And both would runne untill they found a biere
>   To fetch the bodie; both being due to grief.
> But he hath spoil'd the race; and giv'n to anguish
> One of Joyes coats, ticing it with relief
> To linger in me, and together languish.
>   I live to shew his power, who once did bring
>   My *joyes* to *weep*, and now my *griefs* to *sing*.

We have some notion of what "versing" meant to Herbert from "The Flower," where he names it as the first joy of coming alive again: "I live and write" (37), he says there in one breath. In "Josephs coat" he confesses that God has enabled him to write even in suffering and thus to find some measure of comfort. Still, his praise is not direct and full-hearted as it is elsewhere; Herbert offers up thanksgiving indirectly (God is spoken of in the third person) and in a voice choked with bitterness. "But he hath spoil'd the race" is a mordant jest, and even the triumphant "I live to shew his power" betrays his pain. "Josephs coat" is a thanksgiving that remains half a complaint. Although God's love is implied in the title, Herbert's subject here is not love, as in the other thanksgivings, but rather God's "will," his "power" (3, 13).

In "Even-song," "Paradise" and "The Flower," however, Herbert is writing about God's love, the subject for which he is best remembered. "Even-song" is about a need more elemental than music or poetry: the blessing of rest after a day of dust and sin. Summing up at night what he has done by day, Herbert is pained by the waste of self that is also a waste of God's bounty: "What have I brought thee home / For this thy love?" (9–10). As so often, disorderly conduct is met with forgiveness and parental indulgence:

> Yet still thou goest on,
> And now with darknesse closest wearie eyes,
> Saying to man, *It doth suffice:*
> *Henceforth repose; your work is done.*
>
> (17–20)

"What have I brought thee?" is brushed aside with "*It doth suffice*," which has the force of "You shall be he" in "Love, III." It is God's love that enables man to "rest," as it does to "sit and eat."[121] God is not blind to man's "waies," but loving; and man is accepted, despite the plain fact that he is unacceptable. Each night he is kept out of harm's way, "inclose[d]" in God's "ebony box" (21–22), an image of refuge, like "under the shadow of thy wings" (Pss. 17:8, 57:1, etc.), suggesting perfect safety in God's close presence.

In the final stanza Herbert meditates on God's love for man, though he speaks of love in the abstract, with an air of philosophical detachment:

> I muse, which shows more love,
> The day or night: that is the gale, this th' harbour;
> That is the walk, and this the arbour;
> Or that the garden, this the grove.
>
> (25–28)

But then he leaves his "musing" behind in a sudden rush of feeling:

> My God, thou art all love.
> Not one poore minute scapes thy breast,
> But brings a favour from above;
> And in this love, more then in bed, I rest.
>
> (29–32)

---

121. On "rest," see my discussion of biblical "constellations" in chap. 2.

300 · *Spelling the Word*
•

The psalmist too is thankful for rest—"I will lay me downe in peace, and take my rest: for it is thou Lord onely that makest mee dwell in safetie," "for so he giveth his beloved sleepe" (4:9, 127:3)—but nowhere does he make it the subject of an entire psalm. Herbert's poem ends where it begins, praising God's love, but whereas the first line is an impersonal hymn formula, "Blest be the God of love," hardly to be distinguished from the opening of "Antiphon, II," the last line gives thanks for a love intimately experienced.

"Paradise" starts by blessing God for another kind of "inclosure," the gracious protection that enables man to flourish in safety, and that makes life on earth something like life in Eden. We usually associate Paradise with rank and luxurious growth, "Nature boon / Pour'd forth profuse,"[122] but Herbert's Paradise is tidy and trim, with the trees all "in a ROW" as in the nursery rhyme:

> I blesse thee, Lord, because I GROW
> Among thy trees, which in a ROW
> To thee both fruit and order OW.
>
> What open force, or hidden CHARM
> Can blast my fruit, or bring me HARM,
> While the inclosure is thine ARM?
>
> (1–6)

To be a fruitful tree in God's garden is no small thing. When he feels himself dry and despondent, Herbert casts an envying eye at the trees, wishing for himself their natural, untroubled way of flowering and bearing fruit.[123] "Be fruitfull" is God's first imperative to man. Yet only the righteous flourish: the blessed are like a "watered garden" or a "tree planted by the waters," the cursed like a "drie tree" or an "empty vine." "By their fruits," Christ teaches, "ye shall know them."[124] In the first half of

---

122. *Paradise Lost*, bk. 4, lines 242–43.
123. Cf. "Affliction, I," 57–60; "Employment, II," 21–25.
124. Gen. 1:28; Isa. 58:11, Jer. 17:8, cf. Ps. 1:3; Isa. 56:3, Hos. 10:1; Matt. 7:20.

"Paradise," Herbert acknowledges that he "owes" his fruit to God.

In what follows—and here his departure from the psalm model is most evident—Herbert blesses not only God's "inclosure" but also his "knife." Unlike the "case of knives" that he carries around in his head and that wound him to no avail, this knife of a master gardener makes him "more fruitfull." Herbert speaks of God's "inclosure" in the first two stanzas and his "cuttings" in the last three with the same serene thankfulness, knowing them to be related aspects of God's loving care. His pain is evidence that God is taking pains with him:

> Inclose me still for fear I START.
> Be to me rather sharp and TART,
> Then let me want thy hand & ART.
>
> When thou dost greater judgements SPARE,
> And with thy knife but prune and PARE,
> Ev'n fruitfull trees more fruitfull ARE.
>
> Such sharpnes shows the sweetest FREND:
> Such cuttings rather heal then REND:
> And such beginnings touch their END.
>
> (7–15)

Only rarely does the psalmist express this notion (e.g., "It is good for me that I have bene in trouble: that I may learne thy statutes," 119:71; cf. 119:67, 75). Typically he is grateful not for pain but for pain overcome; even the Penitential Psalms are on the whole more plaintive than penitent. But Herbert never sees himself as other than sinful. If in his complaints he is quick to blame himself, in his thanksgivings he blesses God not only for relief from pain but for the pain itself, which he knows to be productive. To Herbert's mind fruit requires order, order means discipline, and discipline is a sure sign of love.

Herbert brings to this thanksgiving the teachings of proverbial wisdom—"For whom the LORD loveth, he correcteth"; "Faithfull are the woundes [= woundings] of a friend" (Prov. 3:12, 27:6)—and, of course, the teachings of Christ. The image of pruning comes from the same chapter of John where Christ calls himself man's "friend" (15:12–15):

> I am the true vine, and my Father is the husbandman. Every branch in me that beareth not fruit, hee taketh away: and every branch that beareth fruit, he purgeth it, that it may bring foorth more fruit. . . .
> Herein is my Father glorified, that ye beare much fruit.
> (John 15:1-2, 8)[125]

Finally, of course, it is the example of Christ himself, in whose person love and suffering meet at their most intense, that inspires Herbert's willing acceptance.

We have seen that Herbert baptizes the psalms by his emphasis on God's love and by his justification of the necessity of suffering. These two motifs come together again in "The Flower," where man's pain is seen as an expression of God's love for him. The great beauty of "The Flower" lies in its joy in "wonders" that God alone can accomplish. The poet celebrates his recovery from a depression terrible as death:

> And now in age I bud again,
> After so many deaths I live and write;
> I once more smell the dew and rain,
> And relish versing: O my onely light,
>   It cannot be
>   That I am he
> On whom thy tempests fell all night.
>
> (36–42)

The sensation of coursing energies, of delight in life, is so marvelously evoked in this stanza that it seems almost a poem in itself. But much of its force comes from its position late in the poem, after Herbert's account of his misery:

125. See Lewalski, *Protestant Poetics*, 97–98, 307–9, on the "garden-husbandry metaphor."

Who would have thought my shrivel'd heart
Could have recover'd greennesse? It was gone
      Quite under ground; as flowers depart
To see their mother-root, when they have blown;
            Where they together
            All the hard weather,
      Dead to the world, keep house unknown.

(8–14)

Vendler writes that Herbert "will not forget the gloomy truth in the springlike experience."[126] In this he follows the Old Testament thanksgiving which in the midst of joy remembers, indeed memorializes, past suffering. Distress in the Psalms is often represented as a kind of death, a descent into the shadowy underworld, and recovery as a kind of resurrection, for example, in Psalm 30: "Thou Lord hast brought my soule out of hell [AV: from the grave]: thou hast kept my life from them that go down to the pit" (30:3),[127] or Psalm 71, used in the Anglican Order for the Visitation of the Sick: "O what great troubles and adversities hast thou shewed mee, and yet diddest thou turne and refresh me: yea, and broughtest me from the deepe of the earth againe" (71:18).

In Herbert's poem, the psalmist's dark "pit" becomes the rich soil of the gardener's flowerbed. As in "Paradise," the garden imagery provides a way of accepting suffering, for the dormant perennial is not what it seems. Herbert's flower quickened by dew and rain, like the tree in Job 14:7–9, is instinct with new life:

> For there is hope of a tree, if it be cut downe, that it will sprout againe, and that the tender branch thereof will not cease.

126. Vendler, *Poetry of Herbert*, 54.
127. Psalm 30 should be compared with "The Flower" also for the notion of affliction as only temporary ("heavinesse may endure for a night, but joy commeth in the morning," 30:5), and the implication that man's hubris is the direct cause of God's anger ("And in my prosperitie I sayd, I shall never bee removed. . . . Thou didst turne thy face from me: and I was troubled," 30:6–7).

Though the roote thereof waxe old in the earth, and the
stocke thereof die in the ground:
Yet through the sent of water it will bud, and bring forth
boughes like a plant.

More commonly, biblical images of growing things signify
mortality: "The grasse withereth, the flowre fadeth."[128]
But having used the flower as a symbol of natural regeneration, Herbert goes on to make it symbolic of the Christian's final triumph over mortality: "Thou hast a garden
for us," "thy Paradise, where no flower can wither" (46,
23).

In "The Flower" Herbert leaves us with a deepened
understanding of love—but not until we have suffered
with him the deaths and rebirths of the spirit. For the first
six stanzas, he attributes those "wonders," so often experienced, to God's power:

These are thy wonders, Lord of power,
Killing and quickning, bringing down to hell
And up to heaven in an houre.

(15–17)

It is only in the seventh stanza, where he contemplates
not the mighty acts of God but their final purpose, that he
is able to see God under the aspect of love:[129]

128. Isa. 40:6–8; cf. Job 14:2, Pss. 37:2, 90:5–6, 103:15–16, Jas. 1:10–
11, 1 Pet. 1:24.
129. Whenever Herbert mentions these attributes together, he does
so in the same order—first power, then love—perhaps suggesting an
order of ascending importance in his mind. "Thy Father could / Quickly
effect, what thou dost move; / For he is *Power*," Herbert writes in "The
Method," "and sure he would; / For he is *Love*" (5–8). He considers the
"supreme almightie power" of God in "Prayer, II" before turning in the
next stanza to his "unmeasurable love"—both guarantees of prayer's
efficacy (7, 13). In "Ephes. 4.30" he finds it inconceivable that the "God
of strength and power" should grieve for him, but then he is moved to
weep when he realizes that it is the "God of love" who is grieving (4, 7).
In "The Church Militant" he starts by addressing the "Almightie Lord,"
who "rulest all things" ("The smallest ant or atome knows thy power")
and quickly adds, "But above all, thy Church and Spouse doth prove /
Not the decrees of power, but bands of love" (1–3, 9–10).

These are thy wonders, Lord of love,
To make us see we are but flowers that glide.

(43–44)

Here is another definition of love to set beside that of "Love, III": God not only accepts us with all our failings but patiently teaches us, guiding our griefs with mercy aforethought so that we will learn to "see." In the life to come God will "look us out of pain," Herbert writes in "The Glance" (21); in this life, he teaches us, through our pain, to understand who and what we are.

"The Flower" is not just an ode to joy, though it is often read that way. It is a poem of insight and acceptance, and its true subject is the subject of all the Psalms: "Thy power and love, my love and trust."[130] In "The Flower" Herbert is learning to spell the word, to see in the confusion of his feelings the shaping force of God's will. To see—and to praise. Like the psalmist, Herbert writes of wonder, frustration, despair, longing and joy, and like the psalmist he insists on turning every motion of the heart into a song of praise.

130. "The Temper, I," 27.

Index of Biblical References

The biblical passages cited below are from the AV with the exception of those from the Psalms, which are taken from the Prayer Book Psalter. Where the numbering of psalm verses in the Prayer Book does not agree with that of the AV, the corresponding AV verse numbers are given in brackets.

Index of Poems Cited

315

General Index

Addleshaw, G.W.O., and Frederick Etchells, *Architectural Setting of Anglican Worship,* 123n
Ainsworth, Henry, 233
Alter, Robert: *Biblical Narrative,* 40n; "Dynamics of Parallelism," 289
Anselment, Raymond A., " 'Church Militant,' " 63n, 140
ApRoberts, Ruth, "Old Testament Poetry," 289n
Aristotle, 154
Asals, Heather A. R.: *Equivocal Predication,* 180n, 259n; "Voice of Herbert's 'Church,' " 231n
Aubrey, John, 34n, 122n, 234
Auerbach, Erich: "Figura," 128–29; *Mimesis,* 40n, 90; "Sermo Humilis," 219–20
Augustine, Saint, xiv, 121, 147, 219; *Confessions,* 29, 172; *On Christian Doctrine,* 219n, 285
Authorized Version (King James Bible), xiii–xiv, 1–2, 11, 15n, 17, 52, 53n, 55, 70n, 135, 211, 245, 250, 256n, 257n, 275, 291n, 292–93, 295, 303

Bacon, Francis, 233, 291
Bainton, Roland H., *Here I Stand,* 53n, 134n, 253n
Baroway, Israel: "Bible as Poetry," 1n; "Hebrew Hexameter," 1n; "Hebrew Prosody," 1n; " 'Lyre of David,' " 1n
Bay Psalm Book, 295–96

Beardslee, William, "Uses of the Proverb," 190n
Bell, Ilona, "Herbert's 'Collar,' " 164n
Bible, 46, 126; accessibility of, 5, 11, 22, 190, 216–20; authority of, 4, 10–13, 20, 42–44; didactic intent of, 5, 34, 174–84, 189–91, 199–209, 217–19; difficulty of, 27–28; etymologies, 208–10; history of salvation, 5, 65n, 113–17, 126–29, 131, 140, 141, 142n, 146, 158, 167, 247; language of, 5, 46–52, 57n, 123, 126, 215–21; narrative style in, 40, 174; parallelism in, 158, 178, 248, 263, 287–90, 291n; rabbinic commentary, 90–91; Reformation attitudes to, 1–2, 4, 9–12, 21–22, 67, 80, 114–15, 131, 233, 245, 273; translations of, 11, 53n, 211, 216, 233–36, 253, 294; unity of, 46–47, 51, 59, 65; used by the believer, 1–2, 4, 9, 11–18, 24–27, 45, 127–28, 238, 265. *See also particular editions; Mashal;* New Testament; Old Testament; Psalms
Bishops' Bible, xiii
Blake, William, *Proverbs of Hell,* 183
Bloch, Chana, " 'Dehumanizing' Herbert," 175n
Blunt, John Henry, *Annotated Book of Common Prayer,* 123n, 237n
Book of Common Prayer, xii, xiv,

Vendler, Helen (*cont.*)
　100, 111n, 116, 137–38, 171,
　172, 173n, 174–75, 195, 197,
　215, 223n, 246, 259, 269, 289n,
　303
Von Rad, Gerhard, *Old Testament
　Theology*, 204n, 209n
Vulgate (*Biblia Sacra*), 77, 245

Walton, Izaak, *Life of Herbert*, 15,
　19–20, 34n, 122n, 173, 228–
　29, 282
Weil, Simone, *Waiting for God*,
　151–52
Whitaker, William, *Disputation on
　Holy Scripture*, 17, 61–62
White, Helen C., *Metaphysical
　Poets*, 123, 240, 272

White, Robert, 193
Whittingham, William, 291n. *See
　also* Sternhold-Hopkins Psalter
Wickenheiser, Robert J., "Herbert
　and the Epigrammatic Tradi-
　tion," 176n
Wilder, Amos N., *Language of the
　Gospel*, 217n
Williams, Arnold, *Common Exposi-
　tor*, 91n
Williams manuscript, 94, 102n,
　153, 245, 257
Wither, George, *Preparation to the
　Psalter*, 233, 239n, 241
Wolff, Hans W., *Anthropology of
　the Old Testament*, 263n
Woollcombe, K. J., "Biblical Ori-
　gins of Typology," 129n, 130n
Wyatt, Thomas, 233, 291

Compositor: Huron Valley Graphics
Text: Palatino
Display: Palatino
Printer: Braun-Brumfield, Inc.
Binder: Braun-Brumfield, Inc.